Principles & Practice of Newswriting

Principles and Practice of Newswriting

Prof. **B.S. Goyal**

SHREE PUBLISHERS & DISTRIBUTORS
NEW DELHI-110 002

Edition : 2008

Published by :
SHREE PUBLISHERS & DISTRIBUTORS
4735/22, Prakash Deep Building
Ansari Road, Darya Ganj,
New Delhi–110 002

ISBN : 978–81–8329–289–4

Printed at Mehra Offset Press, Delhi.

Preface

Principles and Practice of Newswriting has been designed as a text-book for the students pursuing courses in journalism and mass communication at all levels. Newswriting is the heart and soul of all journalism. Therefore a study of the principles of newswriting is essential for anyone who wants to be a journalist or to run the business of journalism.

In spite of rapid changes occurring in the field of journalism because of sweeping advances in information technology, the basic skill in newswriting remains the single most important requirement for every journalist. Today newspapers are facing a great challenge from various media.

The authority of modern newspapers is being usurped by a variety of "new news" forms that combine information, entertainment, persuasion and analysis. (Jon Katz) Katz also claims that the news authority of most prominent daily papers is being challenged by "news" coming from talk shows, television sitcoms, popular films and even music videos. In other words, we are passing from a society in which the transmission of Knowledge depended mainly on books, newspapers and magazines to a society dominated by a mix of print, visual, electronic, and digital information. In the process, the new forms of news have been taking over the roles of traditional journalism, setting the national, cultural, social and political agendas.

Today, a fundamental tension exists between print and electronic conceptions of news. With news-reading habits among young people in decline, T.V. Magazine programmes, talk shows, sit-coms, movies and popular music are sparking public conversation more often than are traditional newspapers, says Richard Campbell rightly. But while smaller nondaily papers tend to play a consensus role in communities, promoting social and economic harmony, national and metro dailies practice conflict-oriented journalism in which news is defined primarily as events, issues, or experiences that deviate from social norms. Under these news orientations, journalists see their role not merely as neutral fact-gatherers but as observers who monitor their city's institutions and problems. They often maintain an adversarial relationship with local politicians and public officials. In telling stories about complex and controversial topics, Journalists under the conflict-model often turn such topics into two-dimensional stories, pitting one idea or person against another. This convention, often called "telling both sides of a story", allows a reporter to take the position of a detached observer.

The present book includes topics like 'understanding the nature of news', 'basic elements of news', 'elements of news writing', 'writing an original and exciting news story', 'techniques of shaping the news stories' 'everydayness of news and audience response', 'qualities of effective news writing,' 'truth and ideology in news making, 'news as cultural politics' 'humanizing the news', 'interviewing for news', 'structuring the news story' and fifty common errors in newspaper writing. All these chapters are based on the best available material an the topics. Essentially, the book is a compilation of the relevant material from different sources to serve the needs of the students and practitioners of journalism.

The book should serve the needs of all those for whom it is meant. I am grateful to all authors from whose books material has been adapted for this book.

Prof. (Dr.) B.S. Goyal

◆◆◆

Contents

◆◆◆

1

What is News?

(A) Understanding the Nature of News

The Nature of News

The most basic, most important and most difficult question in journalism can be asked in three words: What is news? It's a basic question for anyone beginning the study of journalism or for anyone who learns about the word - as most of us do - from journalists. It's an important question because the answer will guide your work as a journalist and will determine what you receive as a consumer of journalism. It's a difficult question because there isn't and can't be a single universal answer. Besides, the answers keep changing.

Even the dictionary, that basic tool of the journalist, isn't very helpful. Webster's defines news as "a report of a recent event; new information; fresh tidings... any matter regarded as interesting to newspaper readers or news broadcast audiences." But just watch the evening news and then read your morning daily, **The Hindustan Times and The Times of India** for the same day. Obviously, not every recent event or every fresh tiding gets reported. Just as obviously, journalists for different news organizations have different ideas about what will be interesting to their different audiences.

If you're a little confused at this point, you should be. Experienced journalists and scholars disagree about what news is and what it ought to be. Don't despair, though. There are broad areas of agreement - guidelines that the best journalists use, and that you can use, to determine which of every day's flood of events are most likely to be regarded as interesting by your particular audience. There are also two principles - accuracy and fairness - that don't change.

What News Was, Is And (Probably) Will Be

For generations journalists have used similar criteria in deciding the news value of each day's tidings; that is, to decide which among the almost infinite number of events, ideas and continuing controversies should be reported in the paper or on the broadcast news on any given day. Various editors, teachers and textbooks use varying labels for those criteria, but almost every journalist's list is similar to this one:

1. **Impact**- how many people an event or idea affects and how seriously it affects them determine its importance as news.
2. **Proximity**- the closer an issue or an event is to your audience, the greater the impact and news value it will have.
3. **Timeliness**- today's news is stale tomorrow.
4. **Prominence**- names make news; the bigger the name, the bigger the news.
5. **Novelty**- the unusual, the bizarre, the first or last or once-in-a-lifetime event is news.
6. **Conflict**- war, politics and crime are the most common news of all.

Just as important as these criteria, however, is the array of events and ideas to which the criteria are applied. Generations of journalists have thought of news as coming mainly from capitals, courthouses, city halls and cops. With a few exceptions, such as murders, sports and natural disasters, news has focused on governmental issues. This was true, for the most part, in the 1950s. It was still true, with the range of subjects starting to broaden just a little, in the 1970s. By the 1990s, however, the broadening had become an explosion while the most important criteria could be boiled down to three: relevance, usefulness and interest.

The explosion of subject-matter resulted from the belated recognition by journalists that government and politics were no longer

- if they ever had been - the most interesting forces in society. Nor were they the only important forces. People needed and wanted to know about everything from the biology of AIDS to the crisis in education, from Japanese business practices to the sex lives of the elderly. The traditional role of the press as school-master of the people had to be expanded to cover the full curriculum of contemporary life.

A 1990 report summarized the findings of a research project intended to create a newspaper for the year 2000:

1. Readers want news in their newspapers.
2. Readers want news to be relevant and to focus on them and where they live.
3. Readers do not want their newspapers to ignore what is going on elsewhere in the nation and the world.
4. Readers are not fooled by gimmicks or fancy designs. They will accept gimmicks and fancy designs only if they seem relevant to stories, make the newspaper easier to use or make the information easier to grasp. If the gimmicks are self- conscious or the designs radical, readers will reject them for interfering with ease of readership.
5. Readers want practical and useful information that helps them live their lives. They want tips and advice. As the lifestyles of readers change, editors must produce newspapers that focus on how they live.

You'll notice a certain repetition: Readers want, readers want.... This is the force that had driven, and will continue to drive, changes in journalists' definitions of news. Those generations of journalists who applied much the same criteria to much the same subjects knew they had readers, of course, and they cared - some - about giving those readers what they wanted. Today's and tomorrow's journalists will care a lot. Why Competition?

When people in the 2000s want new information, fresh tidings or just entertainment, they have dozens of choices- daily newspapers, weekly newspapers, magazines of all descriptions, books, dozens of cable channels, radio, and increasingly interactive computers. Every publication, every voice, every screen is competing for the time, attention and money of people who don't have enough of any of these commodities to go around.

That's why the journalism of the 2000s and beyond must strive for relevance, usefulness and interest.

How and Why News is being Redefined?

Let's look at the new criteria for making news judgments to see how journalists apply them in deciding what news is. Relevant stories are those that have a direct impact on the lives of readers. That impact may be emotional or it may come from war. Or the impact may come from the story's touching on the health or welfare of readers or their children.

When you are assessing the news value of a story or a potential story, your first question should be, "How will this affect the lives of my readers?" Events or ideas that are likely to touch the health, safety, environment of education or significant segments of the public provide the raw material for front-page stories. The more of your readers who may be affected and the more direct the effect, the more relevant-and therefore the more important-the story will be.

Relevant of course depends on your audience. Issues that are relevant to readers in New Delhi may be meaningless to people in Chennai. Journalists who want their work to be relevant can't be content with knowing the subject matter of their stories. They also must know the audiences for those stories.

Many recent studies show that people want news they can use. Usefulness has become an increasingly important criterion for assessing the news value of stories and potential stories as journalists have become increasingly aware of the competition for readers' time. Usefulness takes several forms. In a broad sense, any story that tells readers what is going on in the world is useful to people in a free society. A story whose content can help readers participate in their society is even more useful. You can imagine, for example, the argument and emotion on both sides of the debate over whether cigarette companies should sponsor sporting events. And in a university town such as Allahabad, many readers will take a personal interest in any effort to raise money for education. However, the most direct form of usefulness enables readers to do something directly that they want or need to do- to take some action.

The concept of usefulness has given rise to new newspaper sections and consumer magazines devoted to service journalism, the aim of which is to show people how to solve problems, make better decisions and generally improve their lives. Readers' preference for useful stories is even changing the way journalists write their most serious work, the investigation or analysis. In many cases today- and probably many more tomorrow- investigative and analytical stories include a section or a separate story telling how the problem explained or the abuse exposed can be corrected.

The final criterion for judging news value, interest, is built on relevance and usefulness, but it goes beyond them. Stories that touch readers' lives, especially stories that tell them how to improve life, are likely to be interesting. That isn't guaranteed. As you will realise storytelling is a craft that requires of its practitioners skill not only in choosing topics but in gathering information and in writing clear and compelling prose.

The most interesting stories are most likely to come from reporters who remember that, as the scholar James Carey put it, **"Journalism is a culture's conversation with itself."** That conversation will be painfully dull if it doesn't include some drama, some humour and lots of humanity. In other words, relevance should be defined broadly and not restricted to the grimmer aspects of existence.

The best stories meet all three criteria-relevance, usefulness and interest. Not every worthwhile story does. Some stories worth telling are relevant but useful only in the broadest sense. Some useful stories are interesting only to those who share the particular problem or need being addressed. And some stories are interesting just because of their novelty, the prominence of their subjects, or even because of the skill with which they are told. Today's readers want their newspapers to be complete. (Adapted from **News Reporting and Writing** by the Missouri Group)

Let us consider in more detail the meaning and nature of news.

(1) "News is what people are talking about".

- Anonymous

(2) "News is verified information that is relevant to public life".
- Ellen Hume

(3) "News is what protrudes from the ordinary".
- Walter Lippman

(4) "News is the departure from normal".
- Leo Rosten

(5) "News is what I say it is".
- David Brinkley

Any definition of news would cover all of the above and much more. News is "probably as old as mankind, perhaps older" says Robert E. Park in the essay **News as a Form of Knowledge**. Even the lower animals had some kind of communication which was not very different from news. The 'Cluck' of the mother hen is understood by the chicks as signifying either danger or food, and the chicks respond accordingly In that way, we are all reporters of one kind or another. In the initial stages, news consisted largely of information of interest to the wealthy and powerful people.

When the **News York Sun** appeared in America in 1833, the definition of news seemed to have changed. The character of news changed from being purely political or reflecting the social life of the rich. It began to sample the rich variety of everyday social life in the city- crimes, accidents, the occasions of high and low society. News became a commercial product. The story forms, such as the human-interest story, developed as a kind of marketing tool written to sell papers.

Today news is big business, a multibillion- dollar industry that employs thousands of people. News is the backbone of the thousands of daily newspapers published all over the world. As reporters in the twenty-first century, they will need to use the skills of news-thinking and news- judgment.

Defining what news is has never been more important than it is today.

News is not fiction or poetry or a term paper, although, at its best, it displays the power, beauty and discipline of all three. News is everything from India's score in the Cricket match against Pakistan to a girl's dilemma whether to live with the parents who adopted her and brought her up or her biological parents; from a vote on the foreign policy debates in parliament to the behaviour of the stock market. News is a commodity that is likely to increase in value because people want to know what is going on in the world, in their world, in their neighbourhood.

News is what happened yesterday. It's what's happening today and what will happen tomorrow. News is what somebody wants everybody to know. News is what someone else wants to hide. News is information about the way we live and the way we ought to live. News is what important people say and do. News is what ordinary folks say and do. News is what people should care about. News is information. News is knowledge. News is history. News is negative. News is positive. News is what people chat about at lunch counters and online. (Christopher Scanlan)

News is an ongoing, constantly updatable record of change. News helps people make the choices that citizens face in a democracy-to vote, to petition the government, to exercise constitutional rights. News protects the public from abuses by governments and private institutions. News helps parents, children, students, investors, homeowners, renters and everybody else who has any kind of interest in what is going on in the society, because news is current information about a community that not only informs, but also educates and inspires people.

In its totality, news is the daily chronicle of mankind- people talking, arguing, fighting, trading, planning, building and destroying, winning and losing, making love and making war. It is the story of individuals and nations, humanity and inhumanity; and any definition that omits the human element miss the point entirely. All news concerns human beings. Even when a story is primarily about natural phenomena-storms, eclipses, droughts, floods or earthquakes-we write about their effects on people or how people view them. We are human beings writing about human beings for human beings. (Neal and Brown)

News is not just a story, it's something more

To the writer of fiction, the story is in a sense its own end. But to the journalist, the story is only a container, a form in which news is presented. And it is easier to define the container than its contents. People generally agree on what constitutes a story, but they differ widely over what constitutes news.

News must be timely, factual information which has some value to the reader or listener. It may be enlightening, instructive, or only entertaining. It may be only an interesting tidbit to store away in the mind, something that adds to a person's general knowledge, or it may be information that can be put to use immediately, such as announcements of future events. Regardless of its nature, it can be considered news only if the reader sees some benefit in it.

Indirectly, of course, the public may benefit from almost any current, factual information. The more a person knows, the more he or she can talk about. People who gossip know this instinctively. And some people- salesmen, politicians, and others whose success depends partly on their conversational ability- approach the news consciously with the goal of having something to talk about. Reporters too can benefit from this approach. It they are well informed in several new areas in addition to their own, they seldom lack an "ice-breaker" to open an interview.

News may be defined as:

Anything you didn't know yesterday- If it doesn't somehow add to what you already know, it isn't news.

Whatever interests the reader- If it doesn't interest somebody, it's not news. On the other hand, some highly interesting information- gossip for example – may not be news because it lacks significance.

Tomorrow's history today- This is a good definition of the outstanding stories and even of some less attention-getting stories that are laden with statistics. But it gives news more importance than the bulk of it deserves.

Any change in the status quo – This approach is based on the notion that something must happen or there's no story.

The status quo itself – The prevailing situation which the public may ignore or take for granted, can be important news when it is made visible and analyzed.

A timely, factual report of events, ideas, and situations that interest the public- This may be the best definition of all. It combines timeliness and audience interest, and it is slightly less vague about subject matter. And, unlike the other definitions, it says the news isn't news until it is reported.

The list could go on for several pages. But perhaps the best advice to beginners is that if it's timely, something the general public hasn't heard or noticed before, if it interests you or an identifiable portion of your audience, then it's news.

The Relationship between News and Audience

Telling a story implies an audience. Defining news- which is the content of the journalist's story- involves determining the relationship between events and the interests of your public. Thus the concepts of story and news are inseparable from an awareness of audience or reader.

You may dream of writing the Big Story that will be read by everyone in the world, but it's only a dream. Even the most important international stories reach only a fraction of the world's population. And usually reporters write for a far more limited audience: the readers, listeners, or viewers in a precisely defined geographical area. The newspaper or broadcast station's first goal is to serve its own trade area. Most stories, therefore, are primarily of local or regional interest. The community- its economy, geography, history, traditions, and ethnic composition- plays a large role in determining what constitutes news.

News Holds Everyone's Interest

Regardless of their different interests, all our readers and listeners are human beings, and they are alike in all ways that one human being is like another. No study of the reporter's audience is complete, therefore, without some examination of what writers call "the human condition".

Primarily, people want stories that will:

(1) **Warn of imminent physical danger-** An outbreak of war or local violence, an approaching storm, an epidemic, an unsafe product, or adulterated food.

(2) **Report Developments that promise to extend life-** a peace agreement, a medical discovery, improvement in hospital facilities, a new system of keeping physically fit.

(3) **Expose threats to individual freedom-** political oppression, economic injustice, infringements of civil rights.

(4) **Help them improve their economic or political position-** simple informative stories about business developments and the employment situation, or explanatory or even instructive stories about managing investments, preparing for retirement, juggling the family budget or preparing the tax returns. A political or economic feature even may be a success story about a person the reader dreams of emulating.

(5) **Describe improvements or deterioration in the quality of living-** urban decay, the crime rate, vanishing wildlife, advancements in housing and recreation, changing mores, improvements in clothing and cooking.

(6) **Tell what is happening or is expected to happen to their children-** readers want to know what kind of world their children will live in and how educators are preparing them for it.

The news writer as a watchdog

To help protect their audience, many reporters view their role as that of a public watchdog. They stand ready to detect and report anything dangerous to the public's physical, economic, or political security- a hazardous drug, unsafe toys, business collapses, waste of public funds, political blunders, Pollution of the environment, racial discrimination, violence and injustices of many kinds. They try to provide information that will "keep the establishment honest".

Because of this watchdog function the press often is criticized as a purveyor of only bad news. Yet without this "bad" news, how would be the public warned? How could the average person acquire the information he needs to act with enlightened self-interest? The thoughtful editor realizes that "bad" news is one of his more important commodities, that somehow he must keep the reader informed without becoming a chronic alarmist.

Balanced News Judgment

The first step towards balanced news judgment is to recognize that the press has a responsibility to report progress as well as threats. Arms limitations, cancer treatments, reduced taxes, and shorter work weeks are at least as important as the more depressing stories. Any event or situation that affects the reader's security in any manner, favourably or unfavourably, is top priority news.

Kinds of News

Not all stories deal with life, death, taxes, food, clothing and shelter. And of those that do, not all are concerned with immediate action. Reporters write many "idea" stories about religion and philosophy which deal with universal interests but which are hardly "gut issues". In addition to such stories that appeal to the intellect, they write many that appeal largely to the readers' emotions- their vanity (they like to see their names in print), their curiosity about neighbours, their desire for a thrill, a shudder, or a laugh.

How can we classify such a wealth of subject matter with so many different goals? We could perhaps, talk of "hard" news (that which is immediately useful) versus "soft" news (that which has delayed value). Or "spot" news (highly perishable because of the time element) versus " feature" copy (usable anytime this season). Or we could departmentalize news into sports, home and family, city, state, national, and international. Or we could distinguish between the investigative story, which can require weeks of digging, and the publicity release which arrives without any effort on the reporter's part. We could even classify stories by whether they deal with events, ideas, or situations, or by whether they are informative, explanatory, or entertaining. Perhaps the wise course would be to avoid categorization completely. But to understand how professionals think, let's examine a classification system often used by working journalists. This divides stories into three categories - straight news, interpretation, and human interest. Like all classifications, this system is arbitrary, artificial, and often difficult to apply. Indeed, it is a rare story of any length that is entirely "straight" with no interpretation or human interest. Nevertheless, these three categories are used so commonly that the beginner at least should be aware of them.

Straight News

This often deals only with events. Straight news results from simple surveillance. Most routine stories-obituaries, meeting notices, traffic accidents, crime reports, and weather roundups- fall into this category. When city editors tell reporters to "play it straight", they mean to confine the story strictly to the facts and avoid any attempt to determine motivation or long- range consequences or arouse any emotional response in the reader. On most simple stories, reporters encounter no problem; they play it straight automatically. But on some sensitive development, editors may have to warn them against interpretation because motivation or consequence can't be determined immediately or because of danger of arousing violent public response. In reporting straight news, the reporter summarizes the action but takes special pains to avoid inferences, as in this example:

Uttaranchal to Energise NTPC Hydel Plant

New Delhi: State- owned power utility NTPC is pushing its Rs. 8,500- crore plan to diversify into hydel generation in right earnest, with the laying of the stone for a 600mw hydel project on the Alaknanda river, upstream of Vishnuprayag, at Lohari Nag Pala in Uttaranchal.

The foundation of the project was laid by junior power minister Jaywantiben Mehta and Chief minister N.D. Tiwari at Maneri in Uttarkashi on Saturday.

This will be NTPC's second hydel project after the 800mw project being constructed at Kol Dam in Himachal Pradesh at a cost of Rs. 3,500 crore.

NTPC has an MOU with the Uttaranchal Government for three hydel projects in the state at a cost of 5,000 crore.

The second unit of 360 mw capacity is planned on the Bhagirathi river at Tapovan Vishnughat 10 Km. from Badrinath. The third unit of 108 mw will be built at Lata Tapovan.

The units are to be commissioned in the 11th plan period.

Delhi could be one of the beneficiaries of the extra power that will flow into the northern grid.

NTPC is seeking technical expertise from French consultancy firm EDF.

While 30 percent of the funds will come as equity. 70 per cent through dept. The hydel foray is part of chairman CP Jain's plan to widen fuel base. Hydel capacity will help NTPC improve operational flexibility and optimise use of its generation infrastructure in accordance with demand, saving resources.

Jain feels this will be crucial for NTPC's corporate health once power sector reforms are completed and market mechanisms are in place.

NTPC will execute the hydel projects as part of its Rs. 80,000 crore plan to add 20,000mw capacity in the next 12 years. At present, it has a capacity to generate 19,435mw and produced 130.154 billion units in 2000-01.

NTPC reported a marginal jump in its net profit at Rs. 3,574 crore in 2002-03 against Rs. 3,540 crore in 2001-02.

New regulatory norms in terms of availability based tariffs and same past adjustments restricted the rise in net profit.

Notice that the reporter says nothing on his own authority in this example.

Interpretative News

This is an effort to tell what the facts mean in terms of causes and effects. Even the word "interpretive" is enough to start a controversy in some newsrooms, where editors may argue long and inconclusively over the definition of objectivity. For this reason, many working journalists never speak of "interpretive" pieces? They call them "backgrounders", "stationers" or "depth reports" if only to avoid arguments.

Interpretation, by whatever name it goes, deals more often with situations and ideas than with isolated events. It is explanatory writing, usually arising from analytical coverage of government, the economy, education, or social problems. It requires expert knowledge of the subject and an imposing array of facts, plus the ability to put a complex situation or idea into simple, understandable language. Reporters try to tell what the facts mean without resorting to speculation. Occasionally, when the meaning isn't clear, reporters may be forced to quote the speculation of other observers. If so, they must know the subject well enough to pick sources who can speculate with some authority.

Here is an example of interpretation based on knowledge of background information- facts that have been published before:

Asians Slammed for Filthy Habits

Wellington: The Mayor of New Zealand's largest city has criticized Asian immigrants for "filthy habits" such as spitting on sidewalks, a report said on Monday.

Auckland Mayor John Banks said regional civic and business leaders recently told him they were disgusted by immigrants, mainly from Asia, "using public pavements as handkerchiefs," the **New Zealand Herald** said. "I don't hold back in stopping them in the street and telling them in this country we don't do that", the newspaper quoted Banks as saying.

A reporter sought Bank's comments after the issue was raised by the local Tamaki Community Board at a meeting on February 18, the **Herald** said. Banks said the Auckland Regional Council, Tamaki Business Association and local retailers had also raised the matter of "notably Asians" spitting on footpaths.

"Many of them come from countries where spitting in public is acceptable and when they come here they assume it's the same", the **Herald** quoted Banks as saying. In a telephone interview on Monday, Banks was adamant that his comments should not be interpreted as part of an anti-migrant campaign.

Because the line between interpretation and editorializing is so fine, editors often discourage beginners from any attempt to "interpret". They prefer to assign interpretive stories to reporters who already have demonstrated the necessary knowledge, judgment, and skill to present interpretation fairly and clearly.

Human Interest News

In this kind of news, which usually focuses on an individual rather than a group, the actual subject is a feeling or an emotion. Writers however don't editorialize or express subjective reaction. They achieve their effect best by "putting the reader there", by showing the event or situation that arouses emotions or a sense of humour. This is sensory writing, close kin to fiction, and reporters often use narrative organization and other literary devices, they round out the story with colourful description, anecdote, dramatic quotes, or dialogue; but as in any other reporting, they never go beyond the provable facts.

Many human interest stories focus on an odd or unusual event, as in this example:

Dad 74, Mum 63, 1st Baby, Congrats

Coimbatore: A 63- year - old woman gave birth to a healthy baby boy on Monday at Erode, creating medical history and a new milestone in assisted reproductive technology. The boy has been named Thamathaputhran, meaning 'the son who rises late' in both Sanskrit and Tamil.

'I'm very happy. I never dreamt I would get a child at this age", said Pappathi from her bed at the Maruti Medical centre and Hospital.

"It's a healthy baby by all means. But it's been incubated as it is underweight (it's 1.75kg) at a Coimbatore Hospital for better management," said Dr. Nirmala Sadasivan.

Subramaniam is 74 and the couple had been childless for 47 years of marriage. Rules worldwide discourage assisted reproductive technology for couples beyond the age of 45. Subramaniam brought his wife here a year ago.

"Pappathi had reached menopause some 20 years back but they weren't ready to give up. We discouraged them. Then we thought, who're we to deny them the medical advances which ensures parenthood?" said the doctor.

Nirmala said it's blastocyst culture which made the miracle possible.

"The procedure is the same as for a 'test tube' baby. In that, we normally grow the egg, Zygote for two days in an incubator before placing if back in the uterus. But in blastocyst culture it's grown outside for five days".

Newsworthiness of the News

The evaluation of news is a highly subjective process. One editor may view the events of the day in the broad context of world history while another news to the old - fashioned notion that "a dog fight on main street is worth more than a revolution in Latin America". The first accuses the other of provincialism; the second retorts that the first is guilty of Afganishtanism. Editors are no more agreed on news value than are readers.

Still, no matter how they apply them, all editors measure news values by the same yardsticks. These are:

Significance - whether the event promises or threatens to change the course of history. An event's significance is determined by how many persons it will affect, to what extent, and for how long. The reporter asks *what will be the consequences.*

Magnitude - how much, how many, how big, how fast? Everything else being equal, a million is bigger news than a thousand. A plane crash that kills 120 is bigger news than one that kills five, and a hurricane with 200—mile-an-hour qualifies. The reporter asks how many are dead and **how much will it cost?**

Timeliness - The reader wants information that's new. The reporter asks when did it happen, and ordinarily tries to work the day into the first sentence to let the reader know that it's new. Priority usually goes to the latest action, but even an action that happened long ago may still be spot news if it is only now being disclosed. For example, any new information about Noah's Ark would be news.

Proximity - A two-dollar word for the local angle. If all else is equal, here is greater than there. Readers are interested most in those events closest to them. The reporter asks where.

Prominence - names make news. These are generally names of persons or institutions that already have aroused public interest. The name might be that of the president or a senator, a celebrity in sports or show business or an institution such as Harvard, the Indian Air Force, or the central bureau of investigation. The reporter asks, who.

Human Interest – A quality that every reader can relate to personal experience, recognize as a universal aspect of life. Does the story hit home? Here the reporter can examine only his or her own reaction.

(B) Deciding What is News

Before anything becomes news it must be reported. A professional reporter must be aware of the qualities that characterise a news story, the types of news that exist, and the differences in the way the various media cover news.

Many authors have tried to define news in a sentence or a paragraph. Such definitions help little because they tend to falsely imply that news is a static object rather than a complex process involving many parts (news source, editor, reporter, and the "news hole" or available space, to name a few) which influence each other. To quote one early text, news was "anything timely that is interesting and significant to readers",

Most such definitions stress **change** as an essential element of news. Current or possible future changes that affect a person make up the real stuff of news.

It also seems apparent, however, that certain things merit attention partly because they don't change. The National Advisory Commission of Civil Disorders in USA suggested that race relations remained static in the United States for centuries and the media ignored them. Society might have changed its ways more effectively, and with less pain, had media attention come before the "explosions of the late 1950s and 1960s. Likewise, in the early and mid - 1970s, journalists suddenly realized they'd largely missed stories on energy and the environment for decades. It took the painful "crisis" which doubled or tripled gasoline prices suddenly in 1973-74 to really put the energy shortage on media agendas. Before that, no news peg really drew editor attention to the problem.

In replying to this kind of criticism, many news executives would doubtless argue that magazines and specialized sections within the paper (for example, business news section) should describe that status quo so as to put change in perspective. The regular news columns might then report primarily change.

This argument has some merit. However, current discussions of interpretive reporting suggest the need to put events in perspective as one reports them. The distinction between interpretation and straight news reporting is not as clear as it once seemed. Certainly this issue will receive lively debate for years to come.

In the prevalent news system, reporters serve as agents for the newspaper reader, radio listener or television viewer. The reporter's basic job is to describe and interpret events all over the world (and indeed, the universe). News consumers have very little direct "eye witness" knowledge of most of these events.

Ideally, reporters write without fear or favour, letting the chips fall where they may. The guiding principle is a search for truth. Independence from special interests makes journalism important to every society- so important that some observers have called it a fourth branch of government.

Most often than not, however, reporters themselves are not witnesses to the events reported. And even where they are, they generally cannot fully comprehend these events without help. They must rely on a wide variety of **news sources** in explaining just what happened, why and with what probable results.

For example, in covering a fire, one must often ask firefighters just when and how they got things under control. Hospital officials need to tell the condition of victims. A resident of the burning house may clarify where, when and how the fire started. And so on.

In reporting on a new treaty, it's important to indicate what persons and resources might be committed in case of war. Such points are often more speculative than factual- they may require lots of reading between the lines which only lawyers and diplomats can do. Here again, reporters must depend on news sources.

In a nutshell, the good journalist serves as a critical, independent "middle person" between news source and audience, studying both carefully. Ignoring or forgetting either party is risky.

Those who worry only about appealing to an audience are apt to be sensation- mongers and of little value to community. So-called yellow journalism- dating back to the nineteenth century in America and still alive today- shows what can happen here.

News : A Matter of Judgment?

News is not an easy thing to understand or explain. Nevertheless, newspapers have become so popular that they have become almost a part of routine of every educated person. But life is so busy that the newspaper readers are in a great hurry. Studies show most of the newspaper readers spend less than half an hour on a daily paper. A typical reader is almost certain to skip a particular story unless he or she sees some reason for reading it. It follows that the newspaper which makes a habit of ignoring reader's interest will soon go bankrupt.

Each day, editors must select a few dozen or perhaps a few hundred, events among literally millions all over the world. Of these chosen few stories, only a dozen or so make the front page. The remainders get varied places on inside pages. The news judgment process is a complex one-so complex that it has baffled and worried journalism critics and scholars for decades. In the early 1920s, Walter Lippmann realized journalists must somehow simplify the whole business to survive. Wrote Lippmann: "Without standardization, without stereotypes, without routine judgments, without a fairly ruthless disregard for subtlety, the editor would soon die of excitement... The thing could not be managed at all without systematization, for in a standardized product there is economy of time and effort, as well as partial guarantee against failure."

Only in the 1960s did scholars begin probing the news judgment process with much precision. Here we will review some lessons from these studies. Today we realise the importance of judgment in news more than ever. It should be realised that reporters as well as editors judge the news. It's true that editors assign reporters to cover stories and decide which items go where in the paper. However, reporters must often help for at least three reasons:

(1) In covering a beat, the reporter will often run into a new, unexpected story lead. A city editor may never get wind of such leads unless the reporter thinks enough of them to pursue them further.

(2) Being close to a story, a reporter will normally be in a good position to judge how it will develop and how vigorously it should be pursued. Thus, intelligent editors often ask reporters for news judgment advice.

(3) In writing a story, the reporter must decide what facts merit lead place, what facts may go near the end, and which ones should simply be left out. In light of all this, it is not surprising that reporters influence the thinking of editors as well as the reverse. Sigal, in a recent study of **The New York Times** and **Washington Post**, found this to be the case.

The Rise of 'Objective" Newspaper Reporting

"When a dog bites a man that is not news, but when a man bites a dog, that is news".

(Charles Anderson Dana, editor and proprietor, **New York Sun**, 1982)

"Its primary office is the gathering of news. At the peril of its soul it must see that the supply is not tainted. Neither in what it gives, nor in what it does not give, nor in the mode of presentation, must the unclouded face of truth suffer wrong. Comment is free but facts are sacred.

(C.P. Scott, editor and proprietor, **Manchester Guardian**, 1922)

When we try to answer the question, "What is a newspaper"? We have to go back far beyond the invention of the printing press to a time when news was simply spread by word of mouth. It was during the fifteenth century that the English word 'news' broadly assumed the meaning familiar to us today by displacing the Old English notion of 'tidings.' Spoken news, whether in the form of gossip, sermons, ballads or tales, was an effective form of communication Still, it was always at risk of possible misinterpretation (deliberate or otherwise), to say nothing of faulty memories. Nevertheless, this type of information helped to sustain a shared sense of social order.

The first printing press in Europe astonished members of the public, even frightening some who regarded its capacity to make near perfect copies of texts as the 'black art' of the devil. Printed pamphlets or broadsides, which sometimes presented news narratives in the form of prose or a rhyming ballad, were slowly beginning to replace newsletters copied by hand by the start of the sixteenth century. News books followed next, the more sensational of which were often referred to as canards, which consisted of several pages of news usually about the same topic. Items of public interest included news of state announcements, victories in battle, royal marriages, executions of witches, and the like, as opposed to accounts of everyday events.

Throughout the 1600s, the news-books and related types of publications spoke to an ever expanding audience. Available in town and cities in bookshops and coffee houses, and sold in rural areas by hawkers and peddlers, they 'brought sex and scandal, fantasy, sensationalism, bawdiness, violence and prophecy to their readers: monstrous births, dragons, mermaids and most horrible murders; but they also brought items of news'.

It was not until the early eighteenth century, however, that the daily newspaper, with its wide coverage of subject matter, was fully established in Britain. The first daily was the **Daily Courant** which was launched on 11 March 1702 on premises 'next Door to the King's –Arms Tavern at Fleet Bridge'. The first regularly published newspaper in the American colonies was **The Boston News -Letter** which was established by the town's postmaster, John Campbell, in 1704.

By the close of the eighteenth century, then, the foundations were being laid for a newspaper press which, according to its champions, would come to represent to the world the epitome of democratic power, prestige and influence. Not everyone shared this view, of course, a point expressed rather forcefully in the words of one commentator writing in 1799: "The American newspapers are the most base, false, servile, and venal publications that ever polluted the fountains of writing- their editors the most ignorant, mercenary and vulgar automatons that ever were moved by the continually rusty wires of sordid mercantile avarice".

Most historical accounts of the rise of 'objective' journalism point to a series of crucial developments in the early decades of the nineteenth century concerning the 'pauper press in Britain' and the 'penny press in the USA'. In the pauper press an emphasis was placed on reporting news event which had a distinct 'human interest' angle, as they were perceived to possess a greater entertainment value. For example, in 1834 the publisher of the **Twopenny Dispatch**, Henry Hetherington, promised readers that they would find on its pages: "a repository of all the gems and treasures, and fun and frolic and 'news and occurrences' of the week. It shall abound in Police Intelligence, in Murders, Rapes, Suicides, Burnings, Maiming, Theatricals, Races, Pugilism, and all manner of moving 'accidents by flood and field'. In short, it will be stuffed with every sort of devilment that will make it sell."

The pauper press, mainly made up of weekly titles, stood in marked contrast to the so-called 'respectable press.' This even though these mainstream titles, as Williams remarks, were not particularly respectable: "there had been heavy direct bribery of journalists by Ministers, and official advertising was steered to papers favorable to Government opinion'. In the United States, the penny newspapers championed popular forms of journalism which were very similar to those initially embraced by the pauper press in Britain. **The New York Sun**, Which appeared on 3 September 1833, is generally regarded as the first of the penny newspapers. The contours of 'public opinion' were being quickly redrawn by this new type of newspaper which sought to claim for itself the status of being the people's voice in a society undergoing democratization.

For most of the penny newspapers, reporting 'the news of the day' entailed a commitment to a new, distinctive range of news values. In particular, the local 'human interest story' was to be prized above all others, for it best represented the conditions of contemporary life as they touched the experiences of 'the masses. These newspapers thus tended to restrict their coverage of party politics or issues of trade and commerce to matters of popular interest, electing instead to fill their pages primarily with news about the police, the courts, small businesses, religious institutions, and 'high society'. News from the streets and private households, especially suicides, fires and burglaries, had mass appeal. In this way the line between 'public' and 'private' life was effectively blurred. As James Gordon Bennett, declared: "We shall give a correct picture of the world – in Wall Street- in the Exchange-in the Police Office- in the Opera – in short wherever human nature or real life best displays its freaks and vagaries'. Thus in presenting to their readers a 'gastronomy of the eye' largely made up of 'the odd, the exotic and the trivial', to use Carey's terms these newspapers were expeditiously redefining what could and should qualify as news for 'ordinary people' in the context of their daily lives.

The introduction of the electric telegraph in the 1840s led to the emergence of journalistic 'objectivity' as a professional ideal one based on the presentation of 'unvarnished facts'. The news values of newspapers were being recast by a new language of dailiness, one which promoted a peculiar fascination for facts devoid of 'appreciation' to communicate a sense of an instantaneous present.

Current debates over whether or not journalism properly constitutes a fully fledged profession, one with specialized rules of method and ethical conduct (like medicine, law or engineering), date back at least to the early nineteenth century. It was about that time when the term 'journalist' was becoming widely used, although journalism itself was not held to be worthy of the efforts of a gentleman, let alone a gentle woman, with the possible exception of the writing of editorial leaders for the **Times**. Its gradual climb to 'respectable', if not prestigious, status encountered several difficulties along the way. An example of the sort of attack launched by critics includes that expressed by the philosopher John Stuart Mill: "In France the best thinkers and writers of the nation write in the journals and direct public opinion; but our daily and weekly writers are the lowest hacks of literature which, when it is a trade is the vilest and most degrading of all trades because more affectation and hypocrisy and more subservience to the baser feeling in others are necessary for carrying it on, than for any other trade, from that of the brother keeper up".

In the course of outlining the newspaper policies following his acquisition of the title, Ochs declared: "It will be my earnest aim that **The New York Times** give the news, all the news, in concise and attractive form, in language that is parliamentary in good- society, and give it as early, if not earlier, than it can be learned through any other reliable medium; to give the news impartially, without fear or favour, regardless of any party, sect or interest involved; to make the columns of **The New York Times** a forum for the consideration of all questions of public importance, and to that end to invite intelligent discussion from all shades of opinion.

This quotation highlights a convergence of the discourses of factual journalism with those of professional responsibility *vis-a-vis* the public sphere, in general, and the interests of its affluent readers, in particular. With its new motto of 'All the news that's fit to print', the **New York Times** sought to claim for itself the status of an open forum for debating public affairs. This when the boundaries of its definition of 'serving the public' were recurrently projected in a way which justified existing relations of power and privilege, namely those of wealthy white males, as being consistent with American democracy.

The appeal to 'objective', non- 'biased' reporting was slowly becoming institutionalized to varying degrees, throughout the 1920s in the growing professional culture of US and British journalism. Evidence of the gradual process of institutionalization is apparent in factors such as the following:

1. More reporters began to specialize in relation to distinct news topics (labour, science, agriculture, and so forth) using 'impersonal', fact-centered techniques of observation.
2. There was further refinement in news interview conventions leading to more aggressive questions being asked of public figure (the interview itself being a relatively recent invention)
3. More prominence was given to the by-lined news account.
4. Greater emphasis was placed on new genres of 'investigative' and interpretative' reporting, the latter being increasingly displaced from 'hard news' into political columns.

5. There was a more pronounced reliance on quotation marks for source attribution.
6. Finally, improvements in the relative degree of autonomy from the day-to-day control of both proprietors and editors were being secured.

◆◆◆

2

Basic Elements of News

There are three basic elements of news : Timeliness, Importance and Interest.

(A) News is Timely

The implication of the word 'News' is that it is always 'new', it is the result of the elections that have just taken place, the game that has just ended, the war that has just broken out, the verdict just given by Supreme Court, the fact, event or development that provides what journalists call the peg or reason to publish or broadcast News. It's what you didn't know when you went to bed or when you last turned on the television or went online. It's the fresh angle, the latest word, the most recent development.

The dictionary defines news as "a report of a recent event". Even so, something that occurred long ago may become timely. Archaeological finds routinely make the headlines: At the turn of the last century, an influenza virus killed at least 20 million people worldwide. The long-forgotten 1918 epidemic became front page news in March 1997 after scientists reported that they had found fragments from the Spanish flu virus in the formaldehyde-soaked lung tissue of a man who had died 79 years earlier. But whatever the time frame, news stories need to feel as fresh as bread straight from the oven, not the day-old loaf marked down to half price.

(B) News Is Important

News matters. Reporters, news directors and editors know that readers and viewers will be asking: "So what? Why should I care?" As the world becomes more complex, the job of the journalist broadens to include explaining news. It's not enough to simply report events, the reporter has a responsibility to also help the reader understand why this information matters-or should. When **The New York Times** reported the discovery of genetic material from the 1918 flu, it was quick to discuss the relevance. The story's fourth paragraph points out that researches "hope that understanding the genetic code of the Spanish flu virus might prepare scientists for the next influenza virus, which many scientists think is coming soon". The story provides context. With it, readers can understand why they should care about a pandemic that occurred decades before they were born.

As a reporter, you will have to anticipate readers' demand for relevance, whether it's a story about a burglary on their street or a scientific discovery on another continent. The ability to analyze events, developments and trends, to make connections that help people gain a better understanding of what it means to be alive today, is one of the aspects about journalism that makes it so challenging and rewarding. "Many readers say they look to the paper not for notification that something happened, but for context, meaning, perspective", Overholser says. "They want to know what difference it will make to them: who played, what comes next, what the various views are about, what took place".

Names, the saying goes, make news. People are killed in automobile crashes every day: only Princess Diana's death consumed the news columns and broadcasts for days. People are familiar with celebrities and so will be interested in news about them. Studies have shown that journalists focus principally on well-known personalities. But I believe the lifeblood of news is the ordinary people whose actions influence the news and whose lives are affected by it. Joel Rawson, executive editor of **The Providence Journal**, says journalists need to write the story that reveals a trend through the people who are living it. He calls it making "a new stencil" for the news. News isn't just what officials say and do. It's what regular folks say and do as well.

(C) News is Interesting

"News", an editor once declared, "is anything that makes a reader say, 'Gee Whiz'." In many newsrooms, it's the "Hey, listen to this!"

rule at work, the story that makes a reader, listener or viewer take notice and want to spread the word to a friend. At the heart of the news-gathering process is discovery. Reporters are the explorers of the 21st century, on the hunt for information that will interest people. The reporter has to have a sense of what people find interesting. That means talking to people about what they care about. Use yourself, your friends and colleagues as a barometer of interest.

Let's take a closer look at the kind of thinking that a journalist does when considering whether something is news:

1. It's timely. The news happened yesterday, so chances are good that readers don't know about it unless they witnessed the incident or they had friends or family involved in the accident.
2. It's important. An accident at a busy intersection that injured children riding in a school bus is a serious incident that a community needs to know about, not merely those who have a personal connection.

   Drunk driving is recognized as a serious social problem. It's a significant event that raises issues of important public interest.
3. It's interesting. There's nothing out of the ordinary about a fender bender in a mall parking lot. On the other hand, school buses are not normally involved in serious accidents fortunately. The fact that the students were band members on their way to a concert - an exciting occasion-lends the story an added poignancy.

With any story, you should be able to articulate the thought process behind your news judgment. Being able to do so will help you make the kind of quick decisions that responsible journalism requires. It will also help you produce the kind of stories that provide meaning in a complex world. Remember the three basic elements of news: timeliness, importance and interest. Frame them as questions:

Is it new?

Is it important?

Is it interesting?

How to Find News

Reporters must look beyond traditional sentinel posts to find stories in places that haven't been visited. "There is news in everything if you know where to look for it", John Hohenberg used to tell his students at the Columbia Graduate School of Journalism. I've found stories in the living room of a smoker's window, on a park bench, where an elderly man reminisced about his dead wife and the pain of living alone; at the gate to a state fair, where a boy hoping to make it into the **Guinness Book of World Records** stood shaking hands with all who passed.

This is perhaps the most amorphous side of news gathering. When they get experience, reporters don't need to ask, "What's the news?" They know it when they see it. Reporters see the world through a unique lens.

So how do you, a beginning reporter. Develop the reflexive skill of the veteran, able to pick out the relevant, interesting, important information from the mountains of data in your notebook?

News doesn't occur in a vacuum. Although a newspaper is one day's version of events, good journalism brings to its chronicling of the present a sense of the past and an appreciation for the future.

The reporter sizes up the situation, doesn't wait for the public relations official to dictate the story, and asks, "What do I think the news is?" Start early trying to figure out your story.

You do this by bringing background knowledge and understanding and an appreciation of your responsibility to make sense out of the events, incidents, developments and actions that occur every day. "We're awash in information. Yet at the same time there is less understanding and more difficulty in gaining that understanding", says journalism scholar James Carey.

There will be times, especially at the start of your journalism career, when you will come into a story stone cold, with little or no background. It can be a terrifying experience: walking into a courtroom where you don't understand any of the procedures, can sometimes badly make out what's being said and yet have to figure out what's happening and what it means. Or you are sent to cover a meeting of a group you know nothing about, or a speech, or a strike where you don't know either side the issues or what's at stake.

The only way to give yourself a head start is to begin thinking critically from the first moment, even if it's something you know nothing about.

Once you've found the news, how do you refine it? By asking the questions that place the news in context so your readers understand why the new technologies create new audiences, but fears that one will replace the other have proved groundless. To the newspaper and television watchers in the 1950 scene can be added a new generation who get their news from computer screens, (Courtesy of Library of Congress) being told certain information. The best stories relate a specific incident or event to the larger community. They take the extra step to help readers understand what impact a news event or development might have on their lives. That's why, when you write a story about property taxes, you don't say just that the City Council increased the property tax rate by 10 percent. You describe what the bill of a typical homeowner would be after the rate hike takes effect.

Knowing Your Audience

Audiences today can choose from a seemingly endless buffet of print, broadcast and online sources for news and information, many of which specialize in areas reflecting the interest of specific groups. The challenge for the 21st century journalist is how to analyze audiences and to gather and present news and information that will attract and hold the attention of people chronically confronted with increasing choices.

How can – and should – journalists think about audiences? You can think of them the way market researchers do, as audiences identified by their demographics – age, gender, race/ ethnicity, income, education, occupation, location. Trevor R. Brown, to think of their audiences in light of the varying roles people play in their personal and social lives.

As citizens who are part of "we, the people" on the one hand and as individuals with certain unalienable rights on the other, with responsibilities and interests, need and wants, as they seek to enjoy their liberty and pursue happiness.

As individuals who are children, siblings, parents, lovers, friends, workers, bosses, volunteers, consumers, fans, gamblers, pleasure seekers, investors and so on.

It may help to think of audience by thinking about how you read and react to stories you read or watch. Are you interested because you are a student, a fan of a particular team, a member of a racial or ethnic group, the child of an aging parent? Are you **not** interested because you are **not** a property owner, a registered voter, a member of the armed forces? How do your various roles and identities help determine what news and information you want? How well do your news sources reflect your need and the needs of other audiences?

Talk to your friends, neighbours, classmates and others in your community or on your beat. Ask then what stories news organizations miss, what stories need to be told. What stories move and instruct them. Ask yourself: What stories do you want to read but don't find online, or in the newspaper or on television? Those are the stories that you will probably bring the most passionate interest to and that you will report and write with intensity and integrity. "People resent journalists not because we fail to understand, but because they think we don't try", says Judy Bloch, an editor at the Raleigh **News and Observer.** "Instead of news hounds anxious to learn it all, we're seen as lazy know-it-alls. They don't mind if we ask questions; they do object when we assume the answers".

Seeing News as Culture

What you think is news says as much about you as it does the story you are covering. "Who writes the stories matter", Schudson says, on observation that underscores the need for diversity in the news business. Your view of news also will reflect your background, your community and your sense of audience.

News judgment is often a subjective process, one that reflects the interests, prejudices and mind-sets of reporters and editors.

Your view of news also will reflect your assignment. To the investigative reporter, news is corruption in high places. To the health writer, it's the development of a new surgical technique or the hazards of a new drug. The political writer sees news in the strategies and technique of campaign consultants. To the feature writer new can be found in the lives of ordinary people as well as celebrity interviews. The police reporter finds news, as I did as a new reporter, in the human dramas that occupy law enforcement agencies.

News in the Information Age

Everybody's talking these days about how technology is changing the news business. But that's not new. More than 100 years ago, the invention of the telegraph changed the way news was reported, spawning the so-called "objective" style of reporting that replaced partisan politics with factual coverage of government and business affairs.

What has changed is the public's access to news. In the 1800s you needed a telegraph key and knowledge of Morse code to get instant access to news. Since 1994, when the world wide web appeared, you need only a computer, modem and telephone wire to download news feeds. Cable and satellite television offers dozens of 24-hour channels and even the live (and sometimes raw and unedited) feed of network news operations. More important, the personal computer gives the average citizen access to sources of information that once only journalists had.

The Internet eliminates the role of "middleman" between newsmakers and news consumers. Electronic mailing lists and discussion groups have become a potent source of news. "The technology empowers viewers to determine what they want to know, rather than have that packaged by someone else."

"Yesterday's editors decided what was important and made it so", says Doug Clifton, executive editor of **The Miami Herald.** "Today the consumer is at least an equal arbiter of what is important. In a world of dazzling choices the consumer holds power that once the editor held alone." Despite their increased power, consumers will still need someone to filter news and help make it coherent. Even fierce cities of the media like Michael Crichton- the novelist who created **Jurassic Park** and who predicted in 1993 that the media would be a dinosaur, extinct - see a role for reporters in the future. "They will give me high-quality Information," Crichton says.

Technology changes news, the nature of it, how we get it, how we present it, whether the task is writing for the newspaper, the television or the computer screen, the process of thinking about news remains the same. The tools the reporter may use to collect and deliver the information will undoubtedly differ John Garcia, who created the online journalism program at New York University, predicts the 21st century journalist will be armed with a video camera, tape recorder, digital camera. No matter what the tool, the reporter still has to figure out what the news is. That thought process is what editors demand and consumers need. Bombarded by information, society needs the journalist to help it make sense of the world. "We now have too much information to rationally deal with on a daily basis", says Beth Agnew in an essay titled "Writing for the Third Millennium". "We need skilled professional help to turn that information into the currency of the next millennium-knowledge".

Personal Values in News

Journalists make important decisions on what events, phenomena and issues are reported and which are not. The personal values of journalists determine **which** stories are told and also **how** they are told. Generally these values coincide with the mainstream values of the society in which the journalists live.

Sometimes the concept of news becomes so difficult to define that it is left to the journalist to under stand whatever he wants to understand by it. So he may say, like Chet Huntley: **"News is what I decide is news"**. It seems to imply that events that go unreported aren't news. Regardless of an event's intrinsic qualities, such as the prominence of the people involved and the event's consequence and drama **it becomes news only when it's reported.** – John Vivian

White Huntley emphasizes the point that the journalist's judgment is indispensable in deciding what's news, he also underscores the high degree of autonomy that individuals have in shaping what is reported. While most reporters will agree on the newsworthiness of some events and issues, such as a catastrophic storm or a text proposal, their judgments will result in stories that take different stands and angles. On events and issues whose news worthiness less obvious, reporters will differ even on whether to do a story.

Journalists being humans and controlled by their personal likes and dislike most of the time, tend to reflect their personal values in news reporting. As John Vivian says: "The journalistic ideal, an unbiased seeking of truth and an unvarnished telling of it, dictates that the work be done without partisanship. Yet as human beings, journalists have personal values that influence all that they do, including their work. Because the news judgment decisions that journalists make are so important to an informed citizenry, we need to know what makes these people tick. Are they left-wingers? Are they ideological zealots? Are they quirky and unpredictable? Are they conscientious?

News reporters all over the world by and large adhere to the value system prevailing in their respective countries. Herbert Gans, an American sociologist, who studied stories in the American news media for twenty years, concluded that journalists have a typical American value system. On the basis of the study of Herbert Gans, John Vivian had identified Ethnocentrism, Commitment to Democracy and Capitalism, Small - Town Pastoralism, Individualism Tempered by Moderation, and Social order as the typical American values reflected in the news reporting of American journalists.

Quoting Herbert Gans at length, John Vivian writes, highlighting the above mentioned values:

- **Ethnocentrism** : American journalists see things through American eyes, which colours news coverage. In the 1960s and 1970s, Gans notes, North Vietnam was consistently characterized as "the enemy". American reporters took the view of the American government and military, which was hardly detached or neutral. This ethnocentricity was clear at the end of the wear, which American media headlined as "the fall of South Vietnam". By other values, Gans said, the Communist takeover of Saigon could be considered as liberation. In neutral terms, it was a change in government.

  This ethnocentrism creates problems as the news media become global. During the Persian Gulf War in 1991, CNN discovered that the commonly used world "foreign," which to American audiences meant anything non-American, was confusing to CNN audiences in other countries. Eager to build a global audience, CNN boss Ted Turner banned the word "foreign" and told anchors and scriptwriters that they would be fired for uttering the word. "International" became the substitute word, as awkward as it sometimes sounded to American ears. The semantic change was cosmetic, however, for the CNN war coverage continued, inevitably, to be largely from the American perspective, just as Gans found in his earlier studies. It is hard for all people, including journalists, to transcend their own skins.

- **Commitment to Democracy and Capitalism** : Gans found that American journalists favour democracy of the American style. Coverage of other governmental forms dwells on corruption, conflict, protest and bureaucratic malfunction. The unstated ideal of most U.S. journalists, said Gans, is that other societies do best when they follow the American ideal of serving the public interest.

  Gans also found that American journalists are committed to the capitalistic economic system. When they report corruption and misbehaviour in American business, journalists treat them as aberrations. The underlying posture of the news coverage of the U.S. economy, Gans said, is "an optimistic faith" that business people refrain from unreasonable profits and gross exploitation of workers or customers while competing to create increased prosperity for all. In covering controlled foreign economies, American journalists emphasize the downside.

  It may seem only natural to most Americans that democracy and capitalism should be core values of any reasonable human being. This sense itself is an ethnocentric value, which many people do not even think about but which nonetheless shapes how they conduct their lives. Knowing that American journalists by and large share this value explains a lot about the news coverage they create.

- **Small-Town Pastoralism** : Like most of their fellow citizens, American journalists romanticize about rural life. Given similar stories from metropolitan Portland and tiny Sweet Home, Oregon, editors usually opt for the small town.

Cities are covered as places with problems; rural life is celebrated. Suburbs are largely ignored. This small-town pastoralism, said Gans, explains the success of Charles Kuralt's long-running "On the Road" series on CBS television.

- **Individualism Tempered By Moderation** : Gans found that American journalists love stories about rugged individuals who overcome adversity and defeat powerful forces. This is a value that contributes to a negative coverage of technology as something to be feared because it can stifle individuality. Gans again cited "On the Road," noting how Charles Kuralt had found a following for his pastoral features on rugged individuals.

  Journalists like to turn ordinary individuals into heroes, but there are limits. Rebels and deviates are panned as extremists who go beyond another value-moderation. To illustrate this propensity toward moderation, Gans noted that "the news treats atheists as extremists and uses the same approach, if more gingerly, with religious fanatics. People who consume conspicuously are criticized, but so are people such as hippies who turn their backs on consumer goods. The news is scornful both of the overly academic scholar and the over-simplifying popularizer; it is kind neither to high-brows nor to low-brows, to users of jargon or users of slang. College students who play when they should study receive disapproval, but so do 'grinds'. Lack of moderation is wrong, whether it involves excesses or abstention." In politics, Gans says, both ideologues and politicians who lack ideology are treated with suspicion: "Political candidates who talk openly about issues may be described as dull; those who avoid issues entirely evoke doubts about their fitness for office."

- **Social Order** : Journalists cover disorder-earthquakes, industrial catastrophes, protest marches, the disintegrating nuclear family, and transgressions of laws and mores. This coverage, noted Gans, is concerned not with glamorizing disorder but with finding ways to restore order. To critics who claim that the news media concentrate on disruption and the negative, Gans noted a study of television coverage of the 1967 racial riots in the U.S.: only 3 percent of the sequences covered the riots, and only 2 percent dealt with injuries and deaths. A full 34 percent of the coverage focused on restoring order. Newsweek's coverage, according to the same study, devoted four times as many words to police and Army attempts to restore order as to describing the disturbances.

The journalistic commitment to social order also is evident in how heavily reporters rely on persons in leadership roles as primary sources of information. These leaders, largely representing the Establishment and the status quo, are the people in the best position to maintain social order and to restore it if there's a disruption. This means government representatives often shape news media reports and thus their audiences' understanding of what is important, "true" or meaningful. No one receives more media attention than the President of the United States, who is seen, said Gans, "as the ultimate protector of order".

Journalistic Bias

Critics of the news media come in many colours. Conservatives are the most vocal, charging that the media slant news to favour liberal causes. Liberal critics see it in the opposite light.

The fact is that journalists generally fall near the political centre. A landmark 1971 survey found 84.6 percent of journalists considered themselves middle-of-the-road or a little to the left or right. In 1983 a study found 91.1 percent in those categories. At the same time, Gallup surveys put 90 percent of Indians at the centre or a little left or right. The breakdown as follows:

Political Leanings	Journalists 1971	Journalists 1983*	Indian Adults 1982
Pretty far left	7.5	3.8	0.0
A little left	30.5	18.3	21.0
Middle of road	38.5	57.6	37.0
A little right	15.6	16.3	32.0
Pretty far right	3.4	1.6	0.0
No answer	4.5	2.5	10.0

* Percentages add up to 100.1 due to rounding.

The number of journalists who claimed to be a little leftist dropped considerably during the 12 years. Journalists had moved even more to the middle politically.

Despite such evidence, charges persist that journalists are biased. The charges are all the stranger considering that most Indian news organizations pride themselves on a neutral presentation and go to extraordinary lengths to prove it. To avoid confusion between straight reporting and commentary, opinion pieces are set apart in clearly labeled editorial sections. Most journalists, even those with left or right leanings, have a zealous regard for detached, neutral reporting. Although they see their truth-seeking as unfettered by partisanship, they recognize that their news judgments often are made in confusing situations against deadline pressure, and they are the first, in self-flagellating postmortems, to criticize themselves when they fall short of the journalistic goals of accuracy, balance and fairness.

Considering the media's obsession with avoiding partisanship, how do the charges of bias retain any currency? First, critics who paint the media as leftist usually are forgetting that news, by its nature, is concerned with change. Everybody, journalists and media consumers alike, is more interested in a volcano that is blowing its top than in one that remains dormant. This interest in what is happening, as opposed to what is not happening, does not mean that anyone favours volcanic eruptions. However, the fact is that change almost always is more interesting than the status quo, although it is often more threatening and less comfortable. When journalists spend time on a presidential candidate's ideas to eliminate farm subsidies, it is not that the journalists favour the change it's just that the topic is more interesting than stories about government programmes that are unchallenged. Because conservatives favour the status quo, it is natural that they would feel threatened by news coverage of change and proposals for change, no matter how disinterested and dispassionate the coverage, but this is hardly liberal bias.

The news media also are criticized because of the popular journalistic tradition: a belief that democracy requires the press to serve a watchdog function. Since the founding of the Indian Republic, journalists have been expected to keep government honest and responsive to the electorate by reporting on its activities, especially on shortcomings. Unless the people have full reports on the government, they cannot intelligently discuss public issues, let alone vote intelligently on whether or not to keep their representatives. Sometimes to the dismay of those in power, the news media are part of the system to facilitate change when it is needed.

In short, journalists' concern with change is not born of political bias. It is inherent in the nature of their work.

Variables Affecting News

News Hole

A variable affecting what ends up being reported as news is called the news hole. In newspapers the news hole is the space left after the advertising department has placed all the ads it has sold in the paper. The volume of advertising determines the number of total pages and generally the bigger the issue, the more room for news. Newspaper editors can squeeze fewer stories into a thin Monday issue than a fat Sunday issue.

In broadcasting, the news hole tends to be more consistent. 'A 30-minute television newscast may have room for only 23 minutes of news, but the format doesn't vary. When the advertising department doesn't sell all the seven minutes available for advertising, it usually is public service announcements, promotional messages and programme notes-not news- that picks up the slack. Even so, the news hole can vary in broadcasting. A 10-minute newscast can accommodate more stories than a 5-minute newscast, and, as with newspapers, it is the judgment of journalists that determines which events make it.

News Flow and Staffing

Besides the news hole, the flow of news varies from day to day. A story that might be played prominently on a slow news day can be passed over entirely in the competition for space on a heavy news day.

In a single day in 1989, death claimed Iran's Ayatollah Khomeini, a Central figure in United States foreign policy: Chinese young people and the government were locked in a showdown in Tiananmen Square; the Polish people were voting to reject their one-party Communist political system: and a revolt was under way in the Soviet Republic of Uzbekistan. That was a heavy news day, and the flow of major nation-rattling events pre-empted stories that otherwise would have been news.

Whether reporters are in the right place at the right time can affect coverage. A newsworthy event in Nigeria will receive short shrift if the network correspondent for Africa is occupied with a natural disaster in next-door Cameroon. A radio station's city government coverage will slip when the city hall reporter is on vacation, or if the station can't afford a regular reporter at city hall. When Iraq invaded Kuwait by surprise in August 1990, it so happened that almost all the U.S. and European reporters assigned to the Persian Gulf War, were on vacation or elsewhere on assignment. An exception was Caryle Murphy of the **Washington Post**. Like everyone else, Murphy hadn't expected the invasion, but she had decided to make a routine trip from her Cairo bureau for a first-hand look at Kuwaiti affairs. Only by happenstance did Murphy have what she called "a front-row seat for witnessing a small nation being crushed." Competing news organizations were devoid of eyewitness staff coverage until they scrambled to fly people into the region.

Perceptins about Audience

How a news organization perceives its audience affects news coverage. **The National Enquirer** lavishes attention on unproven cancer cures that the **New York Times** treats briefly if at all. The **Wall Street Journal** sees its purpose as news for readers who have special interests in finance, the economy and business. NBC's **Consumer News and Business Channel** are established to serve an audience more interested in quick market updates, brief analysis and trendy consumer news than the kind of depth offered by the journal.

The perception that a news organization has of audience is evident in a comparison of stories on different networks' newscasts. CNN may lead newscasts with a coup d'etat in another country, while CNBC leads with a new government economic forecast, MTV with the announcement of a rock group's tour, and "A Current Affair" with a six-month-old gory homicide that none of the others covered at all.

Availability of Material

The availability of photographs and video also is a factor in what ends up being news. Television is often faulted for overplaying visually titillating stories, such as fires, or rapes and underplaying or ignoring more significant stories that are not photogenic. Newspapers and magazines also are partisan to stories with strong accompanying visuals, as shown in an especially poignant way when a Boston woman and child sought refuge on their apartment's balcony when the building caught fire. Then the balcony collapsed. The woman died on impact; the child somehow survived. The tragedy was all the more dramatic because it occurred just as fire fighters were about to rescue the woman and child. Most journalists would report such an event, but in this case the coverage was far more extensive than would normally be the case because Stanley Forman of the **Boston Herald-American** photographed the woman and child plunging to the ground. On its own merits, the event probably would not have been reported beyond Boston, but with Forman's series of dramatic photographs, clicked in quick succession, the story was reported in visual media-newspapers, magazines and television-around the world.

Radio news people revel in stories when sound is available. A barnyard interview with a farm leader, with cows snorting in the background, is likelier to make the air than the same farm leader saying virtually the same thing in the sterile confines of a legislative committee chamber.

Competition

One trigger of adrenalin for journalists is landing a scoop and, conversely, being scooped. Journalism is a competitive business, and the drive to outdo other news, organizations keep news publications and newscasts fresh with new material.

Competition has an unglamorous side also. Journalists constantly monitor each other to identify events that they missed and need to catch up on to be competitive. This catch-up aspect of the news business contributes to similarities in coverage, which scholar Leon Sigal calls the **consensible nature of news**. It also is called "pack" and "herd" journalism.

In the final analysis, news is the result of journalists' scanning their environment and making decisions, first, on whether to cover certain events and, then, how to cover them. The decisions are made against a backdrop of countless variables, many of them changing during the reporting, writing and editing processes.

Non-Newsroom Influences on News

While journalists are key in deciding what to report and how, non-newsroom forces in news organizations sometimes play a role too. These forces include advertiser-sensitive executives, who do not always share the truth-seeking and truth-telling agendas of journalists.

Executive Orders

While reporters have significant roles in deciding what makes news, news organizations are corporate structures with the people in charge having the final work on matters big and small. It is publishers and general managers and their immediate lieutenants who are in charge. Some of these executives make self-serving decisions on coverage that gall the journalists who work for them, but such is how chains of command work.

Also appalling is excessive pandering to advertiser interests. It is impossible to catalogue the extent to which journalistic autonomy is sacrified to curry favour from advertisers, but it can occur even at generally respected news organizations. **The Denver Post**, a metro daily of USA once offered a shopping mall 1,280 column inches of free publicity, equivalent roughly to 72,000 words, a small book, as a bonus if the mall bought 30 pages of advertising. The puffery cut into space that might have been used for substantive news.

Some news organizations lean over backwards not to alienate advertisers, which also can undermine journalistic autonomy. NBC once invited Coca-Cola, a major advertiser, to preview a television documentary that reported the company benefited from exploited migrant agricultural workers. NBC then acceded to Coca - Cola's requests to drop certain scenes.

Such policy decisions are more common among smaller, less financially solid news organizations, whose existence can be in jeopardy if they lose advertisers. To avoid rankling advertisers, the Las Cruces, New Mexico, **Sun - News** as on example, once had a policy against naming local businesses that were in the news in an unsavoury way. When police raided a local hotel room, the **Sun-News** offered not even a hint of which hotel was the site of the raid.

Rarely do media owners acknowledge that they manipulate news coverage to their own economic interests, which is why it is difficult to document the frequency of these abuses. Sociologists who have studied newsrooms note that publishers hire managers whose thinking coincides with their own, and these managers hire editors and reporters of the same sort. The result is that decisions made by reporters do not differ much from those that the publisher would make in the same situation. With the sociology of the newsroom shaped by largely like-mined people, seldom does anyone need to order manipulation explicitly.

In fairness, it must be said that media owners generally are sensitive to their truth-seeking and truth-telling journalistic responsibilities and assiduously avoid calling the shots on news coverage. Those who answer to a call other than journalistic soundness are within their court-recognized First Amendment rights, which allow media people to exercise their freedom responsibly as well as irresponsibly. Journalists who are bothered by wrong-headed news decisions have three choices: persuade wayward owners of the wrongness of their ways, comply with directives, or quit and go work for a respectable journalistic organization.

Advertiser Pressure

Special interests try to exert influence on coverage, such as squelching a story or insisting on self-serving angles. Advertiser pressure can be overt. The managing editor of the Laramie, Wyoming, **Boomerang** complied with a request from the newspaper's own advertising manager not to carry a state agency's news release warning people that Bon Vivant vichyssoise, possibly tainted with fatal botulism bacteria, had been found on the shelves at a local grocery. The ad manager was fearful of losing the store's advertising. In fact, the store did yank its advertising from a Laramie radio station when it aired the story, and the station's news director reported that he was warned to back off from the story and later fired.

Generally, advertiser clout is applied quietly, as when the Ralph's grocery chain cancelled a $250,000 advertising contract with the Los Angeles **Herald Examiner** after a story on supermarket overcharging and short weighing. From a journalistic perspective, the sinister result of canceling advertising is the possible chilling effect on future coverage.

Advertiser pressure can be even more subtle. Many airlines insist that their ads be deleted from newscasts with stories about airline crashes. This is reasonable from an airline's perspective, but it also is a policy that has the effect of encouraging stations, especially financially marginal stations, to omit crash stories, which would contribute to listeners having a clearer sense about air safety.

To their credit, most news organizations place allegiance to their audiences ahead of pleasing advertisers, as Terry Berger, president of an advertising agency representing the Brazilian airline Varig, found out from **Conde Nast's Traveler**, a travel magazine. After an article on air pollution in Rio de Janeiro, Berger wrote to the magazine: "Is your editorial policy then to see how quickly you can alienate present and potential advertisers and at the same time convince your readers to stick closer to home? I really think that if you continue with this kind of editorial information, you are doing both your readers and your advertisers a disservice. For this kind of information, people read the **New York Times**. I therefore find it necessary to remove **Conde Nast's Traveler** from Varig's media schedule." Unintimidated, the magazine's editor, Harold Evans, did not recant. Not only did Evans print the letter but he followed with this comment: "Mrs. Berger is, of course, entitled to use her judgment about where she advertises Brazil's national airline. I write not about that narrow commercial issue, but about her assertion that it is a disservice to readers and advertisers for us to print true but unattractive facts when they are relevant. This goes to the heart of the editorial policy of this magazine.... We rejoice in the enrichments of travel, but our aim is to give readers the fullest information, frankly and fairly, so they can make their own judgments."

Pressure From Sources

Journalists sometimes feel external pressure directly. At the court house, valuable sources turn cold after a story appears that they don't like. A tearful husband begs an editor not to use the name of his wife in a story that points to her as a bank embezzler. A bottle of Chivas Regal arrives at Christmas from a sports publicist who says she appreciates excellent coverage over the past year. Most journalists will tell you that their commitment to truth overrides external assaults on their autonomy. Even so, external pressures exist.

The relationship between journalists and publicists can be troublesome. In general, the relationship works well. Publicists want news coverage for their clients and provide information and help reporters line up interviews. Some publicists, however, are more committed to advancing their clients than to advancing truth and they work to manipulate journalists into providing coverage that unduly glorifies their clients.

Staging events is a publicity tactic to gain news coverage that a cause would not otherwise attract. Some staged events are obvious hucksterism, such as Evil Knieval's ballyhooed motorcycle leaps across vast canyons in the 1970s and local flagpole-sitting stunts by celebrity disc jockeys. Covering such events usually is part of the softer side of news, and, in the spirit of fun and games and diversion, is relatively harmless.

Of more serious concern are staged events about which publicists create a mirage of significance to suck journalists and the public into giving more attention than they deserve. For example, consider.

- The false impression created when hundreds of federal workers are released from work for an hour to see an incumbent's campaign speech outside a government office building.
- The contrived "photo opportunity" at which people, props and lighting are carefully, even meticulously arranged to create an image on television.
- Stunts that bring attention to a new product and give it an underserved boost in the marketplace.

Staged events distort a balanced journalistic portrayal of the world. Worse, they divert attention from truly significant events.

Gatekeeping in News

The individual reporter has a lot of independence in determining what to report, but news work is a team effort. No individual acts entirely alone and there are factors, such as gatekeeping, which affect what ends up on the printed page or over the air.

Gatekeepers' Responsibilites

News dispatches and photographs are subject to changes at many points in the communication chain. At these points, called gates, gatekeepers delete, trim, embellish and otherwise try to improve messages.

Just as a reporter exercises judgment in deciding what to report and how to report it, judgment also is at the heart of the gatekeeping process. Hardly any message, except live reporting, reaches its audience in its original form. Along the path from its originator to the eventual audience, a message is subject to all kinds of deletions, additions and changes of emphasis. With large news organizations, this process may involve dozens of editors and other persons.

The gatekeeping process affects all news. A public relations practitioner who doesn't tell the whole story is a gatekeeper. A reporter who emphasizes one aspect of an event and neglects others is a gatekeeper. Even live, on-scene television coverage involves gatekeeping because it's a gatekeeper who decides where to point the camera, and that's a decision that affects the type of information that reaches viewers. The C-SPAN network's live, unedited coverage of Congress, for example, never shows members of Congress sleeping or reading a newspaper during debate, even though this happens.

Gatekeeping can be a creative force. Trimming a news story can add potency. A news producer can enhance a reporter's field report with file footage. An editor can call a public relations person for additional details to illuminate a point in a reporter's story. A newsmagazine's editor can consolidate related stories and add context that makes an important interpretive point.

Gatekeepers at Work

Most gatekeepers are invisible to the news audience, working behind the scenes and making crucial decisions in near anonymity on how the world will be portrayed in the evening newscast and the next morning's newspaper. Here, slightly updated, is how mass communication scholar Wilbur Schramm explained gatekeeping in 1960:

"Suppose we follow a news item, let us say, from India to Indiana. The first gatekeeper is the person who sees an event happens. This person sees the event selectively, noticing some things, not others. The second gatekeeper is the reporter who talks to this 'news source'. Now, of course, we could complicate this picture by giving the reporter a number of news sources to talk to about the same event, but in any case the reporter has to decide which facts to pass along the chain, what to write, what shape and colour and importance to give to the event. The reporter gives his message to an editor, who must decide how to edit the story, whether to cut or add or change. The message goes to a news service where someone must decide which of many hundreds of items will be picked up and telegraphed to other towns, and how important the story is, and therefore how much space it deserves.

"At a further link in the chain, this story will come to a United States news service and here again an editor must decide what is worth passing on to the American newspapers and broadcasting stations. The chain leads us on to a regional and perhaps a state news service bureau, where the same decisions must be made; always there is more news than can be sent on – which items, and how much of the items, shall be retained and retransmitted? And finally when the item comes to a local newspaper, an editor must go through the same process; deciding which items to print in the paper.

"Out of news stories gathered by tens of thousands of reporters around the world, only a few hundred will pass the gatekeepers along the chains and reach a local newspaper editor, who will be able to pass only a few dozen of those on to the newspaper reader".

◆◆◆

3

Elements of News Writing

I keep six honest serving men
(They taught me all I know)
Their names are what and why and when
and how and where and who

(Rudyard Kipling)

These are the components of every news story, the raw material you must collect, interpret, organize, and transmit. On the surface, they may seem simple, merely a list of the questions an inquisitive child might ask about almost anything. But they are precisely the questions many people stop asking when they outgrow childhood. And they are not as simple as they first appear. Getting the five W's and H accurately and completely is a daily difficulty. Learning to express them clearly, gracefully and objectively can be a lifelong project (Neal and Brown)

"The purpose here is to refine our understanding of Kipling's components", continue Neal and Brown. To do this, we must examine attribution, identification, back grounding, motivation, consequence, descriptive detail, style, and word usage everything a reporter puts into a story. For some of these subjects, this chapter can serve only as on introduction to be expanded in later chapters".

What's Happening? And So What?

"Let's see what's happening in the world today..." with these words, millions of readers pick up their newspapers each day expecting to find the answer- not everything that happened, of course, but everything of interest to them. And they expect the reporter to provide the answer as quickly as possible in each story, preferably in the first dozen worlds, as in this example.

Saigon - The last American Combat troops left South Vietnam today.

What happened or what is scheduled to happen is the essence of the story. The central fact that gives it unity and this is how most news stories begin. We satisfy the reader's curiosity and establish the story's point in the first sentence.

What Happened

New Delhi: Mrs. Indira Gandhi the Prime Minister of India was assassinated by her own security men guarding the Prime Minister's House.

What's Scheduled : New Delhi – Live television coverage is scheduled for Thursday night when Sri Atal Behari Vajpayee will be sworn in as the new Prime Minister of India heading the National Democratic Alliances.

Theoretically, the introduction (known as the lead) can be built around any of Kipling's serving men. But in practice, most stories focus immediately on **what or who**, the action or the person or group involved. And usually focuses on the significance or magnitude of a specific action - the most important thing that happened, plus what it means to the reader. The reporter anticipates. The reader's "So what?".

A new postal regulation could cost taxpayers money if its violators aren't informed soon, says a New Delhi postal official.

Instead, the letters are returned to the sender or channeled to the dead letter office.

However, the increase in volume of dead letters may offset the regulation's worth, said R.K. Ruta, customer relations supervisor at the main post office. He said the increased cost of handling eventually will be passed on to tax payers through increases in taxes or postal rates.

The lead paragraph traditionally is only a single sentence, although exceptions are common. The idea is to make a point in the first sentence, then expand upon it throughout the story. The point- the most important action and its significance- usually is summarized in a simple, declarative sentence of fewer than 25 words.

The lead usually makes a positive statement. The story is seldom concerned with a **lack** of action (if nothing happens, usually there's no story), nor is it often concerned with **routine** activities. An organization's day – to – day functions, for example, seldom constitute news, the reader can legitimately ask "So what?" or "Who Cares?"

Negative : Storm clouds of partisan fervour don't seem to be rising over the State capital after a proposal to operate the legislature along party lines.

Positive : Statehouse sources **indicated little support** today for a plan to reorganize the Legislature along party lines.

Who Cares? : The Baptist Women's Society met Thursday afternoon at the home of Mrs. Fred Winter.

Slightly Better : Bandages supplied by the Baptist Women's Society have been sent to foreign missions, members of the organization were told on Thursday.

Emphasis on newsworthy action continues throughout the story. And action is expressed in verbs, which is why Stanley Walker, city editor of the old New York **Herald-tribune**, urged reporters to "give me the verbs- the little verbs that cut and whip and leap and soar". He could hardly have picked shorter, livelier examples. He might have added however, that cutting and whipping don't happen by themselves; somebody causes them. Each action requires an actor. And to make the sentence active, place the actor before the verb; tell who or what cuts or whips, leaps, or soars, for example.

Passive : It is hoped that construction can be started by September.

Active : Jones said he hoped the **firm** could start construction by September.

Despite editors' preference for active voice, a passive lead sentence sometimes is more successful in getting the reader's attention if it places the most important action closer to the beginning of the sentence. This is often accomplished by construction that places the source of the information at the end. For example:

Active : According to the communications minister, Government today awarded a Rs. 5 million contract for a new post office in Culcutta.

Passive, But More Effective: A Rs. 5 million contract has been awarded for a new post office in Culcutta, the communications Minister announced today.

The rule is to place the most important information at the beginning of the lead. In the example above, the contract award is more important than either the person who announced it or the party who made the award.

What Happened : Action may be Physical or Mental

When something happens, the reporter may tell us what a person or a group did or how people were physically affected. In most of the cases, however, what people think, feel or believe is more important than their immediate physical action. This kind of action can only be found out from what a person or group of people said.

It is sometimes found that reporters pay too much attention to what people say and rather little to what they do. There are areas like politics and business in which sometimes actions may contradict public statements. In many such cases the reporter gives the speaker's words exactly as spoken by him without verifying whether they are true. Yet words, even when they are false, can be an important news. It has been physiologically demonstrated that what people say and write are often the most important things they do. Words can start or end wars. They can even be a major factor in turning defeat into victory as happened in the cases of the German dictator Hitler, the British politician Churchill and the American President Roosevelt. Whatever may be the nature of words, the reporter should regard them as a powerful from of action.

The problem lies in determining which words are worth reporting. This becomes a never- ending exercise in judgment, with no absolute rules to guide you. But we can speculate that words are worth reporting when:

(1) They add something new to man's total knowledge.

(2) They come from an expert on the subject or a person with access to important facts.

(3) They come from a person of political or economic power capable of translating words into action.

(4) They express the opinion of a significant number of people.

In summary, the news value of words often depends as much on who says them as on the words themselves. The reporter considers the source: Is he or she an expert? A person in a position of power? One with access to the facts? Does the individual represent the consensus of a large group? How reliable has the person been in the past? What, if anything, does he or she have to gain by these remarks?

No matter how reliable a news source may be, much of what is said must be evaluated carefully. The simple fact that the source is speaking for publication will influence both what is said and how it is said. If the person is talking about himself, for example he will normally portray his actions favourably. This is a distorting factor which reporters can mitigate by careful selection and paraphrase. Also they must consider which of the facts and opinions expressed are of interest to readers- as well as to the speaker. Instead or reporting direct quotations, reporters more often summarize the speaker's thoughts in their own words a technique that enables them to eliminate the irrelevant or prejudicial. But in selecting, summarizing, paraphrasing, or even quoting the speaker directly, reporters constantly must guard against distortion of the original meaning, tone, or emphasis of the remarks being reported.

Who : Identification and Attribution

Every person mentioned in a news story must be identified clearly and adequately. At the minimum, this means first and last names, role in the news, title or occupation, and sometimes age and address. Reporters collect much of the same personal information that is required on a job application. Whenever possible, they get it directly from the person they are identifying, but they also make extensive use of directories, clipping files, and secondary personal sources.

Reporters use the term "identification" as much as low enforcement officers do. In this sense, identification means supplying enough factual information about a person to differentiate him from any other person with the same name.

Minor details of identification that appear in the obituary are likely to be ignored in the **personality sketch.** In this form the writer tries to portray the subject as a living human being, showing him or her in some newsworthy light. his usually requires at least minimal physical description and considerable direct quotation. We bring people to life by showing what they do and telling what they say, characterizing them by their opinions activities, and habits of speech and gesture.

The safest position on identification is that it's always better to have too much, rather than not enough. This is particularly true of **police news** or other stories that involve the possibility of defamation. Identification is an important element in libel law, and the reporter can't afford to make a mistake or even to be ambiguous. We must make certain that the identification is clear, that nobody else by the same name could argue that he has been defamed.

Pitfalls of Identification

In their haste to identify individuals, reporters often distort stories by the way they use labels. These may be titles (Dr., Col.), common nouns of occupation (salesman, banker, dishwasher), or adjectives (blond, black, conservative, radical). Some such labels are unavoidable; without them, the story would lack meaning. But they always must be used with discretion. The reporter not only must make certain that the label is accurate, but he also must determine (1) whether it reflects adversely on the individual, (2) whether it reflects adversely on some larger group, and (3) whether it is pertinent this particular story.

At worst the labeling noun can be libelous. Any identification that imputes crime or moral turpitude is libelous *per se* and must be avoided unless the newsgathering organization is prepared to defend it. Tags of this kind include *killer, prostitute, thief, black-mailer, traitor, racketeer, lecher,* and *deadbeat.* Luckily, most journalists are aware of the danger in name-calling at this level. They avoid such tags entirely unless a person has been convicted of the specific crime. And even after conviction, the tag must be approached with caution. How many persons must an individual kill before we are justified in calling him a killer? How much, and how often, must a person steal before we can call him a thief?

Name-calling is easy to avoid. A more difficult problem, however, is the subtle stereotyping that may result when we classify a wrong- doer as *a black militant, a veteran, a student activist, a draft protester,* or even an *unemployed dishwasher.* By implication we may be convicting the group as well as the individual. Is it important to the story to give the person's race or occupation? Sometimes yes, sometimes no. In any case, however, we can't assume that all blacks are militants nor that all students are activists. Nor can we assume that all black militants or student activists are wrongdoers.

Another common danger is the adjective of inference. *Examples include conservative, reactionary, liberal, radical, outspoken, boisterous, modest, shy, beautiful, and rugged.* Each of these adjectives involves a subjective evaluation by the writer. The traits they suggest have been inferred, a process that must be classified as editorializing. With rare exceptions, such adjectives should be eliminated from all news copy.

Even the concrete descriptive adjective in identification can cause trouble. Is it important that a defendant is long-haired and pimply-faced? or is it irrelevant and potentially prejudicial? Some editors avoid the issue by eliminating virtually all adjectives, objective or otherwise, in every story. This is an extreme position which leads to dull, lifeless copy, but in certain sensitive stories it is perhaps the best approach. In handling adjectives, the reporter must be guided by his subject matter.

The subject of the story- the nature of the action-also influences identification by title. A professor, military officer, or medical doctor may trade on his title to gain public acceptance for views totally unrelated to his field of expertise. For example, a physician who is also a city councilman may express opinions on a proposed ordinance that has nothing to do with medicine. Because he is a councilman, his views are legitimate news. But should he be identified as "Dr."? Some editors say no; others are willing to accord him the title on first mention, then drop it thereafter. Perhaps the best way is to identify him only as a councilman, the role in which he is speaking.

Identifying Organizations and Concepts

Organizations, like individuals, must be identified sufficiently to make them understandable to the reader. Merely giving the name, however, often isn't enough. Proper nouns tell us very little. What is the purpose of this agency or organization? How does it function? How is it financed? Who is in charge? Who are the members? What are their views? Who influence them? Many stories do little more than answer these questions in detail about organizations that the average person reads about daily but never really understands. The reader recognizes a familiar name and often curiosity ends at that point. Investigative reporters dig beneath the noun to get at the verb. They are interested more in what the organization *does* than in what it is called.

An organization is nothing more than a group of persons united in a common activity. A simple appositive phrase of nonrestrictive clause is often sufficient to identify an organization by its activity, its membership, or both. For Example:

The Travel & Tourism Association which promotes tourism in India and abroad. The rural Electrification Administration, which lends money at low interest to rural power cooperatives,.....

Every reporter quickly discovers that many organizations are not all they appear to be. Some espouse one purpose but practice another. Often their goals can be clarified only by a careful study of the individuals who compose their leadership. Other organization exist primarily or paper. They have an imposing letterhead and an impressive list of officers - who may never have met. Such "organizations" may consist only of a file folder at the back of some person's desk drawer. Before a reporter accepts a news release from any organization, he or she should at least verify its existence and determine its goals.

Abstract concepts are difficult to identify for the same basic reasons that organizations are. In each instance, something complex has been reduced to a label which robs it of meaning. We categorize an activity or an idea by giving it a name, tell ourselves that we under – stand it, then quickly forget everything but the label. This is a form of mental shorthand that is sometimes helpful but often crippling. If reporters expect to convey meaning clearly, they must frequently looks at the contents behind the label.

Some concepts have a relatively specific meaning. Parity, for example, was routinely defined for years by the Associated Press as "a price calculated to give the farmer a fair return on his produce in terms of prices he must pay." (One might argue that this is an inadequate explanation, but the AP at least recognized that some explanation was necessary.) The theory of relatively, too, can be defined, although an adequate definition might take several pages.

More abstract concepts-democracy, capitalism communism, human rights dignity of man – have only whatever meaning the user chooses to give them. As a reporter, you should avoid them,·except when you are forced. As a reporter, you should avoid them, except when you are forced to use them in direct quotations. When news sources begin speaking in such vague abstractions, try to bring them back to earth by asking for concrete examples. Then, when you write the story, you can ignore the abstractions and focus on something tangible.

Who Says : Attribution

The body of a news story consists of attributed and documented detail which adds up to, and expands upon, the lead's opening statement. Essentially, reporters show the reader fact after fact and where they got them. Because they must present much information on some authority other than personal knowledge, reporters are constantly telling the reader "who says." They attribute the information to its source, either explicitly or by implication. This gives authority for reporting any event which a reporter didn't personally witness, any fact which isn't already accepted as common knowledge or easily verifiable from public records. And opinion always must be attributed. This means that in speech stories and others dealing largely with opinion and unsubstantiated declarations, almost every sentence must contain some version of "he said".

The primary reason for attribution is fair play. Readers are justified in asking where the information came from so that they can judge its value according to their perception of the source's expertise or proven reliability. Like the reporter, the reader considers the source. And for this reason reporters often attribute information to a source with high credibility even when they could present it on their own authority. They know the reader will be more likely to believe the information when it comes from a person in a position to know.

Reporters also attribute much information to persons simply to keep their channels open. The policeman or minor public official who sees his name in the paper will be more likely to cooperate with the reporter than will the person who is ignored. The wise reporter often tells "who says" even when it isn't necessary.

Specifically, what *must* be attributed? Even professionals disagree, so it's impossible to lay down an all-inclusive list, but these guidelines may help:

1. **All direct quotations** - Unlike the fiction writer, the journalist avoids "orphan quotes". He attributes every direct quotation clearly, usually at the first natural pause, so that the reader has no doubt about who is speaking.
2. **All statements of opinion** - This applies whether they are quoted directly or paraphrased.
3. **Any potentially defamatory statement which libel law allows newspapers to publish in the public interest**- This applies primarily to testimony in court or statements made by MPs or legislators on the floor of their legislative houses.
4. **Anything newsworthy that a public speaker or interviewee says** - There may be an exception to this rule if the speaker is merely recounting background information which either is generally accepted as fact or easily verifiable from other sources.
5. **Anything obtained from another periodical publication** - Even when the publication or the individual story isn't copyrighted,

professional courtesy requires attribution. If the information is spot news, the reporter should attempt to verify it. If it can't be verified, the reporter still may use information from a reliable publication if it is attributed.

Although reporters tend to think of attribution as a protective device, it is no protection by itself in a libel suit. If a public speaker commits slander (oral defamation), the newspaper commits libel (published defamation) if it quotes him. The speaker, the publisher, and everyone who handles the story is legally liable. As a matter of practice, usually only the publisher is sued for damages. Reporters may lose nothing but their jobs- and the chances of getting another.

When in one tense, always in the past

All stories are based on knowledge of past action, even when they concern future events. This is because nobody can predict the future with any degree of confidence. Astronomers, political scientists, and economists may try (always based on their knowledge of the past), but their best calculations could be wiped out at any moment by a nuclear accident. With this pessimistic possibility in mind, journalists seldom attempt to predict the future without considerable qualification.

Reporters know they can't say for certain what will happen tomorrow or even what will be happening at the moment the reader sees a story. Therefore, they write most stories in the past tense or the past participles. Instead of writing that "the President will meet the press Tuesday," they write that "the President has scheduled a press conference for Tuesday", The President may change his mind or die of a heart attack, or the press may decide to ignore him. None of these events may be likely, but reporters can't be sure. They play safe by putting the story in the past.

One dependable way of putting the future into past tense is to add attribution. For example, instead of writing only that "Construction of a new crosstown expressway will begin next week," the reporter adds "Highway Director Sam Johnson announced today." If construction doesn't start, we can then blame Johnson. We didn't say it would start, only that Johnson said it would start.

Reporters who do not understand the reasoning behind editors' insistence on the past tense may produce awkward and illogical sentences. Thinking (wrongly) that every verb must be past tense, a reporter may write:

Manmohan Singh said he thought the war was immoral.

The meaning more likely is:

Manmohan Singh said he thinks the war is immoral.

(If, of course, the war continues and Manmohan Singh survives until press time.) Most of the time, we can assume that any expression of opinion should be put into present tense. Persons who voice opinions seldom change them overnight.

In practice, the general rule of writing mostly in the past tense is often ignored. But the reporter who is devoted to accuracy will be careful when and how the rule is violated. He or she will tell the reader only what is known for certain.

When Needn't Be Today

Most stories for afternoon newspapers or broadcast contain "today" near the verb in the first sentence. Similarly, stories for morning newspapers usually contain the day of the week in the same place. The theory is that the lead should tell the reader not only what happened, but also the fact that it's news.

Many editors have criticized overuse of the "today" lead, especially among news service reporters. They point out that the overall situation often is more important than the most recent action, and that the writer may weaken the story by playing up a relatively minor development in eagerness to be first with the latest. Instead of straining for a "today" lead, the writer should keep the entire story in its proper perspective. If the early action is more important than the later, then perhaps the lead should focus on something that isn't entirely new. Sometimes this is best accomplished by using present progressive tense ("is threatening") or present perfect ("has developed") instead of the traditional past tense. Present perfect (present tense of the auxiliary plus the past participle) is especially convenient. It allows us to eliminate the day of the week, so that we can build a lead around old action without announcing its age.

Expressing Time

Newspapers have developed several conventions for expressing time. The general rule is to be as specific as possible. This rules out such relative terms as yesterday, tomorrow last year, and next month. Instead, we write Monday, Wednesday, 2003 and July. And in an announcement, "this evening" becomes "8 p.m. today."

When an event falls within a week of publication, we normally use the day of the week. If the time is more distant, we use the month and date. The conventional method of expressing time is to write hour, day or date, then place, thus:

The committee will meet at 9 a.m. Thursday at City Hall.

If, however, the meeting is scheduled at a more distant time, it might be more logical to place the date before the hour, thus:

The committee will meet Sept. 18 at 9 a.m. in city Hall.

Time as Context

Each event occupies a place in space and time (or space-time, if you prefer). This context of where and when, the relation of an event to others in space-time, helps give a story meaning. By giving precise time and place, elapsed time, and sequence of events, we enable the reader to make many mental associations. For example, he can relate the event to his own experience ("Why, I was just two blocks away at the time that happened!") or perhaps to his personal schedule ("I'm booked for a night class, but maybe I'll go to that concert instead).

Precise time and Place

The exact hour and place is a necessity in every story of a future scheduled event. If we don't supply the hour, the building or address - and sometimes even the room number - reader who would like to be there won't have the necessary information. The announcement story fails to fulfil its basic function without this specific information.

The exact time also may be important in a story of a past action, especially if it is violent or dramatic. We try to pin down the exact time and place of many such events - fires, disasters, accidents, military attacks, and major crimes. This helps the reader relate the event to his own whereabouts or to other events that were happening elsewhere at the same time. And it often says something important about the event. An armed bank robbery at noon, for example, may be witnessed by hundreds. Many persons may be in physical danger. This makes it a much bigger story than a burglary at 11 p.m. when nobody is around.

Many past-action stories, of course, concern routine events or actions that occur over a span of time- sports events, speeches, or interviews, for example. The exact hour is irrelevant in reporting such stories; we can easily settle for "Tuesday night in Nehru Auditorium."

Elapsed Time

Most of us are aware that a three-day brush fire or a six–hour surgical operation is worth attention. Usually prepared speeches which take some time both to prepare and to deliver are more significant (if not necessarily more sincere) than offhand remarks, and deserve greater attention. We also recognize the news value of speed records, whether they happen to concern sports events, reaction time to emergencies, or six- day wars in the Middle East. The amount of time elapsed during any particular action may or may not be an important factor in the story, but it is something the reporter always should note and consider.

Elapsed time has other aspects which journalists occasionally overlook. If, for example, a year passes without an arrest after a mysterious homicide, it may be time to review the case with a new story. And we probably should pay some attention to any scientific report that results from years of research.

Sequence

The order in which events occur often helps the reader understand them better. For example, in interpreting a politician's strongly worded comment, a reporter might ask: Does it come after a rival's attack? Does it come immediately before election day? Does it come after a reporter's questions? Or was it volunteered?

The fact that B follows A doesn't necessarily mean that B is caused by A, but often their relation in time has considerable significance. For example, if a policeman hits a suspect over the head, the reader will understand the action better if he is told that first the suspect kicked the policeman in the groin. The objective reporter doesn't say that the first action caused the second. He merely relates them in their proper time sequence and lets the reader decide for himself.

And most readers are quick to read cause and effect into a time sequence. For example, if the reporter writes that the chancellor of the university submitted his resignation three days after his wife filed for divorce, who would not assume, rightly or wrongly, some relationship between the two events? If there is any danger that the implications of the time sequence might misrepresent the facts, the reporter should investigate the matter further - or at least exercise caution in the way he or she reports the sequence of events in order to avoid such misrepresentation.

Where : More About Context

As we observed earlier, place often is expressed in conjunction with time. But in the interest of keeping a lead brief and readable, "where" sometimes may be delayed. This is a frequent practice in speech stories. The lead usually consists of what was said, when, and by whom. The second paragraph then sets the scene by telling where, to whom, under what circumstances. The standard procedure for the third paragraph is to return to the lead's central statement and develop it further.

The technique is similar to the "action shot" and "establishing shot" used in film production. We get the reader's attention first with action, then we establish setting.

The extent to which we specify "where" depends largely on the reader. In writing for local readers, we often identify a location by naming a well–known building. But if the building isn't known to nearly all readers, we should also include the address. Sometimes the only "where" necessary is the name of a city.

How : Select Your Verbs Carefully

Telling readers "how" means describing action well enough so they can visualize it and perhaps even "hear" it. This is seldom attempted in straight news stories. Reporters simply write that something happened without trying to describe how it happened. Sometimes how is obvious, sometimes it is irrelevant. Even when it would improve the story, it may require more words than the subject merits.

One problem with telling "how" is that it sometimes requires detailed description that slows the narration. And it may be pointless: why tell how a person crossed the street when we can simply say that "he crossed the street"?

Still, some description of action can be a valuable asset – provided it is accurate, objective, and economical. And much of it can be accomplished by careful selection of verbs. By choosing a specific descriptive verb, we can often eliminate the necessity for adverbs or long phrases of explanation. For example:

The policeman moved down the alley.

The policeman moved rapidly down the alley.

The policeman hurried down the alley.

or

The plane came down low over the crowd at high speed.

The plane buzzed the crowd.

or

Sitting down in a relaxed fashion with one leg draped over the arm of the chair, he explained....

Slumping down in the chair, he explained...

The goal is to make each verb say as much as possible. Writers should avoid long, qualifying phrases or clauses and even look twice at the simple adverb. Adverbs are especially suspect when they modify adjectives. If writers are tempted to use such vague, intensifying adverbs as "very" or "slightly," they probably have picked a poor adjective.

How was It Said?

The verb of attribution deserves special consideration. For the sake of liveliness as well as preciseness, often it is tempting to use one of the many specific verbs denoting the manner in which some thing was said: *exclaimed, shouted, declared, drawled, pronounced, sneered,* etc. Some substitutes for "said" are relatively colourless. These include *added, continued, remarked, and suggested.* But most verbs that tell how a person said something are loaded with connotations.

Thus any departure from the neutral "said" must be considered cautiously. The story can be slanted drastically – often unconsciously – merely by substituting such verbs as *confessed, admitted, protested, jeered, quipped, noted, or pointed out.* "Admitted" implies guilt or error; "pointed out" implies that whatever the speaker said is factual. Even the simple "according to" has a slant: it suggests that the reporter takes no responsibility for what the person has said.

In deciding on a verb of attribution, a reporter must always decide whether the verb he or she has in mind is truly descriptive or merely a personal inference. Whenever there is doubt, the reporter should restrict himself to "said".

How Much and How Many : Be Specific

When editors tell reporters to "be specific," they mean to name and identify everyone and everything, to give the exact hour, the calendar date, exact ages and addresses, even room number. Here are only a few examples:

Vague	Specific
toddler	3- year–old boy
senior citizen	75- year- old man
late in the summer	on Aug. 30
this evening	7:30 p.m. today
holocaust	fire that left seven dead
on Main Street	at 121 W. Main St.
gale	35- m.p.h. winds gusting to 55
a small crowd	50 persons
traffic pileup	six-car collision
large deficit	Rs. 35 billion deficit

A second glance at the list above should make one thing clear: the command to be specific often means to put numbers into your story - ages, dates, addresses, hours, measurements, dollars and cents, exact amounts of anything. Numbers are the most precise form of expression we have.

But don't stop merely with exact numbers. Pay particular attention to numerical change. Whenever possible, compare and contrast. Is the runner's time a record? What was the previous mark? How much time did he shave off it? And this year's Rs. 15 – million city budget - what is the percentage of increase from last year? (If it's a decrease, you have an even bigger story.) Mere numbers without comparison may be meaningless, so do a little simple arithmetic. Don't make the reader figure it out for himself. To give a story meaning, try to relate the new and unfamiliar to what is already known.

Despite the value of figures, you can't use them as substitutes for words. Your goal is to tell the story clearly, and an overdose of statistics may confuse the meaning instead of clarifying it. The reader is slow to absorb numbers, and the radio or television listener often finds it impossible. If numbers can't be spread out readably through a story, then the print reporter should group them into a table. And the television newscaster had better get an artist to prepare a chart. As for radio, the broadcaster can only use round numbers and hope that the ear will absorb them - and distinguish "billion" from "million"

Why : Motivation, Cause and Consequence

The old United Press posted a sign in each bureau to remind staff members to "Always Ask Why." News reporters today are following this advice more than ever. But beginners should be warned that the answer to "why" is only as good as the person who gives it. Wise reporters automatically ask the question but do not automatically present the answer. They weigh the answer with unusual care.

"Why?" almost always calls for a personal judgment. It asks the target of the question (1) to evaluate human motives - often the person's own, (2) to try to determine a cause and effect relationship, or (3) to predict consequences. The source may be totally incapable of doing any of these, but the chances are that he or she will try. Most people try to answer any question put to them, regardless of ability.

Motivation

When "why" requires people to explain their own motives, they generally can be expected to show their actions in the best possible light, portraying themselves as acting unselfishly in the public interest. They may be correct or they may be lying. In any case, they are unlikely to be objective, which is why the self-report is always suspect – whether the interviewer is a policeman, a psychotherapist, or a news reporter.

When the respondent is a public official, the explanation of motives may be a thinly disguised version of "the end justifies the means" or an attempt to gloss over poor results with honourable motives. A pragmatist would observe that means are ends in themselves and that "good" motives recalled after the event can't change the facts of an action.

If the event in no way involves the source, you have a better chance of getting an objective, disinterested explanation of motives – provided the source has any means of knowing the motivation for an event in which he or she was in no way involved.

Cause – Effect Relationship

There are at least three pitfalls inherent in cause-effect reasoning, with a good deal of overlapping among them:

1. **Oversimplification** – This is assigning a single, simple cause to a complex effect. "Poverty causes crime. "Permissive parents have produced a generation with no respect for authority." (The latter statement not only oversimplifies the cause, but also begs the question since it must first be established that we do, in fact, have a generation with no respect for authority).

   If a situation is at all complex, it usually has several causes of varying degrees of significance. When your sources appear to be over simplifying, ask whether they can think of any other factors that may be involved.

2. **Confusing correlation in time or place with causation** – "The Democratic Party has been in power at the beginning of every major war of this century. Clearly that party is to blame for the lack of peace in our time."

   As this example indicates' confusing correlation with causation is often a form of oversimplification. The coincidence in time (or some other factor) is used to justify a cause - effect relationship.

3. **Confusing chronological sequence with cause–effect relationship** Like confusion of correlation with causation, this is the after–that–therefore- because–of- that) *post hoc ergo propter hoc*) fallacy on which a great deal of advertising depends: "She's beautiful. She's engaged. She uses Pond's." It also occurs in many other contexts, sometimes more by implication than direct statement: "After watching three bloody whodunits on television, Smith drew a pistol and shot his wife." The suggestion of a cause–effect relationship in this statement is too strong, unless there is other evidence besides the time sequence to indicate that the television viewing influenced the assault.

Consequences

Closely related to the question of "why?" is the question of "what now?" What will the consequences of this event, action, or situation be? In fact, what promises, or threatens, to result from the action usually is more important than why it happened.

But here again, there is a danger of oversimplification. If a situation is at all complex, it is likely to produce more than one effect. When a speaker asserts that "Recent Supereme Court rulings concerning police techniques only coddle criminals," he or she is overlooking all the effects of these judgements except one. If someone assures us that the election of a particular candidate will mean lower taxes, we must not only ask why, but also what else will result from the election of this candidate.

A request for a prediction of consequences may assume an unlikely degree of clairvoyance. Reporters should consider the respondent's record of reliability before encouraging him to become a prophet. And they should also look for concrete evidence that bears out such predictions. Answering the questions of "what now?" or "what then?" is not an easy matter. But wherever possible reporters, and readers should attempt to evaluate an action by its consequences or probable consequences.

Backgrounding : A Substitute for "Why"

Every story must be written so that it stands alone; that is, it must be complete in itself. Reporters must supply enough information to explain the action fully, even when this means repeating something that has been published dozens of times. The story should never force the reader to go back to previous edition in order to understand the latest action. Supplying this information – telling the reader what has transpired before – is known as "backgrounding".

At the lowest level, backgrounding rehashes only enough recent history to make the story meaningful to a stranger who might be passing through town. A typical example is the brief paragraph in a trial story that tells who was killed, when, and where, none of which might have been mentioned in that day's testimony. Another kind of backgrounding is the compare–and–contrast section that might appear in almost any story: comparing last month's living costs with the figures for the same month a year ago, comparing a new union contract with pay increases won last week in another industry. Another recaps an entire week's developments in a given situation.

Whatever the variety, backgrounding is explanatory writing of a special kind. It consists of factual information, not theorizing. The nature and extent of the content is guided by the axiom that the writer should never underestimate readers' intelligence, but never overestimate their information. We can assume an average education but no specific knowledge of the story at hand.

Backgrounding, by itself, doesn't necessarily tell readers "why." But often it accomplishes that goal at least partially by implication. By recounting related events, we place the story in the perspective of time, often giving readers the information they need to draw their own conclusions.

In a continuing story, the professional may supply the necessary minimum of backgrounding from memory. Sometimes, however a reporter may have lived with the story so long that he or she has lost perspective. The more a reporter knows about the story, the more difficult it may be to put himself in the place of the uninformed reader. Reporters may fall into the trap of assuming that the reader knows everything that they do and inadvertently omit some essential fact. An alert editor usually will spot the omission and throw back the story for an insert. The beginners, often working without an instructor or editor, can test the clarity and completeness of a story on a friend or relative. If the reader doesn't understand, more backgrounding may be required.

Backgrounding in depth means that a reporter must read - reference works, public documents, or at least the back issues of his own newspaper. An explanatory feature may be 90 percent backgrounding obtained by library research, with only the public's current interest as its news peg. (adapted from Neal and Brown).

◆◆◆

4

Writing an Exciting and Origional News Story

If a newspaper reads and looks like the same as yesterday's newspaper or that before the day before yesterday, we begin to wonder if the newspapers, by and large stick to the formula story. Therefore, Neal and Brown tell us in their book **Newswriting and Reporting** that one of the ever-present headaches of journalism is the trite story. "This is the piece written to prescription-the story you seem to have read a thousand times before, with only the names changed. It is "fill-in-the-blanks" writing, with a limited number of standard forms for each standard subject. Once the reader recognizes the subject-an engagement announcement, a wedding, a routine death, a traffic fatalily, or a high school basketball game - he knows almost exactly what information will be presented and in what order. After all, how many ways can you say that Susan Smith became the bride of Jonathan Jones? Or that Samuel Brown died at 86 ? With such material, how can you avoid producing a cliché? Is it even worth the effort to try ?"

Before we answer these questions, let's first try to determine what makes a story trite. Presumably, the problem lies either in the content or in its expression. The prime offender conceivably could be the subject, itself, the list of facts about that subject the overall organization, or the individual words or phrases-any individual element that is dull, commonplace, or worn out by repetition.

Most trite stories, however, are the product of more than one overworked element. A commanplace subject itself is seldom the culprit. Literature amply testifies to the facts that infinite variations can be played upon a familiar theme and works of art can be created out of the most trifling human experience. Nor is the problem simply familiar organization; one can write sonnets or three act plays for a lifetime without being accused of banality. And although many reporters have a penchant for the hackeyed phrase (a weakness fostered by the pressure of deadlines), few readers are offended by common place language. If any one element is more at fault than the others, it is the standard set of facts that we supply for all stories in a given class. But what truly makes the story trite is the total combination - the use of a familiar form and familiar language to present familiar facts about a familiar subject.

In searching for original combinations, beginners may feel defeated from the start. Day after day they must write about the same subject-death, taxes, weather, and violence-and they are limited by law, ethics, style, and the policy of the organization as to what they can say in each story. Further, their best efforts toward originality may be frustrated by old fashioned editors who reject any story that doesn't follow the inverted pyramid form. It is easy to argue that all the words, all the subjects, and all the acceptable combinations already have been used, that journalism is trite by nature. But all this is rationalization. The problem usually is not in the restrictions of journalism; it is in the limitations of the individual reporter's mind, imagination, or methods.

Reporters who continually produce cliches –unless they are observing rigid company policy- are cases of arrested development. They have learned part of their craft, but not enough. And what they have learned has had a tendency to blind them to what they have missed.

The Function of Formulas

Consider how we learn to write. We begin with imitation. As children we watch the teacher's hand movements and try to shape our letters exactly the same. We group the letters into words exactly the way the teacher shows us; we arrange words and punctuation marks into sentences according to the teacher's prescription. We innovate only in a limited sense. We create sentences, essays, stories and poems that are original in content but rigidly stereotyped in phrasing and organization. In other words, we write according to teacher-approved formulas.

Sometime in adolescence, experimentation may replace imitation. Talented young writers aspire to "originality". Perhaps they encounter Faulkner or Joyce- in which case experimentation may be only another form of imitation-or perhaps young writers begin to think for themselves, with no such revolutionary models as guides. At any rate, they begin to fret at formulas. They want to rearrange the language, throwing out every trite word or phrases, every restrictive form. If they succeed, they may become so original that nobody understands them. They may end by talking only to themselves.

Writers who want their stories to be covered repress the urge to revolutionize the language. Instead, they use familiar words in their most commonly accepted meanings. They are aware that only a fine line separates the familiar from the trite. Therefore they organize stories into patterns the reader will recognize and accept. They also trite familiar subjects. The writer gives readers what they want in the form they expect to see it. To do otherwise would be to disappoint the readers, confuse them, and risk losing them.

However, the danger is not in the formula itself, but in the reporter's readiness to accept it for every story that seems to fit the category. Used properly, formulas, like recipes, can be helpful. They enable reporters to check their work to be sure they have put in all the essential ingredients in appropriate order. With the help of a formula, beginners can turn the story out fast, get it past the editor, and tell the reader all he needs to know. And words won't be wasted. Pressed for time or space, beginners may find the solution to all their problems in the formula story.

The formula specifies only those facts that are absolutely essential, and it spells out nothing more than an acceptable way of telling them. Because it provides no guidelines for anything out of the ordinary, either in content or treatment, the result inevitably will be a cliche. And a formula will never do for any story of consequence. Hence, the writer who never gets beyond formula writing remains forever a mechanic, incapable of handling anything more than simple events.

Outgrowing the Recipe

To become more than a word mechanic, you must:

1) **Change Your way of looking at people and events:** Instead of noticing only similarities between one occurrence and another, you also must observe differences.
2) **Collect more information:** Often a formula story is the result of half-done reporting, the reporter simply quite when the minimum requirements were fulfilled. A complete job would have produced a different story.
3) **Increase Your Vocabulary:** As your stock of words grows, so does your total knowledge. And the more you understand, the less likely you will be to oversimplify a story.

Possible Revolutionary Remedy

When the beginner thumbed through the back issues for a story "just like" the one he or she had to write, the motive was better than the logic. Adoption of a model is a sensible step at an early stage, but it is a mistake to assume that any two stories are exactly alike. They may have strong similarities, but each is unique in some respect.

One revolutionary remedy would be quit classifying stories entirely, to approach each event or situation as if nothing quite like it had ever happened before. Instead of saying, "Ho, hum-here's another just like the last", the reporter might try for a while to adopt a wide-eyed attitude of a child who finds everything novel and exciting. But this is neither entirely realistic nor practical, except as a short-term learning experiment. It would be foolish to go through life with a "gee whiz" approach to every minor happening. No editor would tolerate it, for reporters who ignore relationships and similarities are as immature as reporters who see nothing else.

Although professionals continue to classify stories for convenience, they are constantly alert for any clue that the information may be more than routine. Automatically, they look for an "angle", a "different slant", for some hint of a significant departure from the norm. This, after all, is one of the earmarks of a good story-action that is somehow out of the ordinary. And reporters who can't find something different, after searching hard, either have only a formula story or no story at all.

Reporting is the Foundation

Many reporters seem able to spot an "angle" almost immediately. They focus quickly on something unique in an otherwise ordinary situation. If you listen to the questions such reporters ask, you can almost visualize the lead that is taking form in their minds. They find the angle first, then shape the opening questions to develop what will be the lead. Last, they fill in any gaps in the obligatory information by asking routine questions. They have become so story conscious that they ask questions almost in the order that the answers will appear in print.

Reporters who work so quickly and confidently may be geniuses or simply lead-happy hacks. In either case, they are taking a major risk if they fail to explore more than one angle. They are gambling that the angle they so promptly discover is either the only one or the best one. They decide what the story is before they have all the information. They operate more from intuition than from evidence.

Intuition, the celebrated "nose for news", has succeeded so often and so dramatically that it has a permanent position in the folklore of journalism. But it is no substitute for thorough reporting. Reporters who get the most they learn the more different angles they discover. If they are professional, they pursue each to the point where it ceases to be productive. This takes time, but it is the only way to approach an important story. The story developed in this manner may be less spectacular than the one that quickly follows a flash of intuition, but it usually will be more faithful to reality.

The Value of Vocabulary

One of the best protections against trite thinking as well as trite writing is a large vocabulary. When students first encounter the objectivity and shirtsleeve English of journalism, they sometimes get the impression that a reporter's vocabulary is drab and limited. They could hardly be more mistaken. At the least, a reporter's language is (or should be) as lively and varied as the subjects he or she writes about. And this is only the language used to address the readers. It seldom represents more than a small fraction of the reporter's total store of words.

Reporters use words to get stories as well as to tell them. They must be able to understand the special vocabularies of their sources then translate these into everyday English for their readers. They must understand legal terms, medical terms, and the professional languages of civil engineering and government finance. They must be able to decipher the double-talk of politicians, the jargon of social scientists, and the slang of street people.

Yet with all their exposure to varied experiences and language, reporters too often resort to the stock phrases with which the English language abounds. Journalists, no less than other people, are still guilty of the kind of writing George Orwell indicted some years ago: "Prose (now a days) consists less and less of **words** chosen for the sake of their meaning, and more and more of **phrases** tacked together like sections of a prefabricated henhouse..... There is a huge dump of worn out metaphors which have lost all evocative power and are merely used because they save people the trouble of inventing phrases for themselves.... Modern writing at its worst... consists of gumming together long strips of words which have already been set in order by someone else".

Today's cliches are often yesterday's flashes of genius. Their very originality or aptness resulted in overuse- and hence in the yawns with which we greet them now. Many such phrases, as Orwell suggests, are metaphoric:

shot in the dark	shadow of doubt
calm before the storm	fresh as summer's day
rears its ugly head	bitter end
sober as a judge	acid test
budding genius	beat a hasty retreat
grass roots support	more smoke than fire
see the light of day	to coin a phrase
greener pastures	

And most distressing of all perhaps the weary, wordy transitional phrases:

first and foremost	in the final analysis
in the long run	along these lines
last but not least	in the offing

An ample stockpile of words at your command is your best defense against the cliche. Sometimes you will hit on a fresh word or phrase that expresses your point with colour and verve. By trying to see people and things for yourself rather than through the fog of formulas, by trying to find relationships other than those provided by stale metaphors, you may come up with a striking new way of saying something (you may even invent a cliche). But more often you will have to settle for simplicity and precision, qualities of which any writer can be proud.

Words and Knowledge

A large vocabulary, however, means much more than just a stock of synonyms that help us say the same old things in different ways. Words do not just enable us to say things differently; they also enable us to see things differently and to understand things more fully. A small child's perception and understanding of the world is extremely limited by a lack of words and concepts with which to interpret what he or she sees, hears, and touches. Similarly, adults' perception and understanding of the much larger world they live in is directly related to their mastery of language.

In learning a new word, we acquire a new grasp, however small, on the complex worlds that exist both inside and outside of our individual beings. As a student you have learned that each new field you study- psychology, philosophy, anthropology, chemistry, astronomy, music-significantly increases your vocabulary. You cannot understand the concepts on which the discipline is built without understanding the terminology in which they are couched. Vocabulary, then, represents knowledge itself.

For the adult, as for the young child, vocabulary also functions as a tool for developing understanding. When you know the language of psychology, for example, you begin to perceive everyday human behaviour in more complex ways. A word helps us recognize the thing it stands for; and that recognition reinforces and extends our understanding of the word and perhaps of other words as well. The more familiar you are with the myriad shades and nuances of meaning contained in the English language, the better you can perceive the subtle nuances of reality. Words, like mathematical symbols, are tools which allow us to differentiate and integrate to analyze and evaluate.

Justification of Some Formulas

How do we answer the question "is it worth the effort to try to write cliche-ridden formula story?" The answer is no, not always, for several practical reasons. First, the formula is fast. We can get a minimal story into print while the reporter groping for a different angle is still trying to collect more information. And many subjects deserve no more than minimal treatment. They are worth reporting, but they amount to little more than statistics. Time spent trying to avoid the stereotype could be spent better on more deserving subject matter.

Second-and this may be the more important reason-the formula story is democratic; it is a way of treating all stories of a certain class equally. If we treat virtually all obituaries, all weddings, and all engagements alike, nobody will be slighted. And we avoid time wasting arguments with disgruntled families of persons who figure in such stories. We can answer complaints simply by pointing out the equality of treatment and observing that "this is our policy".

Although policy stipulates that most weddings and obituaries shall be treated equally common sense requires many exceptions. A Rashtrapati Bhawan wedding, for example, gets something more than the usual treatment. So does the leader or politician. The reporter dealing with what normally is a subject for a formula story still must be alert to circumstances that lift it out of the ordinary.

Patterns, Practices and Problems

There is a formula approach to almost any kind of straight news story and to much feature material as well. The categories we will examine are:

1. **Notices:** All announcements of future events.
2. **Athletic contests:** The major meets that are covered in some detail.
3. **Contests of greater significance:** political, legislative, and judicial.
4. **Single source - opinion stories:** the speech, the opinion interview, and the political news release.
5. **Meetings:** those that result in agreed-upon action by a governing body.
6. **Controversies:** balanced presentation of opposing sides, with the reporter neutral.
7. **Violent actions:** accidents, assault, homicide and natural disarter.
8. **Outright form stories:** weddings, engagements, obituaries, and high school basketball games.

Notices

All notices tell the reader that a certain action is scheduled at a specific hour, date, and place. Notices include impending tax deadlines, city council agendas, pregame stories, concert programmes - any expected or scheduled action. They range from the single paragraph announcing a club meeting to the long interpretive story announcing an important public hearing. What binds them together is the emphasis on time and place. The notice tells readers where to mail their tax returns and by what hour. It tells them where the game will be played and what time it starts, what time the polls open and close and where they are. It gives them information that is immediately useful. Despite the emphasis on time and place, the lead seldom begins with either of these elements. Instead, the lead usually centres on what is expected or scheduled to happen, and the only reference to time may be the day.

Athletic Contests

When a cricket coach loses a game, he may try to forget the score by talking about character building. After all, he may remind you the important thing is not whether you won or lost, but how you played the game.

Don't believe it. What the fans want to know first is who won and by what score. Next they want to know how this affects the standings they are interested in how the game was played, of course, but first they want to settle their bets. To serve these interests, you must write a lead that names the winner and gives the final score. But you need not limit it to that.

Contests of Greater Significance

In an athletic contest, the only items normally at stake are fans' and players' egos, a few million dollars in bets, and perhaps the coaches' jobs. Win or lose, when the game is over, most people can grin, shrug, and go home and forget about it. The outcome may have no lasting effect on anyone.

Beyond the world of sports, however, are many adversary contests which may yield historic consequences for an entire society. These contests are decided in polling booths, legislative chambers, and court rooms. They are "played" according to rigid rules, and they end-at least ostensibly-in victory for one side and defeat for another. The margin between winning and losing may even be expressed by a "score". But they are not games, nor can they be treated honestly as such, despite their superficial resemblance to sports. They cannot be reported realistically by using the simplistic, melodramatic style of sports writing. Despite the athletic metaphors that politicians themselves are so fond of, it is a disservice to the reader to treat a political campaign as a kind of verbal boxing match.

In political, legislative, and judicial contests, the ostensible winners and losers may be mere figureheads. Who really wins when a certain bill becomes law? The political party that supported it? The legislator who introduced it? Or is the winner some pressure group which shuns the public spotlight? Or perhaps society itself? Proper reporting of such contests requires much more than merely the ability to determine who carried the ball. Even the "Victory" or "Defeat" may be only a beginning. To report the outcome in perspective, we must look backward into the past and forward into the future as well as behind the scenes of the present.

Single–Source Opinion Stories

The single- source opinion story is one of the most familiar fixtures in journalism. We can find it on nearly every page, especially in election years. It may be a speech, an interview or only a political candidate's ghost written handout. In whatever form we see it, it is basically a one-sided story, sometimes filled with accusations and undocumented assertions of so-called fact. It can be either a legitimate news story or an insidious vehicle for propaganda.

What characterizes all these stories is that the reporter presents the source's opinion at face value, carefully attributing it, but taking no responsibility for its validity. Indeed there may be no way of determining validity at the moment. It is only an opinion, with no "right" or "wrong". Depending on one's viewpoint, this practice can be depended as "objectivity" "or presenting a forum for all points of view", or it can be denounced as an abdication of responsibility.

The publication of this kind of story is seldom irresponsible as critics charge, however. Long aware of the dangers of the one-sided story, thoughtful editors are highly selective about those they publish. They do not staff every speech that is presented, nor do they accept every news release that is submitted. And they certainly do not waste staff members' valuable time in interviewing every self-proclaimed spokesman for a cause. They try to restrict coverage to those persons whose opinions appear worthy of publication.

Meeting

Organizing the report of a governing body's actions often is as difficult as getting all the information. Even the meeting of a small-town city council may result in a dozen or more newsworthy actions. Should we round up all of these in a single story ? Or should we treat each action as a separate story with its own headline ?

Much depends on the perceptions of reporters. If they are source oriented, they see all these actions as part of a city council story. If they are action or issue oriented, they see little relationship between the firing of the police chief, the announcement of a new paving project, and the imposition of a city sales tax. They see each as a separate story in which the action is more important than the body responsible for it. Instead of viewing the goal as a "city council" story, these reporters see it as a "sales tax" story or a "police firing" story.

Still, the reporter must deal with reader expectations and the custom of the newspaper. If readers have come to expect meeting roundups, any departure may confuse them. Where can they find all those minor newspaper – off the- record actions, if not in the weekly meeting roundup? Must they go looking all through the paper to find out what happened?

Most editors in smaller cities prefer to make the news easy to find by using the roundup. To write the roundup the reporter must (1) base the lead on the single most important action, subordinating everything else, or (2) summarize the three or four more newsworthy actions in the first sentence, or (3) try to write a lead that summarizes the entire meeting, without focusing on anything specific. Each option has its disadvantages. The single action lead may distort the news by giving the chosen subject more status than it deserves. The multiple action lead may be more honest, but so crowded that it is barely readable. And the overall summary may bury newsworthy specifics and read like a grocery list.

The reporter who gets the outcome into the lead still may miss the story. Is the news only what was said and done at the meeting? or is the real news the effect of that action? Reporters who think all they have is a "meeting story" may be blinding themselves.

Controversies

When a dispute involves points of ascertainable facts, the reporter can and should tell the reader what the facts are. Unfortunately, facts are often difficult to determine, and the only ethical way to serve the reader may be to print the opinions of both sides. Occasionally this is weak journalism, but more often it isn't, In many controversies, fact is not really the issue; there is no "right" or 'wrong" only differing interpretations of "good", "bad", or "Just". In such cases, the only ethical course is to present all sides as fairly and fully as possible.

In organizing such a story, writers should make it clear at the beginning that there are at least two sides to the argument. They must try to summarize the dispute, rather than present either side first in a way that might imply that this is the **only** version of the situation.

Editors differ considerably in their policies on coverage of controversy. At one extreme are a few who refuse to publish anything controversial until it either lands in court to reach a legislative body. At the other are a few who think the newspaper thrives on any difference of opinion. To most, the goal is to keep it in perspective. These editors try to judge each controversy on its merits. They ignore or minimize minor squabbles, discourage disputants, a simple difference of opinion as a confrontation. But they never shy away from a controversy of consequence. They try to treat the major issues fully but dispassionately, always aware that a controversy may lead to open conflict.

Violent Actions

Whether we are writing about an automobile accident, a riot, or a natural disaster, the most important element in any story of violence usually is human death or injury. As a result the formula approach is to begin all such stories with the death toll. This has been criticized by many editors as treating human beings too much like statistics, yet the practice persists because the first question the reader is likely to ask is "How many died?" And the next questions usually are "Who"? and "How"?

In outlawry or warfare the prohibition against placing blame hardly applies. However, questionable statements about guilt must be carefully attributed.

Outright From Stories

Without being cynical, we can observe that death and marriage have a great deal in common. Each is an end and a beginning. Each is the subject for a story about people as individuals; thus names are among the most important ingredients. Each is a scrapbook story: it will be clipped from the paper and placed in the family album. Therefore you had better make certain that all the names are spelled right.

Using Your Judgment

Every situation, every event, every newsworthy item is different from every other for the same reason that a person never steps twice into the same stream. Sometimes these differences are important and should determine the approach you take to the story. Sometimes you do not have enough information to distinguish a given story from many others like it. Sometimes the story is too minor to merit more than routine formula presentation, but stressing a unique detail can inflate a trivial matter beyond its proper proportions. In short, sticking to formulas can be dull and misleading, but departing from them can be difficult, undemocratic – and also misleading.

The solution to this daily dilemma lies in experience and judgment. If reporters are to fight the formula story reasonably and effectively, they must learn how to do these things: they must be able to see or dig out the distinctive elements in every situation they encounter; they must be able to evaluate these distinctions and, decide how much attention, if any, they merit, and they must be able to vary the formula story accordingly- sometimes only slightly, sometimes moderately, sometimes dramatically. Developing these three abilities takes time, effort, and experience. But what they add up to is skilful reporting and skilful writing.

◆◆◆

5

Techniques of Shaping the News Stories

Stories need a shape, a structure in the same way a building needs a frame and our bodies a skeleton. Ernest Hemingway, a one-time reporter who became one of America's most influential novelists, had this in mind when he said, "Prose is architecture, not interior decoration." Effective writers understand this and make sure their toolbox contains a variety of story shapes. This chapter introduces traditional story forms widely used by news writers – inverted pyramid, hourglass, nut graf and narratives-and describes the late 20th century renaissance of a popular 19th century form: the serial narrative.

Story Forms

Architects and writers follow the same rule: Form follows content. That means before you design a container you determine what you need to put inside. You wouldn't try to ship an elephant in a shoebox.

The best stories create their own shape; writers consider their material, determine what they want the story to say and then decide on the best way to say it. But journalists, like all writers, sometimes rely on tried-and-true forms and formulas. You need to be familiar with these forms whether or not you decide to write your story in a completely new way. Depending on the news organization you work for, you may be expected to report the news following one or more journalistic conventions of story form. The forms described in this chapter have been used for a long time, the oldest ever since humans began telling stories. But they remain relevant even to those on the cutting edge of new media.

"It's difficult to overestimate the importance of Hemingway's point about stories being written in established forms," says Bill Mitchell, a veteran journalist and pioneer in online journalism who puts great faith in the importance of story forms. "Formulaic writing," he argues, "has gotten a bad name. Done right, it diverts creatively from formula in ways that serve the needs of the story at hand. Tying the reporting, as well as the writing, to the form lends a discipline and focus that produce better stories."

Mitchell's point is an important one for 21st-century journalists: All story forms evolve from previous forms. If you're intent on breaking new grounds or work for a news organization where the forms are changing, your knowledge of tried-and-true story forms will be of great use.

Inverted Pyramid

From the Top Down

Developed more than a century ago to take advantage of a new communications technology, the inverted pyramid remains a controversial yet widely used method of reporting news and will have a future in the 21st century, journalists in all media agree.

The inverted pyramid puts the most newsworthy information at the top, and then the remaining information follows in order of importance, with the least important at the bottom.

Historians argue over when the form was created. But they agree that the invention of the telegraph sparked its development so that it had entered into common use by newspapers and the newly formed wire service organizations by the beginning of the 20th century.

One of the first inverted pyramid leads was written by an Associated Press reporter after Abraham Lincoln was assassinated in April 1865:

To The Associated Press

Washington, Friday, April 14, 1865

The President was shot in a theater to-night

and perhaps mortally wounded.

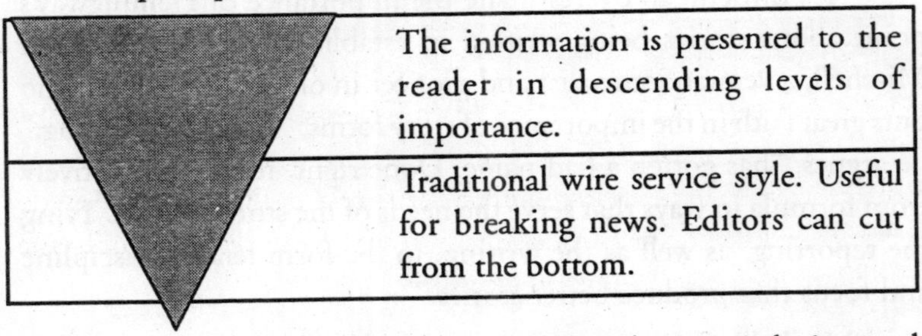

Popularized by newspapers during the 20th century, the inverted pyramid is a mainstay of online news reporting. The most newsworthy information goes at the top of the story.

The pyramid has to be big at the top because it must answer all the questions that readers have. Remaining information is arranged in diminishing order of importance. The conventions of the inverted pyramid require the reporter to summarize the story, to get to the heart, to the point, to sum up quickly and concisely the answer to the question: What's the news? The pyramid approach addresses the most important questions at top of the story. It states the thesis and then provides supporting material.

Journalism has a love-hate relationship with the inverted pyramid. Its supporters consider it a useful form, especially good for breaking news. The inverted pyramid, or at least its most substantial element- the summary lead is used widely and is one of the most recognizable shapes in communications today. You'll find it on the front and inside pages of most newspapers as well as in stories distributed world wide by The Associated Press, Reuters and other news services. The inverted pyramid is also the dominant from in the news sections of America Online and on news sites elsewhere on the Internet.

"The inverted pyramid organizes stories not around ideas or chronologies but around facts," says journalism historian Mitchell

Stephens in A History of News." "It weighs and shuffles the various pieces of information, focusing with remarkable single-mindedness on their relative news value."

Critics of the inverted pyramid say it's outdated, unnatural, boring, artless and a factor in the declining readership that newspapers have been grappling with for decades. The inverted pyramid, its critics say, tells the story backward and is at odds with the storytelling tradition that features a beginning, middle and end. Rather than rewarding a reader with a satisfying conclusion, the pyramid loses steam and peters out, in a sense defying readers to stay awake, let alone read on. Despite the criticism, the pyramid survives.

In the memorable phrase of Bruce DeSilva of The Associated Press "The inverted pyramid remains the Dracula of journalism. It keeps rising from its coffin and sneaking in the paper."

There are good reasons for this staying power. Many readers are impatient and want stories to get to the point immediately. In fast-breaking news situations, when events and circumstances may change rapidly, the pyramid allows the news writer to rewrite the top of the story continually, keeping it up-to-date. It's also an extremely useful tool for thinking and organizing because it forces the reporter to sum up the point of the story in a single paragraph. Journalism students who master it and then go on to other fields say it comes in handy for writing everything from legal briefs to grant applications.

The inverted pyramid can be a challenging form for some journalists. Summing up three hours of a school board meeting or trying to answer the five W's about a fatal car accident in a single paragraph, then deciding what other information belonged in the story – and in what order is arduous and frustrating, especially with the clock ticking to deadline. Also as a beginner a reporter usually does not have the knowledge of the subjects he covers to easily answer the central question posed by the event: What is newsworthy about it, and in what order? The reporter resists the disciplined thinking the pyramid demands, and like many reporters, scorn the form as uncreative and stilted. He prefers the storytelling approach of the fiction writer to the "just the facts" style of the reporter. Over time it becomes easier, and the reporter comes to see that the form helps develop the powers of critical thinking, analysis and synthesis that the form helps develop the powers of critical thinking, analysis and synthesis that are the foundation of clarity in thinking and writing. **The inverted pyramid is a basic building block of journalistic style.**

In the days of "hot type" printing, when stories had to be trimmed to fit a finite space, the inverted pyramid allowed editors, even the compositors who made up the pages in the back shop, to cut stories from the bottom up: no news judgment required. Technology continues to wield its influence. With studies showing that those who get their news from computers don't want to look at more than screen at a time, it's not surprising that the inverted pyramid is widely used by online news organizations. Like it or not, the reporter of the 21st century must master this form.

The Hourglass : Serving the News, Serving the Reader

In 1983, Roy Peter Clark began to notice something new as he read his morning paper. It wasn't the news; it was the way the news was being told. In their stories, reporters seemed to be combining two forms: the inverted pyramid and the narrative. Clark was a likely discoverer. A college English literature professor-turned-newspaper writing coach and reporter, he used his skills as a literary scholar and his experience in the newsroom to deconstruct the form. In an article published in the Washington Journalism Review (since renamed American Journalism Review), he described this form and gave it a distinctive name: the hourglass. News writers who adopted the hourglass were combining narrative elements that contained the power of storytelling with the inverted pyramid. It provided an alternative, Clark said, "that respects traditional news values, considers the needs of the reader, takes advantage of narrative, and spurs the writer to new levels of reporting."

The hourglass story can be broken into three parts:

The Top : Here you deliver the news in a summary lead, followed by three or four paragraphs that answer the reader's most pressing questions. In the top you give the basic news, enough to satisfy a time-pressed reader. You report the story in its most concise form. If all that is read is the top the reader is still informed. Because it's limited to four to six paragraphs, the top of the story should contain only the most significant information.

The Turn : Here you signal the reader that narrative, usually chronological, is beginning. Usually, the turn is a transitional phrase that contains attribution for the narrative that follows – "according to police," "eyewitnesses described the event this way," "the shooting unfolded this way, law enforcement sources and neighbours agree."

The Narrative : The story has three elements: a beginning, middle and end. The bottom allows the writer to tell a chronological narrative complete with detail, dialogue and background information.

The hourglass is a form that satisfies editors who prefer a traditional approach to news writing as well as impatient readers who tire easily of leisurely approaches to stories that take forever to get to the point. Readers who want a more complete story, who like to see a story unfold as they read it, are happy as well. The hourglass serves readers' need for news and their natural desire for story.

The hourglass can be used in all kinds of stories: crime, business, government, even to report meetings. It's best suited, however, for dramatic stories that can be told in chronological fashion. In the rights hands, as the following from The Miami Herald illustrates, the hourglass is a virtuoso form that provides the news-conscious discipline of the inverted pyramid and the storytelling qualities of the classic narrative.

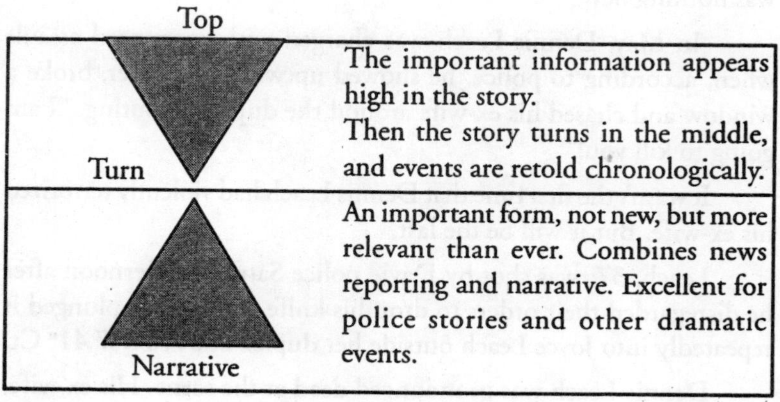

The hourglass form summarizes the news, then shifts to narrative. The top delivers the news, the turn acts as a transition, the narrative tells the story.

Behind the Hourglass

1. The Top : In the first five paragraphs, the story conveys all the information the time-pressed reader needs to know: Police shoot to death a man who refuses their commands to drop his knife and stabs his ex-wife instead. The top answers several of the five W's: who, what, where, when, why; as well as how. A special feature of this lead is the first paragraph, which departs from the usual summary lead: Police shot and killed a 37- year-old Davie man after he disregarded their orders to drop his knife. Instead the writer draws in the reader with an indirect approach that sums up the situation with chilling finality.

Hourglass Example

Shots fired While He stabbed Ex-wife.

"Why did you shoot him?" as she was loaded into the ambulance, was taken to Memorial Regional Hospital in Hollywood, where she was listed in stable condition.

The Mayhem was witnessed by Dennis Leach's parents and some neighbours. The neighbours said turmoil at the Leach home was nothing new.

In May, Dennis Leach was charged with aggravated assault when, according to police, he showed up with a hammer, broke a window and chased his ex-wife around the duplex, shouting, "I am going to kill you!"

It wasn't the first time that Dennis Leach had violently terrorized his ex-wife. But it will be the last.

Leach, 37, was shot by Davie police Saturday afternoon after he disregarded their orders to drop his knife and instead plunged it repeatedly into Joyce Leach outside her duplex at 6110 SW 41st Ct.

Dennis Leach was pronounced dead at the scene. His ex-wife, who asked police,

2. The Turn

The Transition is short, alerting the reader that the news report is shifting to story telling form and indicating the sources for the chronicle to come.

Police and neighbours gave this account of the latest domestic violence.

3. The Narrative

Now it's time to tell the story of what transpired the night Dennis Leach died. The writer tells the story chronologically, drawing together information gleaned from interviews with the sources identified in the turn. As with all stories, the narrative section has a beginning, a middle that describes the main action and an end, with the climactic cry of the abused ex-wife, "Why did you shoot him?" The conclusion wraps up the story with background about the couple's troubles and then, like many good stories, ends on a note that echoes back to the beginning. Note how the writer uses dramatic quotations and vivid details, such as the yellow tarp that covers Dennis Leach's body, to show the narrative scene that the reader is merely told about in the top.

Dennis Leach became angry with his 37-year-old ex-wife after he went to a neighborhood bar Friday night. He stormed into her duplex Saturday afternoon and threatened her with a butcher knife.

A terrified Joyce Leach dashed next door to the adjoining home of Leach's parents.

"He's got a knife, and he's gonna kill me!" Leach's mother, Reba Leach, said her daughter-in-law screamed.

At the same time, 15-year-old April Leach, one of their six children called from a convenience store blocks away.

"Your father is going to kill me!" Joyce Leach yelled.

April Leach hung up and dialed 911.

When officers arrived at the duplex, Dennis Leach was chasing his ex-wife with a knife.

Police ordered him to drop the weapon, said Davie Capt. John George.

Instead, Leach started stabbing her.

An officer fired at Dennis Leach, striking him around a knee but he wouldn't stop plunging the knife into his ex-wife, neighbors said.

An officer or officers fired again, this time hitting Leach in the chest. He collapsed and died on the side of the road. His parents were watching from inside their home.

Davie police would not say whether more than one officer fired at Dennis Leach, nor would they identify the officer or officers.

Neighbours say they heard at least five shots.

As police carried Joyce Leach to an ambulance, the knife still struck in her right shoulder, she turned to police and said: "Is he dead, is he dead... Why did you shoot him.? said next-door neighbor Shannon Schmitzer.

As Joyce was hoisted into the ambulance and police places a yellow tarp over Dennis Leach's body, April Leach and a brother arrived.

The two siblings cried and tried to run to their mother and father but were escorted away.

Police later drove them to Memorial regional Hospital to be with their mother.

Dennis and Joyce Leach lived for years in the duplex owned by Leach's parents.

"They've had a lot of trouble in the past." Schmitzer said.

As the couple's problems escalated, the Department of Children and Family Service stepped in. The state took custody of the children for a while, placing them in foster homes, neighbors said.

He got out Tuesday night and returned to his family's house, his mother said.

"We weren't supposed to let his stay here," his mother said. "But he just showed up."

Joyce Leach got a job at Dunkin donuts, just blocks away, but Dennis Leach couldn't stay out of trouble.

In May, Davie police charged him with domestic violence and aggravated assault after the incident with the hammer. He was convicted and jailed for 90 days.

The Miami Herald
August 9, 1998

The Nut Graf : Giving Readers a Reason to Care

Barney Kilgore was tired of today. He was sick of yesterday. And in 1941, he had the power to do something about it. "It doesn't have to have happened today to be news," he declared. "If a date is essential, use the exact date." From now on, he decreed, The Wall Street Journal would no longer use the words "today" and "yesterday" in the leads of stories.

With that single act, Kilgore, the new managing editor to The Wall Street Journal, paved the way for a revolutionary treatment of news. Journalistic story forms, like many creative ideas, are often linked with the places where they originated or where they reached their zenith. That's why the inverted pyramid, popularized by the newspaper wire services started before the U.S. Civil War, is often referred to as an "AP story" or a "wire service approach." In the same way, The Wall Street Journal is home to a form best known as the "nut graf" story, although it is also identified as the "news feature" and the "analytical feature." This genre's hallmarks include anecdotal leads that hook the reader, followed by alternative sections that amplify the story's thesis and provide balance with evidence that presents a counter thesis. But its chief hallmark is the use of a context section, the "nut graf" in newsroom lingo. Now newspapers and magazines around the world publish stories following the form that emphasizes explanation over information and under standing over knowledge. Online news sites also rely on this form.

The nut graf tells the reader what the writer is up to; it delivers a promise of the story's content and message. It's called the nut graf because, like a nut, it contains the "kernel," or essential theme, of the story. At the Philadelphia Inquirer, reporters and editors called it the "You may have wondered why we invited you to this party?" section.

Nut Graf	The lead is an anecdote or scene or portrait. The news value is communicated in the third or fourth graph. The rest of the story delivers the promise in the nut graf.
	Wall Street Journal style. Excellent for news analysis or trend stories. Forces writer to consider the most interesting information and the essential news value.

The "nut graf" story invites readers into a story, often with an anecdote or scene, and then by the third or fourth paragraph provides context by summarizing the essence, or "nut," of the story's theme.

The nut graf has several purposes:

- It justifies the story by telling readers why they should care.
- It provides a transition from the lead and explains the lead and its connection to the rest of the story.
- It often tells readers why the story is timely.
- It often includes supporting material that helps readers see why the story is important.

Ken Wells, a writer and editor at The Wall Street Journal, described the nut graf as "a paragraph that says what this whole story is about and why you should read it. It's a flag to the reader, high up in the story: You can decide to proceed or not, but if you read no farther, you know what that story's about."

As the name implies, most nut grafs are a single paragraph long. In the following example, Julia Malone, a national correspondent for Cox Newspapers' Washington Bureau, begins her story about pork barrel politics with a specific case that illustrates how politicians use tax dollars for pet projects that have dubious value.

Blacksburg, Va.- High on a mountain overlook, construction crews blast through solid rock on a 20-hours –a-day rush schedule to build the first two miles of an expressway that, for the next few years, will lead only to a turn around.

Malone then immediately provides the context for this scene and solves the puzzle of a two-mile-long expressway.

But for promoters in this Appalachian university town that's of little concern. Dubbed the "Smart Road" and designed to double as a high-technology research site, this federal-state project shows how a little "pork" tucked into a federal transportation bill can buy a whole hog for a community.

(The Atlanta Journal-Constitution)

Wisely, Malone doesn't make her intrigued readers wait any longer to find out what the story is about and why they should bother reading it. The nut graf has done its job: given readers enough information early on to see where to story is heading so they can decide whether they want to keep reading.

Student Example

Rookie reporters can use the nut graf form to good effect, too. Jeremy Schwartz, a reporting student at The Poynter Institute, used two short vignettes to begin his story about the problem elderly residents in a St. Petersburg neighborhood were having with Super Soakers, oversized water guns wielded by local kids. In his lead, Schwartz described how Avita Berry, 62, watched as the occupants of a car "let loose with thick streams of water, soaking anyone unlucky enough to be in range," and Annie Lee, 72, saw a group of pre-teens open fire with massive water guns filled with bleach, "strong enough to turn her grass white."

Then it was time to step back from the specific cases and clue the reader in on the whole story:

Berry and Lee are victims of a new urban weapon in South Sr. Petersburg: Super Soaker water guns-high-powered, bubble shaped, neon water guns that can extend to three feet and hold up to two gallons of water. They tell stories of guns filled with bleach, hot pepper and even. garlic and say that neighborhood youths have taken the game too far. This summer has seen an explosion of Super Soaker use on the South Side, say residents, local retailers and police.

First, Schwartz identifies the women in the lead as representatives of a larger group: neighborhood residents victimized by Super Soaker water guns. Then, he anticipates the readers' question by immediately describing the weapons, using details that paint a vivid picture. Nut grafs often use summary language to bring together disparate events to reveal trends or long-running situations. "They tell stories of "specific examples- "guns filled with bleach, pepper and even garlic" to convey a fad gone out of control.

The nut graf can be longer than one paragraph but never more than two or three. Longer than that, and the story can bog down. In chapter 4, you read this emblem lead on a story about pre-teen dieting:

Nut Graf Example

Worried about her weight, Sarah swore off dessert and cut back on meal-portions. Eventually, she began skipping breakfast and was just nibbling at lunch and dinner. Within six months, she dropped 13 pounds.

A weight-loss success story? Not at all. Sarah is only 10 years old. Her diet cost her 20 percent of her weight.

By now, the reader is sufficiently intrigued: **"Hey, when I started reading I thought it was a story about a woman dieting, but actually, it's about a kid who lost an alarming amount of weight. What's going on here?"** At this point, unfortunately, too many writers might continue on with the story about Sarah, either by providing biographical details- Sarah lives in Philadelphia with her mother. Her dieting began three years ago when her parents divorced.- or a quote- "I wanted to look like Kate Moss," says Sarah. "The only way I could do it was to stop eating."

What the writer needs to do a instead is anticipate the reader's reaction, every step of the way. That's where the nut graf comes in, stepping back from the individual case or scene or person to show where it fits into a larger picture. As Jack Hart, editor and writing coach at **The Oregonian,** described it so well, the nut graf is " a core statement that answers the basic question lurking in the mind of every reader: 'Why should I bother with this story?"

In this dieting story, the two-paragraph anecdotal lead is followed by three paragraphs designed to answer questions raised by the lead and provoke further interest:

Children such as Sarah, a Philadelphia fourth-grader who's too embarrassed to let her real name be used, are at the forefront of a disturbing new trend affecting the health of U.S. children: dieting.

Around the country, children as young as 6 are shedding pounds, afraid of being fat and increasingly being treated for eating disorders that threaten their health and growth, health specialists report,

It trying to correct one problem- one in five children is now overweight doctors, parents, schools and the media have unwittingly caused another.

Behind the Nut Graf

The first paragraph identifies Sarah further and discloses that her identity is being concealed and the reason why. Normally, news organizations identify subjects of stories, so it's important to explain when and why you depart from the norm. It also foreshadows a key theme explored later in the story: The stigma that being overweight carries in our society. The sentence then connects Sarah to a larger problem-dieting by children. Nut grafs must be economical. Notice how one word-new-conveys the story's timeliness.

Paragraph 2 anticipaptes the reader's reaction: "Kids are dieting! Really? What do you mean?" It answers it by amplifying the description of the trend: specifying the age of youngest weight-conscious children and telling of an increase in children under treatment for eating disorders. Attribution of this conclusion, to health specialists, is an important feature of this paragraph, anticipating the reader's questions: **"Oh, yeah? Says who?"**

Paragraph 3 concludes the nut graf section by building to a strong conclusion. Using the dash allows for insertion of a telling statistic that communicates the extent of the problem.

Using parallel construction-"correct one problem... caused another"-creates ironic tension that the writer hopes will prompt the rader to now say: **"That's interesting. I want to know more."**

After the lead and the nut graf, this story form now consists of alternating sections, all designed to support the story's focus.

Section 1: Quotes from experts support her story's thesis.

"This whole pressure to be thin has backfired on children, "said Joanne Ikeda, a dietitian at the University of California at Berkeley who counsels parents and health professionals about children and weight issues.

"It's a national crisis," said Frances Berg, editor of Obesity and Health a North Dakota journal that reports the latest scientific research on obesity.

Section 2: The story now provides balance by introducing a section that contrasts the problem of dieting children with the very real problem of obesity among America's youth.

No one denies that many American Children, like adults, have a problem with weight. American Children are fatter than ever before, experts agree. Among children 6 to 11, obesity increased 54 percent in the past two decades, according to a 1987 review of four national nutrition and health surveys. The number of obese youths rose 39 percent in the 12-17 group.

Obesity a Health Risk

Obesity poses serious health risks for children.

The condition is linked with high blood pressure and future problems with diabetes, heart disease and colon and breast cancer, said Dr. Gilman Grave of the National Institute of Child Health and Development.

In recent years, public health officials, doctors and the nation's schools have preached the importance of reduced fat and cholesterol and more exercise for children as well as adults.

Section 3: This chunk returns to the main theme of the story. It buttresses the thesis by citing medical evidence and experts. The last sentence provides a transition to the next section.

But now many health professionals are sounding a new warning: Children should never diet.

Dieting can lead to anorexia nervosa, bulimia and other eating disorders that cause death, serious illness, stunted growth and other health problems at a vulnerable stage when extra protein is needed for a child's healthy development.

It can also affect a child's learning, ability to concentrate and performance in school.

"Even with fat children you can stunt their growth so that instead of ending up with a slender child you end up with a short fat child," dietitian Ikeda said.

Children go through stages when they are heavier, especially during puberty, and often grow into their weight, dietitians say.

Children, whatever their size, need a healthy diet low in fats and sugars and high in fiber and a active life, health professionals say. Exercise is the key to preventing and controlling obesity, experts agree.

But that message apparently has not reached many children, recent surveys show.

Section 4: The following section amplifies the nut graf. With statistics drawn from a medical study, it tells the reader about widespread dieting among young people.

Pre - Teen Dieting

In a study published last summer, researchers at the Medical University of South Carolina reported dramatic evidence about the problem of pre-teen dieting. In the largest study of middle school children to date, they surveyed 3,175 boys and girls between 10 and 13. More than half the girls in the fifth to eighth grades who were surveyed felt they looked fat and wanted to lose weight.

One-fourth of the boys had similar attitudes. Among all the students, one out of three had dieted, and almost 5 percent said they had vomited to lose weight.

"The heavier the kids were, the more anxiety they expressed about their weight," said Elizabeth Hodges, who treats children with eating disorders and is one of the study's authors. "But even normal weight kids were dieting."

Unhealthy dieting is even more widespread more teen-agers. More than two third of high school girls are dieting, one in five has taken diet pills, and many girls as well as boys are using laxatives, diuretics, fasting and vomiting in a desperate effort to become slim, according to a 1992 study of students in 10 Cleveland high schools.

Section 5: The next section shows another face behind the numbers. Nut graf stories should never rely on the example.

"If you want to look pretty, if you want to be popular, if you want to stand out, you have to be thin," Said Katie, 13, who lives in a Chicago suburb.

Katie's order began at 7 when she looked at the girl sitting next to her on the school bus. "I just thought my things were a lot bigger than hers. I was shocked because I thought I was fat." Her parents were dieting, and Katie said she was "afraid I was going to be like my mom."

What followed was a typical pattern, experts say. The 75-pound third-grader cut out fat from her diet and began refusing food. She began spending hours exercising to lose weight, often waking at 4:30 a.m. to jog in place in her bedroom.

42 Pounds at 11

By 11, when she was admitted to a psychiatric hospital for treatment of anorexia nervosa, she weighed 42 pounds.

Section 6: In the following two sections, the story alternates between the close-up and the wide shot. Specific examples are always related to the larger context.

Today's children face a cruel dilemma. They are growing up in a society that condones eating too much of the wrong food and exercising too little, while at the same time clinging to unreasonable ideals of thinness and beauty. Fat children are often shunned and taunted by their classmates, who reflect society's prejudice against obesity.

Children today are merely reflecting a national obsession about diet and weight among adults, Hodges said, They are, in effect, the post-weight Watcher generation.

"These children have always been exposed to the diet culture," said Hodges.

It's a fact of life. Everyone's running and exercising and dong Nordic Track and step machines and watching their weight and what they eat. Kids get the message that the be thin is what's most important."

Section 7: The story comes full circle, returning to Sarah, the child in the lead. It avoids a common flow: introducing a character in the lead who is never seen or heard from again.

That message is so overpowering, doctors say, that even children of normal size, like Sarah, who weighed 66 pounds when she began dieting, are driven to lose weight. "I couldn't control it," she said.

Sarah's mother recalls her daughter "starting to read labels, counting the calories, reading about the fat content. I thought it was a stage."

But her daughter quickly moved from avoiding snacks to skipping entire meals.

"She was beginning to look like a concentration camp victim. You could see her ribs. She had lost so much on her thighs there was a big gap between her legs.

"It was heartbreaking," her mother said. Under therapy, Sarah and Katie both regained weight.

Section 8: Now that the problem has been fully explored, the story concludes with a section designed to answer the question on the reader's mind:

What can be done?"

Therapist Ellyn Satter, author of **How to Get Your Kid to Eat... But Not Too Much**, advises "carefully indirect" methods of weight control that divide responsibility for eating between parent and child. "Parents are responsible for what, where and when (the child eats); the child is responsible for how much and whether," she said. She advises against allowing children to "pan handle" for food between mealtimes and recommends drinking water, rather than juice or soda, between meals.

Besides fostering good eating and exercising habits, what's needed most is acceptance of a child's weight, experts say.

The emphasis on being thin "sets up a dilemma for kids who are normally heavier to try to diet themselves down to a biologically impossible state," Hodges said.

"The question should not be how do we make fat kids thin. It should be how do we make fat kids healthy," said Sally Smith, executive director of the National Association, Calif.

Attitudes that parents hold about obesity must change, Berg said. "They're conveying the message: There's something wrong with your body, and we've got to fix it. They need to give the message that you're great the way yu are, and we love you."

Knight Rider
February 18, 1994.

Many reporters, both students and professionals, have a hard time writing a nut graf. The nut graf requires the writer to summarize the story in a way that may seem like editorializing. It's not. The critical thinking and analysis that the form demands must be supported by rigorous reporting. The nut graf makes a case, but it must be supported by evidence. The story about pre-teen dieting is based on numerous interviews with children, parents, doctors, nutritionists, psychiatrists and other health professionals and on extensive research of medical literature.

Magazine editors like Evelynne Kramer at **The Boston Globe Magazine** describe the paragraph as "opening the aperture." As members of a video generation, you may find it helpful to think of this form's lead as a close-up. The nut graf is a wide-angle shot. Theme has been defined as "meaning in a word". In a nut graf story, it's the meaning in a paragraph. William E. Blundell, a former **Wall Street Journal** writer who coaches writers, and whose stories illustrated the approach in its finest form, calls "the main theme statement the single most important bit of writing I do on any story."

The Wall Street Journal's approach redefined news, transforming it from events or actions that happened today or the day before to trends or situations that had been developing over time but that had not been noticed by a news media focused on the now. Most important, **The Wall Street Journal's** reporters were following a news rule: Write a story that keeps readers reading rather than provides a built-in-excuse to stop, a complaint made by the inverted pyramid's critics.

At the same time, the nut graf required in every story served the function of the inverted pyramid's summary lead: providing readers with the gist of the story up high. If they chose to stop then, they at least knew the broad outlines of the story. If they chose to continue, however, they knew they would be rewarded with even greater understanding and enjoyment.

Although the nut graf approach is most often associated with trend stories, analytical pieces and news features, reporters also employ it to bring drama and context to breaking news. An example of this approach is this prize-winning deadline story by Mark Fritz of The Associated Press.

KURUBAMBA, Rwanda (AP)- Nobody lives here any more.

Not the expectant mothers huddled outside the maternity clinic, not the families squeezed into the church, not the man who lies rotting in a schoolroom beneath a chalk-board map of Africa.

Everybody here is dead. Karubamba is a vision from hell, a flesh-and-bone junkyard of human wreckage, an obscene slaughterhouse that has fallen silent save for the roaring buzz of flies the size of honeybees.

With silent shrieks of agony locked on decaying faces, hundreds of bodies line the streets and fill the tidy brick building of this village, most of them in the sprawling Roma Carholic complex of classrooms and clinics are Karubamba's stilled heart.

In those first four paragraphs, Fritz sets a horrific scene, bringing the reader face-to face with the massacred victims in an African village. The vivid details answer the questions "Where?" and "What?" and "Who?" in a powerful fashion that draws the reader into the story. Fritz's lead leaves unaddressed the "How?" and "Why?" Had he continued to describe the massacre there's a good chance the reader would become frustrated. That's where the nut graf comes in.

Karubamba is just one breathtakingly awful example of the mayhem that has made little Rwanda the world's most ghastly killing ground.

Karubamba, 30 miles northeast of Kigali, the capital, died April 11, six days after Rwanda President Juvenal Habyarimana, a member of the Hutu tribe, was killed in a plane crash whose cause is still undetermined.

The paranoia and suspicion surrounding the crash blew the lid off decades of complex ethnic, social and political hatreds. It ignited a murderous spree by extremists from the majority Hutus against rival Tutsis and those Hutus who had opposed the government.

This awesome wave of remorseless mayhem has claimed 100,000 to 200,000 lives, say U.N. and other relief groups. Many were cut down while cowering in place traditionally thought safe havens: churches schools, relief agencies.

The Associated Press
May 12, 1994

Here, Fritz backs up to provide context for the scene in the lead, like a filmmaker drawing back from a close-up to a wide-angle shot. This is the "nut section" that provides the background by addressing "How?" and "Why?" the scene described in the lead came to be.

Without context the reader who is hooked by an arresting lead may feel left dangling. The image of the nut works whether we think of it as plant life or an industrial device. Consider what happens, for example, if you leave a lug nut off a car wheel; you run the risk of the car careening off the road. In the same way, a story that intrigues without providing context can quickly leave a reader feeling derailed.

When the nut graf became popular in the 1970s, many reporters and editors believed that a nut graf had to include a phrase that indicates the source of the conclusion- "officials say" or "neighbors and friends of the victim agreed." Although the paragraph provided context and meaning for a story, it needed to rely on some authority other than the reporter to do so. Otherwise , they argued, the story read more like an editorial. Although that mindset still lingers in some newsrooms, by the 1990s even The Associated Press permitted its reporters to draw conclusions when it was based on their reporting and expertise. Thus, Mark Fritz delivers his interpretation of the Rwandan massacre in the nut graf without attribution but for one exception-the casualty estimates that he, appropriately, attributes to relief workers. Because the nut graf is designed to provide context for the story and then should always be followed by the evidence supporting the conclusion, attribution is often unnecessary.

A word of caution about nut grafs form James B. Steward, a former **Wall Street Journal** front page editor and successful nonfiction writer: Don't let nut grafs tell the reader so much about the story that they have no incentive to keep reading. In his book, **Follow the Story: How to Write Successful Nonfiction,** Stewart argues for nut grafs that accomplish the goals of the device, including "selling" the story to the reader by conveying its timeliness and importance while "preserving every bit of the suspense and curiosity so carefully cultivated in the lead." Stewart's guidelines to enhance rather than crush the story you want to tell include:

- Never give away the ending of the story.
- Anticipate the questions that readers might be asking early in a story, and address them.
- Give readers a concrete reason or reasons to move on.

Here's a quick way to produce a nut graf for your next story: Make up your mind what the story is about and why people should read it-and then type that conclusion in one or two sentences. Experienced reporters say they find it helpful to constantly write and rewrite the nut graf through the course of reporting the story: Doing so tends to reveal holes earlier in the process and helps you avoid too many intriguing but tangential side trips.

The Narravtive : The way we tell stories

Most of us learned about stories as children. That early reading experience stimulated a lifelong appreciation for stories. That certainly is the case for many and that makes it especially difficult to learn journalistic forms, such as the inverted pyramid, that turn the traditional story form on its head. What are the lessons about stories we learned as children?

Stories have characters, settings, themes, conflicts, plots with climaxes and resolutions. Storytellers don't give away the story in the first paragraph the way news writers do. Instead they set up a situation, using suspense or the introduction of a compelling character to keep the reader turning pages. Rather than put the least important information at the end the way an inverted pyramid writer might, the storyteller waits until the end to give the reader a "big payoff"- a surprise, a twist, a consummation.

As a writer one always finds the hard news story to be the most challenging to write. It feels unnatural. One realizes that as a writer one wants to create the dramatic tension that one found as a young reader. One wants to be caught up in the suspense of fiction that swept him away.

Narratives are often long stories. Readers find long stories off-putting. They will read them when the subject matters to them or the presentation is compelling. But for the most part, readers find a long story hard to take. If a block of gray stares a reader in the face, it's possible he will give up. So if you're going to write a long story, you'd better have a good reason.

No matter what the length, the rules are the same. The story has to be clear and compelling. The reader should not be allowed to stumble. Dot's put all your work into the lead and then start flinging stuff around in the middle. As with a short story, a long story should say one thing, convey one dominant impression.

Even the most fervent champions of narrative journalism are cautious about its use. "Not every story merits it, nor can every reporter be trusted with it," said Jon Franklin, a two-time Pulitzer Prize winner whose book **Writing for story** continues to influence long-form writers. "Most stories should be short, to the point and written in traditional journalistic style. A cop round-up, written in fake Joan Didion, makes the reader wonder if the journalistic world is asleep at the switch." Franklin believes most stories would be "better handled as inverted pyramid stories or at most, delayed lead features. What could have been good stories come off instead as underreported and overwritten fluff."

If you want to write long stories that people are unable to stop reading, ask yourself: Have I got the material, the scenes, some dialogue, details about lives? Narratives must grab readers' attention quickly, intrigue them, then satisfy their natural curiosity. Storytellers reveal story with dialogues and images.

To a good reporter the story endings that are most satisfying reverberate like a Chinese gong. They conjure up images from throughout the story, then take you back to the beginning. In a story about the Navy's insensitive handling of a young seaman's unexplained death, it ended with a scene of a grief-stricken mother getting a letter sent to her son from the recruiting station a few days after he died. Unaware that the young man was dead, the recruiters wrote, "We liked your stuff, shipmate. We'd like to have you back." Most reporters might have used that the as the lead. When a reporter gets something that is powerful and reinforces the story's theme, his impulse is generally to save it for the end.

The importance of reporting for a long story is critical. Look for details. Use the best. Here is an example of a narrative followed by an account of the writing.

Five Boxes Story

Good writing comes from an overabundance of information. But collecting notebooks full of observations and computer screens of interview notes can pose another problem: where to put it all. Faced with that problem, many reporters and students swear by the **"five boxes" story approach**

The five boxes approach works as follows:

1. **Lead** : The first box contains the lead, the image, the detail that draws the reader into the story. It can be a single paragraph or several.
2. **Nut Graf** : A paragraph (or paragraphs) that sums up the story and provides the reader with context and background is the second box.

3. **Retelling** : This box is almost a second lead, based on a new scene, detail or strong image, which allows the writer to begin retelling the story that began in the lead and draws the reader into the bulk of the story. Length can vary.
4. **BBI** : Shorthand for "boring but important," this box contains less compelling material, such as quotes from experts or data bolstering the main theme. It rounds out the story and provides balance.
5. **Kicker** : The story ends in this box. It may be quote, an image, a comment; whatever you choose, the best endings resonate. Says Bragg: "I'm a strong believer that you can't have a decent story if it doesn't leave you with a strong feeling or sense or image."

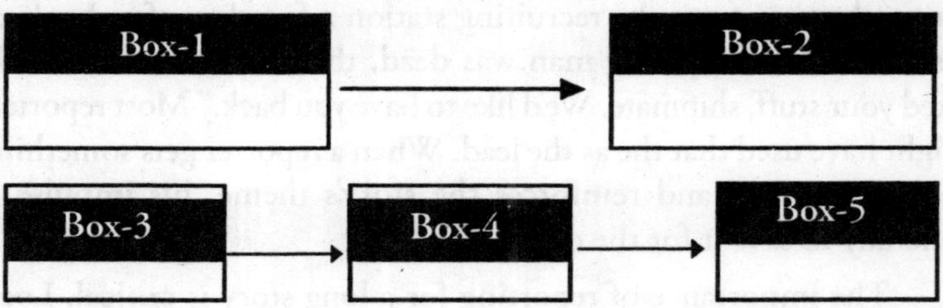

Dividing material into "five Boxes" is an efficient and graceful way to organize information, especially on a deadline.

The five boxes approach is the easiest method for quick organization of material. Using the boxes you can select and arrange information, settle on the beginning and ending of the story and decide what the story is about. Armed with this rudimentary outline, you can flesh out your story. It breaks the story into components that can be developed and refined.

An Illustration

Another Battle of New Orleans: Mardi Gras

By Rick Bragg

New Orleans, Feb. 18- the little shotgun house is peeling, and the Oldsmobile in front is missing a rear bumper, but Larry Bannock can glimpse glory through the eye of his needle.

For almost a year he has hunkered over his sewing table, joining beads, velvet, rhinestones, sequins, feathers and ostrich plumes into a Mardi Gras costume that is part African, part Native American.

"I'am pretty," siad Mr. Bannock, who is 6 feet tall and weighs 300 pounds. "And, baby, when I walk out that door there ain't nothing cheap on me."

Most days, this 46-year-old black man is a carpenter, welder and handyman, but on Mardi Gras morning he is a Big Chief, one of the celebrated-if incongruous-black Indians of Carnival. He is an important man.

Sometime around 11 a.m. on Feb. 28m Mr. Bannock will step from his house in a resplendent, flamboyant turquoise costume complete with a towering headdress, and people in the largely black and poor 16th and 17the Wards, the area known as Gert Town., will shout, cheer and follow him through the streets, dancing, drumming and singning.

"That's my glory," he said. Like the other Big Chiefs, he calls it his "mornin' glory."

Box 1: Lead

The first box contains the lead, the image, the detail that draws the reader into the story. It can be a single paragraph or several. Bragg focuses on Larry Bannock and the contrast between his shabby surroundings and the glory of his role as a black Indian of Mardi Gras. The section concludes with a brief but-vivid quote. Note how Bragg separates the quotation with a description of Bannock: a technique that provides pacing and a vivid counterpoint.

He is one of the standard-bearers of a uniquely New Orleans traditions. The Big Chiefs dance, sing and stage mock battles-wars of words and rhymes-to honor American Indians who once gave sanctuary to escaped slaves. It is an intense but elegant posturing, a street theater that some black men devote a lifetime to.

But this ceremony is also self-affirmation, the way poor blacks in New Orleans honor their own culture in a Carniyal season that might otherwise pass them by, said the Big Chiefs who carry on the tradition, and the academics who study it.

These Indians march mostly in neighborhoods where the tourists do not go, ride on the hoods of dented Chevrolets instead of floats, and face off on street corners where poverty and violence grip the people most of the rest of the year. The escape is temporary, but it is escape.

"They say Rex is ruler," said Mr. Bannock, referring to the honorary title given to the king of Carnival, often a celebrity, who will glide through crowds of tourists and local revelers astride an elaborate float. "But not in the 17th Ward.' Cause I'm the king here. This is out thing.

"The drums will be beating and everybody will be hollering and" he paused to stab the needle through a mosaic of beads and canvas-"and it sounds like all my people's walking straight through hell."

Box 2: Nut Graf

A Paragraph (or paragraphs) that sums up the story and provides the reader with context and background is the second box. Bragg steps back now from the close-up scene of Bannock working in his house to place him in the larger context. The phrase "He is one of the ..." is signal that the nut section is beginning. Here the writer provides an analysis, which he attributes to the Big Chiefs and academics. The section ends on a dramatic quote, a useful method of narrative as punctuation.

A man does not need an Oldsmobile, with or without a bumper, if he can walk on air. Lifted there by the spirit of his neighborhood, it is his duty to face down the other Big chiefs, to cut them down with words instead of bullets and straight razors, the way the Indians used to settle their disagreements in Mardi Gras in the early 1900s. Mr. Bannock, shot in the thigh by a jealous old chief in 1981,

By tradition, the chiefs must sew their own costumes and must do a new costume from scratch each year. Mr. Bannock's fingers are scarred from a lifetime of it.

His right index finger is a mass of old punctures. Some men cripple themselves through puncture wounds or repetitive motion, and have to retire. The costumes can cost $ %5,000 or more, a lot of cash in Gert Town.

The rhythms of their celebration, despite their feathered headdresses, seem more West African or Haitian than Indian, and the words are from the bad streets of the Deep South. Mr. Bannock said that no matter what the ceremony's origins, it belongs to New Orleans now. The battle chants have made their way into popular New Orleans music. The costumes hang in museums.

"Maybe it don't make no sense, and it ain't worth anything," said Mr. Bannock. But one day a year he leads his neighborhood on a hard, forced march to respect, appears to be the last to have been wounded in battle.

"I forgave him," Mr. Bannock said.

The tribes have names like the Yellow Pocahontas, White Eagles, the Golden Star Hunters and the Wild Magnolias. The Big Chiefs are not born, but work their way up through the ranks. Only the best sewers and singers become Big Chiefs doing battle at every turn with other chiefs who are out trying to do the same.

Jimmy Ricks is a 34-year-old concrete finisher most of the year, but on Mardi Gras morning he is a Spy Boy', the man who goes out ahead of the big. Chief searching for other chiefs. He is love with the tradition he said, because of what it means to people here.

"It still amazes me," he said how on Mardi Gras mornings the people from the neighborhood drift over to Mr. Bannock's little house on Edinburgh Street and wait for a handyman to lead them.

"To understand it, you got to let your heart wander," said Mr. Bannock, who lead the Golden Star Hunters. "All I got to do is peek through my needle."

I'm 52 inches across my chest And I don't bow to nothin'

'Cept God and death

– from a battle chant by Larry Bannock

Box 3: Retelling

This box is almost a second lead, based on a new scene, detail or strong image, which allows the writer to begin retelling the story that began in the lead and draw the reader into the bulk of the story. Length can vary. In this section Bragg's reference to an Oldsmobile is an echo of the lead. It is a clever technique that acts as a transition from the nut section to a new one that continues with the story of Bannock and the Big Chiefs.

The more exclusive party within the party- the grand balls and societies that underlie the reeling, alcohol soaked celebration that is Carnival-have always been By Invitation Only.

Organized parades in the 1830s. One of the oldest Carnival organizations, the Mystick Krewe of Comus, staged the first organized parade. Today, Mardi Gras is not one parade but several, including that of the traditional Zulus, a black organization. But Comus, on FAT Tuesday, is still king.

The Krewes were-some still are-secret societies. The wealthier withstand Creoles, many of whom are descendants of people of color who were free generations before the Civil War, had balls and parades while poorer black men and women cooked the food and parked the cars.

Mardi Gras had no other place for them, said Dr. Frederick Stielow, director of Tulane University's Amistad Research Centre, the largest minority archive in the nation. And many of these poorer blacks still are not part of the party, he said.

"These are people who were systematically denigrated," said Dr. Stielow, who has studied the Mardi Gras Indians for years. So they made their own party, "a separate reality," he said, to the hard work, racism and stark poverty.

It might have been a Buffalo Bill Wild West Show that gave them the idea to dress as Indians, Dr. Stielow said, but either way the first "Indian tribes". appeared in the late 1800s. They said they wore feathers as a show of affinity from one oppressed group to another, and to thank the Louisiana Indians for sanctuary in the slave days.

By the Great Depression these tribes, or "gangs" as they are now called, used Mardi Gras as an excuse to seek revenge on enemies and fought bloody battles, said the man who might be the biggest chief of all, pictures of Indian scenes, painstakingly beaded by hand. The feathers are brilliant yellows, blues, reds and greens.

The winner is often "the prettiest," Mr. Montana said, and that is usually him.

"I am the oldest, I am the best, and I am the prettiest," he said.

The origins of Carnival, which climaxes with Mardi Gras or Fat Tuesday, are found in the Christian season of celebration before lent. In New Orleans the celebration reaches back more than 150 years, to loosely 72-year-old Tootie Montana. He has been one for 46 years.

Mr. Bannock said, "They used to have a saying, 'Kiss your wife. hug your momma, sharpen your knife, and load your pistol'".

Even after the violence faded into posturing the New Orleans Police Department continued to break up the Indian gatherings. Mr. Bannock said New Orleans formally recognized the Indians rig hum a tiny piece of Mardi just two years ago.

Shoo fly, don't bother me.

Shoo fly, don't bother me.

If it wasn't for the warden and them low-down hounds.

I'd be in New Orleans' fore the sun go down & Big Chief's battle chant, written by a chief while in the state prison Angola.

They speak a language as mysterious as any white man's Krewe.

In addition to Spy Boys, there are Flag Boys- the flag bearers- and Second Line, the people, sometimes numbering in the hundreds, who follow the chiefs from confrontation to confrontation.

They march-more of a dance, really-from Downtown, Uptown, even across the river in the poor black sections of Algiers until the Big Chiefs meet at the corner of Claiborne and Orleans Avenues and, inside madhouse circle of onlookers, lash each other with words. Sometimes people almost faint from the strain.

But it is mainly with the costume itself that a man does battle, said Mr. Montana. The breastplates are covered with intricate.

A few are well-off businessmen, at least one has served time in prison, but most are people who sweat for a living, like him.

Some chiefs do not make their own costumes, but pay to have them made-what Mr. Bannock calls "drugstore Indians." Of the 20 or so people who call themselves Big Chiefs, only a few remain true to tradition.

Box 4 : BBI

Shorthand for "boring but important," this box contains less compelling material, such as quotes from experts or data bolstering the main theme. It rounds out the story and provides balance. Here Bragg includes material from an academic expert, hoping that by this time the reader is sufficiently engaged and interested to care about the event's history. Writers often make the mistake of including this kind of information earlier in the story before the reader is ready for it.

Mr. Bannock sits and sweats in his house, working day and night with his needle. He has never had time for a family. He lives for Fat Tuesday.

"I need my mornin' glory," he said.

A few years ago he had a heart attack but did not have time to die. He had 40 yards of velvet to cut and sew.

The New York Times
February 19, 1995

Box 5 : Kicker

The story ends in this box. It may be a quote, an image, a comment; whatever you choose, the best endings resonate. Now Bragg comes full circle, returning to the scene in the lead. Many writers might end with the "mornin' glory" quote, but Bragg chooses to end the story with a detail that strikes the chord of his theme: one man's devotion to a tradition larger than himself.

The Serial Narrative : "To be Continued..."

Newspapers have been home to serial narratives since a young reporter for London's Morning Chronicle named Charles Dickens published the first one in 1836. A serial narrative is "any story, whether told with words, visual images or drawings, that is broken up into segments and is revealed gradually," says Tom French, who has written several award-winning serial narratives for the St. Petersburg Times.

A serial narrative can run for a few days to several weeks. It can range in length from 200-inch instalments about a murder investigation and trial to stories about life along the 45th parallel in Oregon. Ranging from short instalments designed to be read in five minutes to segments consuming several newsprint pages and large chunks of a reader's time, this form provides what one writer called a "drip-feed of narrative satisfaction."

Newspaper writers such as Tom French and Donald Drake at **The Philadelphia Inquirer** have been writing book chapter-length serial narratives for two decades, and there has been a revival of the form in a briefer version.

Hoping to repeat the 19th –century success of Charles Dickens, newspapers in the mid-1990s embraced the serial narrative, with more than 25 series published around the country.

Instalments of these serial narratives are designed to be short-800 to 1,000 words long. "That's a five-minute read. Your breakfast serial," notes Roy Peter Clark, senior scholar at The Poynter Institute. In 1996, Clark published two serial narratives, "Three Little Words," a 29-day series about a family's struggle with AIDS, and "Sadie's Ring: A Journey of the Spirit," a poignant 11-part chronicle about his experience as a young Catholic man experiencing his family's Jewish roots.

Greg Lampman, a reporter for the **Norfolk Virginian-Pilot** who is credited with writing some of the first serial narratives in the 1980s, turned to the form when editors stopped making room for his long feature stories. He researched the form by studying microfilmed copies of stories published in Norfolk at the turn of the century, when the city had 11 daily papers and when luring readers "wasn't a matter of increasing circulation; it was a matter of survival." The absence of international copyright laws gave newspaper publishers license to pirate serial narratives written by Europeans such as Dickens, Thackeray and de Maupassant. (Interestingly, because the papers could get these fiction serials free, many American writers turned to factual reporting, the only writing they could get paid for.)

Lampman wondered, "could we use these techniques in modern newspapers? What about taking dramatic stories I'd been writing at 300 inches and doing them as a serial?" He realized that the common thread of the 19th century serial was not curiosity but rather something stronger-"suspense"-that created a need in readers-"you had to know." For Lampman, the serial was "born of necessity because it was the day of the designer. With newspapers choosing shorter stories as a way to stem readership decline, I couldn't get a long story into my paper." But, Lampman adds, "Writing these stories is a lot more than cutting them into pieces."

Boosters of the serial narrative point to immense reader response thousands of Website "hits" as modern readers exhibit the same intense interest as did readers of Dickens' serials.

Jan Winburn, who edits serial narrative at **The Baltimore Sun,** identified four elements needed for a successful serial:

1. The Engine : The unanswered question that drives the story-and the reader-forward. In **Wizard of Oz,** the question is whether Dorothy will get home to Kansas. In **Jurassic Park,** it's who will end up in the digestive tract of the dinosaur. In mysteries, it's whodunit.

Although every narrative needs an engine-a narrative thread that drives the story and pulls the reader along-the serial narrative imposes extra burdens. If the narrative is a mountain that the reader is climbing, a serial requires what Winburn calls "switchbacks," things you didn't expect, lots of twists and turns, which give you the opportunity for cliffhangers.

In the opening section of his award-winning serial, "A Stage in Their Lives," Ken Fuson of **The Baltimore Sun** introduces the story's engine-the suspense surrounding the mounting of a high school play-and its theme- a rite of passage:

Spellbound she sits, her mother on one side, her boyfriend on the other, as another young woman performs the role that will someday be hers.

Since she was little, Angie Guido has dreamed of standing on stage, playing the Puerto Rican girl who falls in love with the Polish boy named Tony.

Maria.

She will be Maria in West Side Story.

Say it loud and there's music playing.

"That's me, Mom," she said.

Say it soft and it's almost like praying.

It won't be long, Angie thinks as she delights in a touring company production of West Side Story at the Lyric Opera House in Baltimore. She and 20 members of the Drama Club from North Country High School in Anne Arundel Country attend the December show with a few parents. This is a prelude; there is expectant talk they will stage the same show for their spring musical.

Someday soon, Angie hopes, she will own the role that is rightfully hers. She has been a loyal drama club soldier, serving on committees, singing in the chorus when she yearned for a solo, watching lead roles slip away because she didn't look the part. But Marie is short, as she is, and dark, as she is, and more than that, Angie is a senior. This will be her last spring musical. Her last chance to shine.

But on the very next night, in that very same theatre another girl from North Country High sits spellbound, her mother on one side, her best friend on the other.

She, too is captivated by the Puerto Rican girl with the pretty voice.

She, too, wonders: What if that were me?

Two months later, in the middle of February, two dozen students gather in a dark and cavernous auditorium at North Country High School to plan the spring musical.

You don't know them. Not yet.

Find a seat-there, in the middle, close to the stage- and watch.

You will meet tow girls. One will have her dream come true, the other won't, and the experience will change them both.

You will meet a boy who can't sing but refuses to quit trying.

You will meet another boy, the leading man, who falls for one of the leading ladies. But so will someone else.

You will meet a girl who wants to be a star, then chooses a new destiny.

Come to the practices. Laugh at their goofy jokes. Encourage them when they flab their lines.

Soon you will know them.

And you will know this:

The high school musical is a rite of passage that will shape – and-reveal-the adults they will soon be.

And nothing ever produced on stage can possibly match the drama of growing up.

By Ken Fuson
The Baltimore Sun
June , 1997

2. Access : You need good access for any narrative story, but you can't have any reluctant sources for a serial narrative. When Fuson wrote his serial narrative, he attended scores of rehearsals, interviewed the students, teachers, their parents. Tom French of the St. Petersburg Times dressed up in a toga to follow the high scholars he profiled in his serial narrative "South of Heaven."

3. A "Gold Mine" Source : Someone who knows all the answers, has all the details the reporter needs to craft a believable, dramatic story. Usually it's the subject of the narrative, but it can also be a detective or prosecutor privy to workings of a criminal case or a doctor overseeing the care of a cancer patient. Of course, the reporter should make every effort to verify the source's account with documents and interviews.

4. The Big Payoff : A resonant ending : The unifying feature of a serial narrative is not length. Rather, "the serial forces the reader to wait, and that quality, that sense of enforced waiting, is what makes serial narratives different," says French.

Serial narratives have focused on a variety of subjects: ordinary life, crime, personal crisis, quests, and rites of passage, including the first year in the life of a widow and the making of a high school play.

A Serial Narrative Glossary

At a 1998 conference on serial narratives at The Poynter Institute, reporters and editors responsible for producing the more than two dozen narratives published since 1996 created a glossary of terms:

The Three Dragpms : The main character in a serial narrative needs to face a series of challenges, just as medical knights had to slay not just one but three dragons before reaching their goal. In a news serial, the main character can't kill all the dragons in the first chapter. He or she must kill one, then another, then another, in an increasingly more dramatic way.

Cliffhanger : A dramatic point at which to conclude a chapter, encouraging the reader to come back tomorrow. "At the end of each chapter, there has to be that, 'I want to go on'" Example: Study how fusion accomplishes that goal at the end of the first instalment of "A Stage in Their Lives" by returning to the question posed in the lead: Who will get the part of Maria?

Casting Maria is Just as easy. When the choice is finally made, there is no discussion about who has her heart set on the role, or who will be crushed with disappointment, or who has dreamed of playing Maria since that December night when she saw it on stage.

Only one question matters: Who can do it best?

Mr. Shipley writes the winner's name on a piece of paper.

Narrative ARC : The curved line that connects the beginning of the story to the end. In **Romeo and Juliet** it is a boy and girl from feuding families falling in love, their deaths showing their families the cost of such hatred. In "Angels and Demons," Tom French tracks a murder from the crime to the killer's conviction.

Switchbacks : Surprising reversals of fortune, plot twists that shock the reader.

Gold Mine Source : Court records, a diary, a willing source with a great memory, a trunk of letters.

Stakeholder : A key character with something important at stake.

BIG PAYOFF. A satisfying ending to a long series: a resolution, revelation or exaltation.

Conclusion

"Can you imagine Hemingway or Steinbeck or Mark Twain-journalists all sitting down to figure out whether an inverted pyramid or an hourglass structure would be the best formula for one of their stories?" asks writing coach Richard Andersen. "Good writers let their stories determine their own structures, but each course brings with it a new set of formulas."

Avoid formulas by reading widely. Andersen continues, "reporters have to read more-not just the best writers in their field, for they, too, are often limited by preconceived ideas of what constitutes good writing-but our world's best writers, the ones who write what we call literature. They are the writers whose narrative techniques are as multiple and various as life itself- the way newspaper writing should be-and they are also the people who, at least in their writing, refuse to compromise their human integrity." Finally which shape should the reporter select? the accompanying table provides some guidelines.

Story form Guide-Lines

Story Structure	Story Type
Inverted Pyramid	Breaking news: police and crime news, accidents, meeting Coverage, elections
Hourglass	Breaking news: stories with strong dramatic appeal that can best be told with a chronological narrative.

Story Structure	Story Type
Nut graf	Breaking news: News analysis, opinion pieces, news features, features, trend stories
Narrative	Stories that rely on characterizations, action line, rising action, climax and resolution
Five boxes	News features. Trend stories, profiles, breaking news

Whichever form you choose, remember Associated Press Enterprise Editor Bruce DeSilva's point that none of journalism's forms "inherently requires a writer to sound pompous and dull." The most important thing to remember is "don't report a form; report a story." The more and better reporting you do through interviews, research, observation and analysis, the more likely you are to write a story that conveys more than just the five W's, no matter what shape the story assumes.

Shaping the News : The Coaching way

- Make a list of everything you think belongs in your story. Number the list in terms of importance.
- Every story, no matter what form, has a beginning, middle and end. Make three piles, labeled B, M and E, and separate your list of separate elements by the part they belong in.
- Put yourself in your readers' or viewers' place. What question do you have about the story? Can you organize your story so that each paragraph answers the readers' or viewers' questions in the order they ask them?
- Plan your ending first. What do you want your readers or viewers to do when they finish your story? Register to vote?

  Get an AIDS test? Open an individual retirement account? account? Rethink their opinions on an important issue? What do you have in your notes- a detail, a statistic, a quote-that might provoke such a response? Write it and show it to someone and ask his or her reaction.
- Plan your beginning. What's the news?

What's the story?

- The next time you're stuck on a story, employ the "five boxes" method of story organization suggested by Rick Bragg or **The New York Times.** But don't feel bound to stick with it. "Even if you just completely scramble it later on," Bragg says, "at least it got you going.

Glossary of Important Terms

"Five boxes" story approach. A way of organizing a story in five parts: a lead, nut graf, a retelling of the story, background and kicker.

Hourglass : A story form that delivers the news value of the inverted pyramid and the storytelling power of the narrative. Composed of three parts: a four-to five-paragraph "top" that reports the most important news elements; a transition paragraph called the "turn" that shifts the story from a report to a story and contains attribution indicating the source of the information to come; and the "narrative," usually a chronological retelling of the story reporterd in the top using dialogue and scenes.

Inverted Pyramid : A story form that puts the most newsworthy information at the top, and then the remaining information follows in order of importance, with the least important at the bottom.

Kicker : Newsroom jargon for a story ending that delivers a resonant conclusion with a detail, example or, most often but often least effective, a quote.

Narrative : The classic story form, featuring a beginning, middle and end, characters, theme, plot, climax and resolution. Scenes are the building blocks of narrative.

Nut graf (sometimes spelled "graph"). One to three paragraphs that summarize the theme as a story and tell the reader what the story is about and offer a reason to read it. Usually follows anecdotal lead.

Serial Narrative : A narrative broken up into segments that unfolds in instalments.

◆◆◆

6

Everydayness of News and Audience Response

I have to believe that a better informed world is more civilised, more compassionate, more ready to act and to help. But I do not think it is my place to tell the audience what to do.

(Kate Adie, chief news correspondent of the BBC)

Serious, careful, honest, journalism is essential, not because it is a guiding light but because it is a form of honourable behaviour, involving the reporter and the reader.

(Martha Gellhorn, foreign news correspondent)

Pronouncements about how the 'average person' relates to the news media often invoke a continuum of sorts, one where the drowsily indifferent 'couch potatoes' are positioned at one and the hyperactive 'news junkies' are at the other. Somewhere in between, it follows, is where most news consumers can be situated, particularly where televisual news is concerned.

It is surprising to note how few news organizations conduct regular, systematic research into who makes up their audience, a problem which parallels the insufficient number of investigations being undertaken within an academic context. A number of the studies which have been launched do point out, however, that care needs to be taken to avoid thinking of 'the news audience' at too abstract a level. Such a phrase, after all, defines people who may or may not actually choose to define themselves in this way and, in any case, risks transforming them into a fixed, rigid totality of individuals on the basis of only one aspect of their engagement with the media. Accordingly, just as the claim that journalists are participants, knowingly or not, in some sort of wilful conspiracy to encodify the dictates of a 'dominant ideology' in the newsroom may be safely dismissed, so may the corresponding assertion that news viewers, listeners and readers be regarded as passive, alienated dupes indoctrinated into a state of 'false consciousness'.

At issue here is the need to elucidate how the materiality of news culture is intimately imbricated in the varied realities of everyday experience. With this aim in mind, our attention first turns to a series of issues raised in critical investigations of newspaper (both broadsheet and tabloid, respectively) readership. In the course of mapping a number of the most salient features of this research terrain, particular attention is given to exploring the ways in which the cultural dynamics of newspaper reading are interwoven throughout the cultural fabric of our everyday realities. Next, analyses of the televisual news audience are centred for critique, in the first instancy by drawing upon Hall's (1980) highly influential encoding-decoding model. This conceptual model is examined with an eye to its impotence for investigating how televisual news discourses encourage the viewer to negotiate or 'decode' the fluidly contradictory dynamics of their 'preferred meanings' as being inferentially consistent with the dictates of 'common sense'. The ensuing discussion focuses on the need to situate the televisual newscast within the household in order to discern how the profuse flow or its sounds and images are negotiated by the viewer on an ordinary, 'lived' basis.

Mapping the newspaper audience

Attempts to 'measure' the audience for a particular newspaper usually begin with its daily circulation figures. These figures provide an indication of each newspaper's relative share of the market, although distortions can creep in where copies have been given away for free or sold at a reduced price in order to give the numbers an upward boost. In any case, circulation is different from readership as more than one person typically reads a single copy of a given title. As a general rule, it is assumed in most industry calculations that between two and three people may be counted as readers per copy. Interestingly, according to Kent's research, in Britain the so - called 'average person' spends about 20 minutes a day reading a newspaper (in contrast with about 3.8 hours a day watching television, and around 3 hours listening to the radio). Precisely how best to quantify a 'reading threshold' for a given newspaper, however, is itself hotly disputed. For some industry studies, 'reading may simply refer to the availability of a newspaper in a household, for others it means that some of its pages have at least been scanned, while others define reading as a through engagement with its contents (the reader's recollection of which may then be assessed the next day).

The Most typical methods employed to collect data about newspaper audiences are interviews, conducted either face-to-face or over the telephone, and opinion surveys, usually involving a questionnaire circulated via the post. In addition, newspapers will often survey their own readers by including a questionnaire for them to fill in and return, possibly in exchange for a chance to win a prize. A range of different groups have a direct interest in knowing more about the characteristics associated with a newspaper's readership. These groups include, in the first instance, the owners of the newspaper, its editors and marketing people. Readership data, as Brown argues, serve 'as evidence of the success (or otherwise) of attracting the size and profile of audience aimed for via a particular policy on editorial contents and their treatment'. In the second instance, groups which also have a vital stake in acquiring information about a newspaper's readers include advertising agencies, market research organizations and, of course, potential advertisers.

It is almost always the case that the price listed on the front page of a 'quality' broadsheet newspaper generates only a relatively small share (usually about one-third) of the revenue necessary for the title to meet the costs of publication. The principal source of revenue is the sale of advertising space; the number of advertisements sold determines the size of the 'news hole', not the other way around. Newsworkers are all too aware of the status of the newspaper as a commodity, the financial success of which depends on attracting the type of readers of interest to specific advertisers (several of the tabloid titles, in contrast, depend primarily on sales revenue because their readers are less 'desirable' in marketing terms). In light of the demands of advertisers, then, it is not surprising that the 'upmarket' broadsheet's projection of an 'average' or 'typical' reader is likely to prefigure a middle-class, educated male who is middle aged and interested in public affairs. It is precisely this type of person whom many advertisers would define as their 'target audience', hence their aspiration to purchase the attention of this reader being sold by the 'serious' press.

Beyond these types of generalized assumptions, however, most newsworkers actually know very little about their readership, and tend to be highly sceptical of claims made on the basis of market research. After some forty years as a newspaper journalist in Britain, Alastair Hetherington maintains that 'very few journalists have more than a hazy personal view of their public.' He supports his point with quotations from a number of reporters:

> Oh, we're writing for the editor of course. He's the audience.
>
> My wife, she's the critic.
>
> Will it get people talking over the breakfast table or in the pub? That's what I ask myself.
>
> If I like it, that's the only quotient I put on it. I reckon that I'm an average reader.

Analyses based on interviews with newsworkers recurrently suggest that forms of direct audience feedback, such as letters and telephone calls, have only a limited impact on the newsworker's rudimentary impressions of their readers. Indeed, these types of respondents evidently tend to be dismissed as being 'atypical' or 'unrepresentative' due to a general conviction among newsworkers that 'the bulk of audience reaction is from cranks, the unstable, the hysterical and the sick'.

Academic studies of newspaper readerships have been undertaken via an extensive array of conceptual and methodological approaches, some of which entail extremely complex sociopsychological model in their attempts to quantify 'audience behaviour'. Of particular interest, however, are those investigations which have sought to explore the actual ways in which readers engage with their newspapers as an ordinary part of everyday life.

We many characterize newspaper reading not as an 'isolated, individual process', but rather as a 'collective process' typically transpiring 'in the context of the family, friends, colleagues'. The contents of newspapers, like those of other media, are 'materials for conversation', the precise meaning of which is the subject of discursive interaction among readers. Clearly, then, 'A bit of wild thinking is needed to catch and describe this complex world in all its rational irrationality'

Sceptical laughter? Reading the tabloids

Critical investigations of newspaper audiences typically focus on the 'quality' end of the market, that is, on the 'respectable', daily broadsheets of national prominence. The reason for this tendency, in part, is because these publications are usually deemed to have the greatest impact across society, especially in terms of their influence on the governmental sphere. Studies of the 'tabloid', 'popular' or 'mass consumption' press are growing in prominence, however, as increasing numbers of researchers seek to realign their analyses so as to address journalism as a form of popular culture. In Britain, daily tabloid titles like the **Sun** (about 3.8 million circulation) or the **Mirror** (about 2.5 million circulations), for example, secure far greater circulation figures than do their elite rivals, such as **The Times** (about 0.8 million circulation) or **The Guardian** (about 0.4 million circulation). Additional points of comparison include differences in their respective size, news values, mode of address, language (both written and visual), readership and price, all of which inform distinct strategies of representation.

If more than one tabloid editor prefers to use the phrase 'unpopular press' to describe the 'quality' titles, for some members of the latter the tabloids symbilize journalism sunk to its lowest depths. To be called 'the greatest tabloid journalist of all time', media commentator Clive James once remarked, is 'tantamount to calling a man the greatest salesman of sticky sweets in the history of dentistry'. In any case, there is little dispute that the ways in which the popular newspapers treat matters of public concern stand in marked contrast with the 'serious', 'high minded' reporting of the 'qualities'. As sparks argues: "the popular press embeds a form of immediacy and totality in its handling of public issues. In particular, this immediacy of explanation is achieved by means of a direct appeal to personal experience. The popular conception of the personal becomes the explanatory framework within which the social order is presented as transparent ... [T] he 'personal' obliterates the 'political' as an explanatory factor for human behaviour."

This overemphasis on the 'personal' as it is defined in relation to the immediate issues of daily life leads Sparks to maintain, in turn, that readers of tabloid newspapers are being denied the means to recognize the structural basis of power relations in society as a totality. News which is highly personalized in its representations of reality makes it that much more difficult for readers to identify means of articulating their resistance to these power relations.

There is a distinction between the 'official' and 'tabloid' news. In the USA, 'Official' news, prefigures a top - down definition of information based on convictions regarding 'what the people ought to know for a liberal democracy to function properly'. That is to say, official news promotes a certain form of knowledge, one which is largely defined in relations to public sphere events, by matters of policy, and not by the particularities of everyday life. 'The social reality it produces is the habitat of the masculine, educated middle class, the habitat that is congenial to the various alliances formed by the power – bloc in white partriarchal capitalist societies.' Significantly, this type of knowledge produces what may be called a 'believing subject', that is , a reader who generally accepts its claims as being self- evidently true. It is at this level, then, that its difference from tabloid news is most apparent: "The last thing that tabloid journalism produces is a believing subject. One of its most characteristic tones of voice is that of a sceptical laughter which offers the pleasures of disbelief, the pleasures of not being taken in. This popular pleasure of 'seeing through' them (whoever constitutes the powerful **them** of the moment) is the historical result of centuries of subordination which the people have not allowed to develop into subjection":

Where official news accounts normalize rational definitions of reality through appeals to 'objectivity', tabloid journalism subverts the very idea of rationality.

Examples of headlines taken from various weekly US 'supermarket tabloids' included in a study conducted by Hogshire support this latter point all too clearly:

Sex – Change Woman Makes Self Pregnant!... Scientists confirm 'first of a kind' case

(Sun)

John Lennon is Alive! Electrifying recent photo

(Sun)

Family Claims 500-IB. Space Alien Raided Their Refrigerator!

(Weekly World News)

Dolly the Cloned Sheep Kills A lamb - And Eats it!

(Weekly World News)

Not only is 'objective' journalism's appeal to value –free, neutral information disrupted, but also the very ideological disciplines regulating what counts as 'truth' are being flagrantly transposed. For news to be pleasurable, and thus popular, Fiske suggests, it needs to provoke conversation: 'it is by taking up and recirculating the issues of news orally that the people construct aspects of the public sphere as relevant to their own.' The apparent irrelevance of much 'official' (or 'top-down') news for many readers is thus directly linked to its repression of alternative or oppositional knowledges. 'Unlike official news,' Fiske maintains, 'popular news makes no attempt to smooth out contradictions in its discourse; indeed it exploits them, for unresolved contradictions are central to popular culture.' It is this contradictoriness, he argues, which the 'ordinary' reader can identify with as being consistent with their daily experience of trying to copy with inequalities of power: 'Knowing when to dissemble and go along with the system and when not to is a crucial tactic of everyday life'.

In her study **For Enquiring Minds: A cultural study of supermarket tabloids**, Bird similarly refuses to dismiss tabloid news as trivial 'trash', arguing instead that researchers need to understand why it is the case that millions of readers across the USA 'find a valued place for the papers in their lives'. It was with this end in mind that she arranged to place a notice in the **Examiner** inviting readers to share with her their experience of reading it and other tabloids, such as the **National Enquirer**, the **Weekly World News**, the **Globe**, the Sun and the **Star.** Fifteen members of this self–selected group (114 letters were received), as well as one other person, were then interviewed. Bird is quick to acknowledge that her respondents did not constitute a scientifically representative sample, yet believes that they were nevertheless reasonably close to the 'typical buyers' envisaged by the **Examiner's** staff: that is, 'mostly white, predominantly female, and middle- aged or order's. Interestingly, few of these respondents use the world', tabloid' to refer to publications like the **Examiner**, generally preferring terms like 'paper', 'magazine or an affectionate 'tabs'. The style of the tabloids tends to be described as 'fun', ' exciting', 'newsy', 'interesting' or 'gossipy'.

Although most of Bird's respondents consider the news stories to be well researched and verified, none of them accept everything presented on the pages of their tabloid as being true. That Said, some find pleasure in assuming an 'as if' stance, playing along with the item's truth claims to see how far their own willingness to believe can be stretched. Most readers, however, appear content to 'pick and choose' what they believe according to their existing interests and beliefs, while only a small minority or 'self - conscious' or 'ironic' readers stated that these 'sleazy' and 'vulgar' titles were an enjoyable kind of 'slumming'. Apparent across the range of responses is a perception that the tabloids provide a means to counter the constant flow of 'bad news' being presented in 'proper' newspapers and television newscasts. As Bird Writes: "an important element in their readings is indeed a form of resistance to dominant values - an awareness, for example, that they 'should' be reading about news and current affairs but find these studies boring and irrelevant. The perception that tabloids offer 'untold stories' about any thing from government waste to a movie star's romance is important to them because is suggests some sense of knowing and control over things that are really out of control." Still, as she quickly points out, the sense of pleasure derived from a felling of control is very different from actually having control and, moreover, 'resistance is not subversion'. Bird suggests that tabloids, as an endless 'source of laughs', help readers 'cope with their lives and feel good about themselves, but they do not give them power to change their lives'.

The word 'tabloid', signifies a very different meaning in a British context. The vast majority of readers in Britian purchase their newspaper in a tabloid format; there are currently five national daily tabloid titles being published: the **Sun, Mirror, Daily Mail, Express** and **Star.** Although these titles share certain characteristics with their weekly US namesakes (including common ownership in the case of those titles controlled by Rupert Murdoch's companies), none would consider regularly publishing the types of stories identified by the headlines listed above. The one national daily publication which might be so inclined, the **Daily Sport**, is not generally regarded to be a newspaper. Instead, these five tabloids provide - to varying degrees of depth - 'straight' news coverage of public affairs, although each arguably places a premium on entertaining, as opposed to informing, the reader. Their preferred modes of address draw on distinctive styles of language (everyday vernacular, direct 'straight talking;) and presentation (snappy headlines, provocative photographs, visually compelling forms of layout) so as to enhance their popular appear. As several analyses have documented, however, their 'light and breezy' news items can often be shown to anchor, in hegemonic terms, an array of prejudices (sexist, racist, homophobic, xenophobic and so forth) as being synonymous with 'public opinion' or 'what our readers think'.

Notable among the small number of studies conducted with British tabloid readers to data is Pursehouse's analysis of interview data gathered with regular readers of the **Sun.** This study, although somewhat preliminary in that it is based on only thirteen in – depth interviews (the people chooses were deemed to fulfill the ideal reader role set down by the title furnishes a series of intriguing insights into how this the most popular of Britain's dailies may be typically negotiated by its readers. By encouraging his interviewees to discuss their routine use of the newspaper in the context of their own personal lives, Pursehouse is able to situate the activity of sun reading in relations to work and domestic arrangements. In both spheres, he suggests, the tabloid offers a 'temporary respite' of sorts from the monotony of labour, an important form of distraction from specific tasks requiring concentration. As a resource, the Sun can be used as a shared talking point with others or, alternatively, as a site of 'private' leisure space in order to avoid such interactions. One thing that it is not, however, is a reliable source of fair or balanced reporting. In the words of three of the interviewees, for example:

> I find a lot of pleasure in the way that a lot of **The Sun** articles are written... I read a story like- like the classic ' Freddie Starr Ate My Hamster' and nobody in their right mind is going' to believe that- but as a piece of journalism to me -it's fun.
>
> (Julie)

> I watch the news on telly: so you get it straight.
>
> (Ian)

> I usually see the news once a day ... it's a truer report
>
> (Helen)

Far from being ' passively acquiescent' or 'misguided' about the truth- value of the tabloid's news coverage, then, most of these readers simply claim to look to television for their 'real news'.

Important aspects of the **Sun**'s popular appeal identified by this group of interviewees evidently include its humour, 'street credible' sociability and simplifying 'common sense'. As Pursehouse observes: 'It gains credibility, almost becomes friends with readers, through appearing to "talk the same language".' The basis of this 'friendship', he argues, is on the grounds of ' a shared joke', although much of what counts as the **Sun**'s fun persona' is gender-specific in that the tabloid typically positions itself as 'one of the lads'. At the same time, forms of ethnocentrism are recurrently discernible in its projection of whiteness as a norm in its 'humour'. Not surprisingly, however, the tabloid claims for itself an apolitical status, one consistent with its appeals to the 'down-to-earth' qualities of its 'fun-loving' readers who take pleasure in photographs of topless female models on 'page three', 'saucy' and scandalous tales, the problem pages, and so forth.

According to Pursehouse, the tabloid characteristically rejects 'politics' in favour of 'entertainment', leading him to suggest: "[In] some ways the horoscopes, crosswords, cartoons, sport pages and television chat say the most about **The Sun**'s politics. It is a world of 'entertainment', consumerism, easy self-pleasure, rather than social concerns or active, productive contributions to society... **The sun**] during the period of the interviews] was able to turn far-reaching 'public', ideological values into accessible personal stories... Above all, **The Sun** involved in the apparent depoliticising of politics itself and public life, turning all into individual issues, personalities and choices... as larger senses of social groups were denied or fragmented."

This language of depoliticization was implicitly reaffirmed by many of the interviewees, as indicated in quoted statements such as: 'Oh I don't like polities' (Sam), 'I am not a political animal' (Julie) or '[politics] don't interest me' (Jackie). Comments such as these are evidence for pursehouse of the success the **Sun** enjoys in making 'ordinary' its most entrenched cultural assumptions in a way which enables them to be taken up and lived by its readers as being consistent with a seemingly apolitical self-identity.

'Decoding' television news

Turning our attention now to the televisual news audience, it is advantageous to retain this important commitment to investigating the complex ways this medium is actually used by individuals in their day-to-day lives. The televisuals news account, far from simply 'reflecting' the reality of an event, actually works to construct a codified definition of what should count as the reality of the event. It follows that this dynamic, if inchoate, process of mediation is accomplished in ideological terms, but not simply at the level of televisual news as a discrete text. By focusing on how this text is consumed or 'decoded', the fluidly contingent conditions under which it is negotiated as 'meaningful' will be centered for analysis.

It seeking to address the moment of viewing of 'decoding' televisual news, it is crucial to recognize how the production or 'encoding' of the actual news accounts structures the hegemonic rules by which social reality is to be negotiated by the news audience. To clarify how analyses may best discern the extent to which the codes of televisual news discourse are embedded in relations of hegemony, many researchers have drawn on a conceptual model introduced by Hall. The encoding- decoding model, as it was quickly dubbed at the time, remains to this day the singularly most influential attempt to come to terms with these issues within cultural and media. By situating televisual news discourse in relation to the variable conditions of its encoding and decoding within the continually evolving limits of common sense, these critical modes of inquiry provide us with a far more dynamic understanding of meaning production than those efforts which treat it as an object in isolation, removed from its ideological context.

It follows, according to Hall, that while the encoding and decoding of the televisual news message are differentiated moments (that is, they are not perfectly symmetrical or transparent), they are related to one another by the social relations of the communicative process as a whole. Before this form of discourse can have an effect, however, it needs to be appropriated as a personally relevant discourse by the televisual viewer, that is, it has to be 'meaningfully decoded' It is this set of decoded meanings which' influence, entertain, instruct or persuade, with very complex perceptual, cognitive, emotional, ideological or behavioural consequences'. The ideological form of the message thus occupies a privileged position vis-a-vis the determinate moments of encoding and decoding. These moments each possess their own specific modality and' conditions of existence', for while their respective articulation is necessary to the communicative process, the moment of encoding cannot 'guarantee' that of decoding. That is to say, the moments of encoding and decoding are' relatively autonomous': they are inextricably bound up with one another, but there will be highly varied degrees of symmetry ('understanding' and 'misunderstanding') between the encoder-producer and the decoder- receiver.

Hall outlines three hypothetical positions from which decodings may be constructed. These 'ideal-typical' reading positions, all of which are available at the moment of decoding, may be distinguished as follows with regard to televisual news.

1. When the viewer of a televisual news account decodes its message in alignment with its encoding, the viewer is occupying the 'dominant-hegemonic position'. From this position, Hall argues, the 'authoritative', 'impartial' and professional' signification of the news event is being accepted as perfectly obvious or natural. The compliant viewer, operating inside the dominant subjectivity that the news account confers, thereby reproduces the hegemonic' definition of the situation' in ideological terms.
2. In what Hall characterizes as the 'negotiated position', the viewer understand the preferred definition being mobilized by the televisual news account, but does not relate to it as being self-evidently 'obvious' or 'natural'. Although viewers recognize its general legitimacy as a factual report, certain discrepancies, contradictions or 'exceptions to the rule' within their own (personal) situational context are identified. The news account is seen to be encouraging one interpretation over and above other, more appropriate possibilities.
3. The final reading position is that which is consistent with an 'oppositional' code. That is to say, the viewer apprehends the logic of the dominant-hegemonic position in such as manner that the authority of its definition is directly challenged. Hall offers the example of viewer who follows 'a debate on the need to limit wages but "reads" every mention of the "national interest" as "class interest". In this way, the dominant code has been reinflected within a resistant, counter-hegemonic framework of reference.

Here it is important to note that these 'ideal-typical' reading positions are begin marked for purposes of analytical clarity, and that they are not to be conflated with actual empirical or lived positions. In other words, researchers have recognized the need to try to interrogate the precepts underpinning the rather abstract neatness of these decoding positionalities. The viewer's engagement with an actual televisual newscast is likely to engender a complex range of (often contradictory) positionalities as the social relations of signification in operation.

Despite the rather abstract nature of its postulates, the encoding-decoding model allows for the issue of textual determination to be addressed as a fluidly heterogeneous process without at the same time, losing sight of the ways in which it is embedded in relations of power. The status of the televisual news viewer is not reduced to that of a victim of false consciousness (one who passively acquiesces to the dictates of a dominant ideology being imposed via the text), nor is it to be celebrated such that the viewer is to be accorded with an ability to identify freely with multiple interpretations of the text in a wildly immaterial fashion. Instead, by situating this dynamic activity as a negotiated process within certain conditional, but always changing, parameters, the encoding- decoding model succeeds in highlighting a spectrum of potential positions to be occupied, however fleetingly, in a determinant manner.

Central to the encoding- decoding model , then, is a recognition that the codification of meaning in televisual news discourse is necessarily constitutive of a particular politics of signification. What is at stake is the need to clear the conceptual space necessary for the investigation of the specific cultural relations at work in the discursive legitimation of certain hegemonic definitions of reality. From this vantage point, the communicative strategies utilized in televisual news to construct a sense of the very taken-for-grantedness of hegemony may be shown to be structuring 'in dominance' what is, at least in principle, a polysemic text. More to the point, once it is acknowledged that the full range of meanings potentially associated with a given message do not exist 'equally' (true polysemy), then new questions arise as to why particular meanings are being preferred over other possibilities. The ideological dynamics of hegemony may therefore be explicated, at least in part, through an examination of the integration of televisual news into everyday routines within the household. For a news narrative to be 'read' as an impartial reflection of 'the world out there', its explanations of the social world need to be aligned with the lived experiences of its assumed audiences. Critical efforts to document arguments of this type in relation to the decoding of televisual news discourse have utilized the research strategies of ethnography to considerable advantage. Evidence drawn from these ethnographic accounts often suggests that how people watch televisual news is much less determined by the actual content of the newscast than it is conditioned by the social relations of its consumption. In tracing the contours of the social contexts of viewing characteristic of domestic life in the household, the varied social uses to which televisual news is put have been examined in association with the (usually unspoken) rules by which the very 'normality' of everyday life is defined and reproduced.

The everydayness of news

In attempting to situate television news within the habits, rituals and taken-for-granted routines of everyday life, Silverstone's research makes a significant conceptual contribution. In examining the rhythmic ordering of the day's activities, he argues, it is necessary to discern the (often mundane) practices in and through which people sustain a personal sense of continuity from one day to the next. He points out that this feeling of constancy, of confidence in the stability of the world around us, is an important aspect of what Giddens has described as the project of' ontological security'.

Shaping a viewer's engagement with television, it follows, may be a deeply felt need for continuity as a kind of defence against the fears, worries or threats typically associated with an increasingly stressful world. Silverstone suggests that of the various genres of programming on television, it is the news which most clearly demonstrates ' the dialectical articulation of anxiety and security'. It is precisely this dialectical tension between televisual news's creation of apprehension and its narrative resolution which encourages the viewer to find in the newscast a sense of reassurance. This sense of reassurance, as Silverstone proceeds to elaborate, is more closely tied to the form of the news programme than to the item within it: "Reassurance is not provided only, of course, in the content of reporting. On the contrary. Yet the levels of anxiety that could be raised (and of course may well be either inevitably or deliberately raised) are ameliorated both in terms of the structure of the news as a programme (the tidying of papers, mutual smiles and silent chat following a 'human interest' story complete news bulletins, except under exceptional circumstance of crisis or catastrophe, all over the world), and in terms of its reliability and frequency."

The embeddedness of television news in the cultures of everyday life thus corresponds to the structured regularity of its ritualized 'flow' of information. More than that, however, the daily repetition of its preferred ways of mediating society's risks and dangers generates a comforting sense of familiarity and predictability. Consequently, it is the combination of these factors which, according to Silverstone, underpins the creation and maintenance of the viewer's sense of well-being and trustful attachment to the world beyond the television screen.

To further develop this line of inquiry, the scheduling of newscasts over the course of the day is deserving of critical attention. Several researchers have argued that these structures presuppose a representative domestic pattern within the household (current sub-genres being variations of breakfast news, lunchtime news, early evening news or suppertime news, the evening news, late- night news, and so forth). This inscription of television's institutional basis in its programming protocols is also revealed in the strategies employed to build and hold an audience throughout the day. Paterson's discussion of the scheduler's lexicon identifies several of the key formulations in play, including 'inheritance factor' (a programme which follows a particularly popular one is likely to inherit a proportion of that audience), 'pre-echo' (people tuning into a programme often watch the end of the preceding one, and thus may be encouraged to watch it in future) and 'hammocking' or 'tentpoling' (a less popular programme is placed bewteen two popular ones in order to benefit from inheritance and pre-echo), among others. Newscasts thus provide the scheduler with a means to facilitate the structuration of programming flow, namely by serving as points of transition in the routines of daily life and between different genres of entertainment.

Morse illustrates some of the potential implications of these dynamics for those people who work both inside and outside of the household when she writes: "Morning and prime time news occur at key thresholds in the day between work and leisure. Morning news precedes the transit from the privacy of the home, where one kind of reality prevails, to the realm of work, a reality with entirely different roles, hierarchies and rules. Morning news can be used as an alarm and packing device to speed the viewer- auditor into the rhythms of the work world; the news, however lightly attended, may also orient her/ him in social reality... In contrast, the evening news has a more hierarchical 'work' structure in its anchor-reporter relations, and the set, dress and demeanour of the news personalities are from the world of work and its imposed roles... The evening news is a mixed form... which aids the transition between one reality and another – between the attentiveness demanded by the world of work and the relaxation promoted by the TV fare of prime time drama and entertainment and the exhaustion of work".

A number of these themes are echoed in Hjarvard's account of how news programmes perform a ritual function: by tying together the different elements of the schedule, news 'provides variation as well as continuity'. The privileged status of the news as a 'reality-oriented genre' tends to be exploited by schedulers: 'the openness of the news structure creates the impression that the earlier reported events continue in a parallel time, but "behind" the screen while we watch other programmes'. This is an illusion, 'since social reality is not made up by a limited number of events, but by an infinite number of social interactions', and yet it is an illusion which has arisen because 'the reports of events have already been initiated as continuous stories'.

By accentuating this sense of the lived nature of the televisual news experience, Morley demonstrates why this medium needs to be located as an integral part of everyday life in the household and as such acknowledged as one of several sites of contestation. Televisual news, as his work and that of Hobson illustrates, can be the object of a micro politics of domestic power, the material nature of which may be shaped by the hierarchical dictates of familial ideology.

'How come they call it news if it's always the same?' is a rather intriguing question posed by a child in a **New Yorker** magazine cartoon. Somewhat curiously given the amount of public debate concerning the possible 'effects' of television on young minds, investigations into children's engagement with televisual news in the household are few and far between. Much of the available research tends to suggest that televisual news (and current affairs) programmes are unlikely to be watched by children by choice. That is to say, typically they watch because that is what happens to be on at the time (who holds the 'remote control' or the 'zapper' is a question of power) or because they are under pressure to do so by their parents and teachers (or indirectly by their peer groups). Newscasts are generally seen to be lacking the qualities which those programmes actually popular with children possess to attract and hold their attention. Indeed, some research suggests that children are likely to consider televisual news to be 'too serious' and 'boring', and that when they do watch it they often find it both difficult to follow and emotionally unsettling. In taking issue with the claim that the very process of watching televisual news may be properly conceived of as a politically oppositional activity in and by itself, Jensen argues that counter-hegemonic decodings are not in themselves a concrete materialization of political power. 'Resistance', he argues, 'is always resistance by someone, to something', for a purpose, and in a context'. It follows that in addition to questioning whether or not the 'preferred meanings' of the newscast are accepted (or not) by the viewer, attention needs to turn to consider the designated social uses of this genre of discourse and how they have evolved over time. Equally important, as well, are the changing forms of its actual relevance to viewers in terms of their lived experience of the everyday.

Briefly, Jensen identifies four general types of 'uses' which the viewers in his study ascribed to televisual news in terms of its significance for their daily lives.

First, televisual news has **contextual uses**, that is, the (usually gendered) roles and routines of ongoing activities in the household, especially with regard to domestic labour, are often partially structured by news viewing. The daily rhythms associated with news times, he argues, have become naturalized: 'There are no arguments [among the respondents], for example, that the evening news might be scheduled differently, fitting news to every day life rather than vice versa'.

Second, there are **informational uses** of televisual news for the viewers, particularly in their roles as 'consumer, employee, and, above all, as citizen and voter'. Here Jensen discerns a tension in the interview material from his respondents between 'the active and public uses that are associated with the news genre in a political perspective and ... its more limited practical relevance for audiences in terms of "keeping up" with issues for the purpose of conversation or voting in political elections'. One respondent, identified only as a 'printer', is quoted by Jensen as making a typical statement about the opportunity for political participation: "Well, I can vote. As far as taking any further, I don't know. I guess the opportunity will have to arise. Being, you know, I feel I'm just the average person out here."

Third, the implications of this tension for the social definition of news are even more pronounced with respect to what Jensen calls the **legitimizing uses** of televisual news. His interview material indicates that the political relevance of news to the viewer may be characterized in terms of the twin concepts of control and distance: 'The news may give its audience a sense of control over events in the world which would otherwise appear as distant... it is the feeling of control which is crucial, even if "you can't do anything about it"'. To the degree that televisual news is seen by the viewer to offer a 'generalized sense of community', then, it is equally likely to be considered to be an adequate forum for the articulation of public issues.

Finally, Jensen pinpoints the diversional uses of televisual news as discussed by his respondents, namely the variety of its visual pleasures for the viewer. The designated social uses for news, while generally defined by the respondents as distinct from those of entertainment, nevertheless share with them several important features. In particular, the 'holding power' of the visual narrative is deemed to be significant. The respondents attached salience not only to the visuals of the news events, which were seen as communicating ' a sense of experiential immediacy' (words such as 'pleasing', 'enjoyable', 'easy', 'vivid' and 'exciting' are used by the respondents), but also to the actual performance of the news. In the case of newsreaders, for example, both journalistic competence and personal appeal are stressed, while other respondents emphasized the appeal of 'nice, trivial information'.

Together, Jensen's four types of 'uses' suggest that although individuals make thier own sense of what the political significance of the news is for them, their perceptions are constrained by the ways in which what counts as 'politics' is being represented. "The reception of television news, accordingly, can be seen as an agent of **hegemony** which serves to reassert the limits of the political imagination... Even though the social production of meaning may be seen as a process in which the prevailing definition of reality can be challenged and revised, the conditions of that process are established within particular historical and institutional frameworks of communications. The polysemy of mass media discourses is only a political potential, and the oppositional decoding of mass communication is not yet a manifestation of political power.

From this perspective, it follows that news research strategies need to be adopted so as to further explore the extent to which televisual news discourse operates to 'reassert the limits of the political imagination' through the lived conditions of the everyday after all, as Jensen contends: 'If audiences do not perceive news as a specific resource for political awareness and action, then, arguably, the legitimacy of the political process and its institutions is called into question'.

Conclusion

These explorations of the everydayness of news culture provide us with a rich starting point for further research. By engaging with the apparent 'normality' of how readers, listeners and viewers 'make sense' of the news, we are better able to look beyond the fixed text-audience dichotomy indicative of so much previous research on news audiences.

Moreover, it has been shown that by situating the lived materiality of news culture within an evaluative context, we can begin to discern a conceptual pathway through, on the one hand, a deterministic model of the audience as passive onlookers whose thinking is controlled by a 'dominant ideology' and, on the other hand, a model which celebrates an active audience free to pick-and-choose any possible interpretation from a news text in an indeterminate manner. As we have seen, an alternative approach which recognizes the need to investigate people's deeply engrained habits of interacting with news discourses as part of their lived experience of the everyday, resists a rigid analytical separation of news discourse from the conditions of its decoding. In its place is a conceptual commitment to interrogating the fluidly contradictory cultural relations of textual negotiation in all of their attendant complexities. The materiality of news discourse, it follows, is made 'real' within certain variable yet determinant limits. That is to say, it is contingent upon the embodied experience of power relations as they traverse the contested terrain of ordinary culture.

◆◆◆

7

Qualities of Effective Newswriting

Words are really tools for making distinctions. Perhaps because we use them so much and so easily, we come to take them for granted. The resultant sloppiness has helped create some of humanity's worst problems. For example :

- Social scientists have suggested that the use of labels can help turn a person into a stutterer or a criminal. Call someone bad or stupid often enough and you may lead him or her to feel just that. A person has little to go on in defining himself or herself except words uttered by others. The school of thought which emphasizes this most strongly is symbolic interactionism.
- Race prejudice stems in large part from fallacies of labeling. As has been obvious the mere use of a world like Nigger, Wop or Nip calls attention to derogatory stereotypes of vast groups of people. Actually people of any ethnic, racial or religious group vary greatly, and careless use of labels obscures these differences. By so doing, it adds credence to beliefs that "all blacks are lazy" and "all Jews are aloof." Such beliefs, in turn, provide fertile soil for hatred and prejudice.

In this chapter we will lay a foundation for two important rules of newswriting. The rules go hand in hand in the sense that when you obey one, you are very likely to obey the other. They are:

1. Write factually, leaving your own opinions out of copy.
2. Write concretely, avoiding undue abstractness.

At first glance, the meanings for concrete and factual seem fairly obvious. However, there is a geat deal more to both words than meets the eye. This chapter analyzes each one carefully to help keep the reader on guard by driving home the fact that one can never be completely factual or concrete, but a reporter must keep trying (within certain limits)

We now turn to the rather sticky question of what a fact is.

Three Types of Meaning

Ogden and Richards- two semanticists-have noted that anyone who uses language is using symbols (words, pictures, graphs or drawings) to refer to something (perhaps a physical object, an abstract ideal like Christian love or a characteristic like beauty). The following diagram, simplified version of one presented by Ogden and Richards, shows how these three parts of the meaning process fit together.

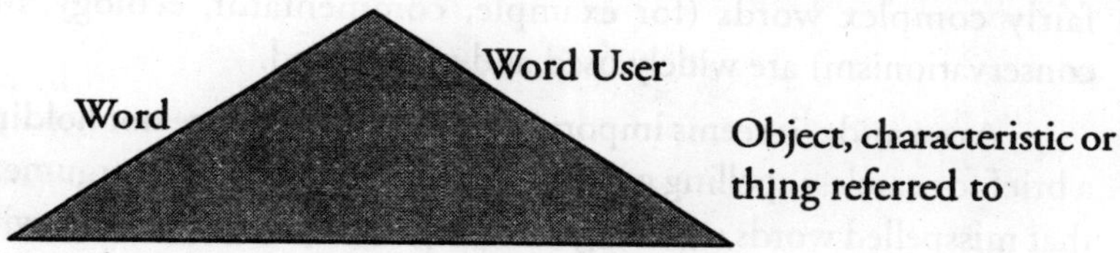

The dashed line indicates that the connection between symbol and object is an arbitrary one chosen by the word user. Granted, on rare occasions, a word may physically resemble an object (for example, the word "whiz" seems appropriate partly because it sounds like the speeding objects it often refers to). However, this is rare. And even in such a case, the word user could talk about a "shreeming" object. There is no law of nature which makes one say 'whizzing.'

By now, the reader may have raised an eyebrow slightly. Sure, one could call a whizzing object a shreeming object, you might say. But what good would it do ? It would simply confuse the readers and listeners, most of whom have not heard the word "shreeming" before and do not know what to make of it.

This point would be well taken. A writer and a reader would have the same meaning for "shreem" only if they have had similar experiences with that word. People get along and understand each other largely because they have had similar experiences with a great many words. Practically, when, you cannot use just any word you wish without losing your audience.

In a deeper sense, however, this analysis really supports the validity of the "dashed line" in the Ogden-Richards diagram. Meanings are in people, not in words. Dictionaries are useful because they report common word spelling and usage within a society at a certain time. They do not reflect natural or God-given standards of proper usage.

The important thing is for the reporter to use words which will be understood. His or her job is to communicate with readers. Whether a given word is understandable depends more on whether readers are familiar with it than on its length or complexity. To be sure, often-used words tend to be short and simple. However, some fairly complex words (for example, commentator, ecology and conservationism) are widely used and understood.

As an aside, it seems important to stress that we are not holding a brief for careless spelling grammar and word choice. The argument that misspelled words are all right so long as they don't interfere with understanding (anyone would know that "alright" really means "all right") has no place in journalism. A misspelled word tells your readers that you are careless and/or illiterate. No journalist can achieve genuine success with this kind of reputation, since newspapers do serve as educational instruments.

Following Ogden and Richard then word meaning really has three aspects-one centering on each element in the above diagram.

First, denotative meaning centers on the referent or object. The statement that Joel Smith is 6-feet-10 tall give us denotative information. Such a sentence may be true or false. In either case, it is highly denotative because it provides information about Joel which we can check. Generally accepted measurement procedures insure that we will agree on Joel's height, whether we chance to love or hate tall people.

Second, connotative meaning centers on the word user. The statement that the Taj Mahal is beautiful, really tells us more about the observer than about the Taj Mahal. Most people feel it's beautiful, but some can stand only building with sharp turns and corners. Taj Mahal lovers really have no basis for arguing that deviants are in error. Beauty is in the eye of the beholder.

Third, structural meaning centers on the word itself as related to surrounding words. The sentence "Azlnx pounded Zlvbn" looks like nonsense. Yet the sturcture of the sentence tells us something about Azlnx and Zlvbn. It indicates they are both things. It also shows that Azlnx was capable of pounding Zivbn, and that Zivbn was capable of being pounded by Azln.

Structural meaning often provides cues about denotative and connotative meanings. A note in an operatic piece has beauty partly because of surrounding notes (hence context provides connotative meaning). And the statement, "Mike Schmidt hit a long .... over the left field wall" gives us denotative information that he probably hit a round object called a ball (after all, few other things are hit over left field walls very often).

The demand that a reporter stick to the facts seemingly requires emphasis on denotative meaning. Semantic analysis makes it clear, however, that there is no such thing as pure denotative meaning-as perception without perceiver.

A simple example should drive this last point home. Someone might be unable to make any use of his or her senses. To such a person, poor soul, the phrase 6-feet-10 would be meaningless. He or she cannot experience it in any way. Obviously, then, an object's height has no meaning without reference to the senses and skills of the observer.

How can one avoid Editorializing?

Journalists have learned from other professional communicators' mistakes to avoid overusing highly connotative words. Perhaps the bestknown abusers of such words, by the way, are diplomats. In a typical U.N. Security Council debate, charges against aggressors and imperialists abound. At best, such debate seldom leads to solutions (if they are to be found at all, solutions generally come in secret session where each side can talk specifics without using highly emotional words to impress the world). At worst, public debate may worsen a crisis by hurting diplomats' feelings.

Freedom of the press is a highly connotative expression that causes journalists many problems. To the westerner, freedom of the press implies the right to criticize even top government officials. Only when fully informed about news of the day, including mistakes in high places, can citizens look out for their own interests at the polls, in twon meeting and elsewhere.

To avoid confusion, the young reporter must work hard to seek out the subtle editorializing that can creep into a story. Eventually, sticking to the facts will become second nature. In the meantime, however, one must remain on guard.

Perhaps the worst-offending words are loaded adjectives like beautiful and good. The reporter's job is to describe things like a person's physical characteristics (for example, thinning hair or a height of 6 feet 8 inches) and accomplishments. That provides information needed to judge attractiveness. Yet the reader does the judging. It's important to remember that one can objectively report a statement by another person that something is good or beautiful. Joan's beauty is a matter of opinion but the fact that Robert said that she's beautiful is not.

Adjectives such as unique, strong, active and dynamic carry more or less hidden implications of goodness or badness. Such words require special care becuase their meaning varies from usage to usage. For example, we expect politicians to be dynamic, but we may care very little whether druggists are or not. It follows that a dynamic politician may seem better than a dynamic druggist. Furthermore, in a story about politics, one should make it clear in what way a person is dynamic. Does the term mean giving lots of speeches and kissing hundreds of babies each year ? Without such concrete elaboration, the word dynamic is dangerously vague.

A reporter is often tempted to insert some commonly used, subtly loaded words and phrases because of habit. A well-earned rest is one example. (To say that one is taking such a rest implies that he or she has worked hard and done a good job on something.) Reporters generally have no business making such judgments.

In the same vein, many people often use the word lady in conversation out of deference. However, woman generally suits the reporter's needs better because it lacks certain connotative meaning (good manners, social respectability and high moral character to name a few) generally associated with lady.

The phrase "passed on to one's reward" is inappropriate in obituaries for at least two reasons. It sounds flowery. And it implies the deceased has shown good character and has gone to a pleasant life in the hereafter. A desire to honor the dead is understandable, but reporting specific accomplishments is the way to do it. Further, using a loaded phrase routinely in all obituaries-even for the worst of scoundrels-will eventually make the words seem meaningless. In much the same way, Hollywood has gradually drained adjectives like "outstanding" and "spectacular" of meaning.

Editorializing can also creep in with adjectives like large, heavy and long. At first glance, such words seem quite objective because they refer to dimensions (area, weight and height) which one can measure scientifically. Howeyer, heavy and long do not specify weight and height in measurable units. That which is heavy to a weakling may be very light to a champion weightlifter.

Lest the reporter feel too restricted, we pause to note that some subjective adjectives can be used where their application in a given story is clear. For example, one may safely call Miss America beautiful because she is chosen by a panel of authorities on beauty. Many people might argue, in fact, that the Miss America pageant helps determine the way in which Americans define beauty.

It's not accurate to equate objectivity with avoidance of connotative meaning. In fact, there's a growing belief that today's reporter must handle such meaning clearly and forcefully, rather than to ignore it or treat it subjectively. The National Advisory Commission on Civil Disorders put the point as follows:

> By and large, news organizations have failed to communicate to both their black and white audiences a sense of the problem America faces. ... the media report and write from the standpoint of a white man's world. The ills of the ghetto, the difficulties of life there, the Negro's burning sense of grievance, are seldom conveyed.

Ills, difficulties and senses of grievance are not easily measured. they center on the way people feel. The commission seems to be saying that the press cannot help people share meaning about complex problems in human relations without going beyond traditional, highly denotative reporting.

What can the journalist do to convey connotative meanings- as the Kerner Commission asks-without entering a semantic fog ? One approach is to adopt the methods of the feature writer, who reports facts but does it in such a way as to make readers laugh, cry and feel anger. Good feature writers do not use loaded, unclear words. Second, the reporter can use modern social science techniques to measure opinions, fealings and frustrations with some objectivity.

By now the reader should have some feel for the great care required to be factual. We turn next to our second rule-good writing should, within limits, be concrete.

The Ladder of Abstraction

The continuum from abstract to concrete includes many shades of grey.

One of the authors has asked hundreds of students which word is more abstract, cow or animal. All agree on animal, but few can explain just why. To understand, we must remember the three parts of the meaning process-symbol, symbol user and symbol referent. Cow and animal differ in at least two ways with regard to these parts.

First, animal refers to a larger, more varied class of referent objects than does cow. Tiny insects qualify, as do whales and elephants.

Forgetting such variation can lead us astray. When we give something a label, we lump it and other things into a class designated by the label. As used here, the word object is defined very broadly to refer to any entity. Entities can vary from physical objects like a table to concepts like freedom to concept systems like democracy. In an oft-quoted example, people who know little about ancient Greece may assume that Socrates was masculine because he was a man. Actually, however, Socrates was effeminate in some ways.

Second, a concrete word like cow conveys lots of information. Say you have a cow and one immediately knows your animal has four legs, four stomachs and probably eyes that look large and mournful.

Moving a few rungs up the ladder, the word democracy has a great deal of emotional or connotative meaning for many people. Hundreds of thousands of Americans have died to preserve democracy. The word's history has made it "loaded." Its mere mention stirs the adrenalin in many people-particularly political conservatives. Animal, by contrast, is a very bland word.

People from several nations and backgrounds view democracy differently. They disagree about its denotative meaning. (Some people feel democracy refers to specific events like casting a secret ballot, but others would include civic freedom more broadly defined.) And they differ on its connotative meaning. (In the United States during the 1970s, many young leftists hated the thought of American democracy about as strongly as their parents loved it.)

It's interesting to note that, while animal is more abstract than cow, the two words differ little in connotative meaning. Both are quite bland. However, as we move further up the ladder of abstraction, a growing number of words tend to have lots of emotional loading. Even highly educated people let such meaning get out of hand. For example, "aggressor" has become a fighting word in the United Nations.

Concrete words can have emotional wallop, too. Take a sentence like, "Lying face down in the mud, Sam crawled inch by inch toward the edge of the battlefield." Fortunately, we can decide and agree on the denotative meaning of a concrete word-on its referent. This, in turn, helps us control and harness the connotative meaning to fit our needs. The moral to the journalist-be specific and don't write in broad general terms.

Dead-Level Abstrating

The general semanticists make one point that many of us overlook. Interesting writing tends toward the lower end of the ladder of abstraction, all right, but concreteness can be overdone.

One of the authors once attended a convention at a small college. Roommates were assigned more or less at random, and the author drew a talkative but seemingly harmless partner. Trouble was, this fellow had a great penchant for the little things. He went on endlessly about the blue wallpaper in the dormitory room, the soggy corn flakes in the cafeteria, and so on. A few hours of such ultraconcrete minutae can make the poor listener or reader scream.

To be sure, extremely abstract writing can be just as boring. One sociology book contains 470 pages of statements like the following:

> It is true that seen from the logico-experimental point of view the theories involved in ritual prescriptions involve either error or unverifiable statements or both. The former element is by no means negligible. But in a positivistic context the tendency is to jump directly from proof of the existence of error to the conclusion that it is explained by a nonnormative, nonsubjective drive, or something of the sort.

Concreteness depends on the content of a passage and the choice of words describing specific events which we can all easily imagine. The above sociological passage is bound to be quite abstract because of its content. However, the author could have added some concreteness by choosing words that clearly describe certain specific ritual prescriptions and the errors made in their interpretation.

General semanticists have coined the phrase dead-level abstracting to denote remaining steadfastly at one level-any level-on the ladder of abstraction. It is generally wise to stay on the lower rungs in the news business. Yet one needs to stand back occasionally and say something about how reported facts relate to what is past and what's apt to come later. This involves at least a dash of abstractness.

It's possible, for example, to write a brief story which does nothing more than quote an American black separatist leader calling for militant action, for a black nation quite separate from white America. The story takes a greater interest, however, when the reporter stops to contrast the leader's rhetoric with the emphasis on integration which dominated the civil rights mevement 10 to 20 years earlier. Such, analysis revolves around a fairly abstract issue-separation vs.

integration as a primary goal of black people. Without moving a step or two up the ladder abstraction, the story would be incomplete, unclear and perhaps boring.

At the opposite extreme, young reporters doubtless tend to plant their feet near the top of the ladder of abstraction at least as often as near the bottom.

Abstract words are dangerous because they help build stereotypes, which in turn contribute to prejudice. Such words as oriental and Hindu suggest images which are bound to be inaccurate because one is tempted to apply the same image to each person within a broad class.

Orientals are a varied lot, as are Hindus. Careless use of abstractions tends to gloss over each person's own unique character.

One way to avoid being too abstract is to define terms by analogy with some object or process familiar to the reader. One of the authors has frequently done this in reporting on agricultural science. Here are two examples from his files:

- Elasticity of demand puzzles people. However, it helps to remember that an elastic rubber band or garter stretches. By analogy, people almost quit buying a product with highly elastic demand when the market price goes up. In other words, they make a little bit of such a product stetch or go further. Thus defined, demand elasticity becomes clear to a newspaper audience.
- The root system of alfalfa seems rather unexciting at first glance. Yet one can add punch to a story about alfalfa roots by likening them to a food cellar. Mow or pasture alfalfa in September and you empty the cellar by forcing plants to spend the fall living off material stored in roots. As a result, alfalfa might starve during the long winter that follows.

A second approach to insuring against too much abstraction is to define clearly long, unfamiliar words or leave them out entirely. Treatment of a phrase like broadcast seeding requires special care. Writing for a metropolitan Philadelphia paper, a reporter would need to define it in parentheses (scattering seed on top of the ground).

however, the farm editor of a Fargo, N.D., paper probably need not define the term. Broadcast seeding would be very clear to Fargo farmers.

A third way of moving down the ladder of abstraction is to describe how an event happens and not just the end results of that event. A science writer once tackled what seemed to be a drab story on a rat poison called dieldrin. The result of dieldrin use-a bunch of dead rats-seemed less than appetizing. However, a little reading revealed that dieldrin is applied as a kind of dust. Rats get it on their fur, then eat it inadvertently while using their tongues to clean themselves. The picture of a rat being hoodwinked into licking itself to death seemed rather touching (perhaps humorous to some), and this formed the basis of the story lead.

Another story discussed a survey on those who skied in Michigan. Statistics such as gross annual income for ski resorts looked dry until the author hit on the idea of using them to portray an average skier and how he or she spends a skiing weekend. Some arithmetic revealed that the typical skier spent $58.40 per weekend trip and traveled 580 miles per round trip to and from a ski area. Such figures painted a picture that readers could relate to themselves. After all, it's rather enjoyable to compare oneself with another person-even a hypothetical one.

Clear, interesting presentation of number takes ingenuity, but it's fun for both the reader and the writer. For example, a certain fast-food chain claims to have sold over 10 billion hamburgers. That figure seems mind-boggling and rather dry. But one enterprising writer brought the statistic to life by noting that 10 billion hamburgers piled one on top of another would reach from the earth to the moon with 40,000 hamburger miles to spare! Also, one burger measures about four inches in diameter. That means that 10 billion laid side by side around the globe at the equator would form a hamburger belt 8½ miles wide.

At a somewhat different level, many journalists need to present several numbers at once so as to clarify trends among them. The recent growth of specialized magazines and journals has made this more important than ever before.

Presenting Numbers

Tables and graphs help. The latter appear only in a few specialized publications. So this section concentrates on constructing and explaining numerical tables.

To begin, a number usually seems dry and meaningless without a standard of comparison. A journalist often needs to provide a context. For example, a question arises in reporting that America's average income per family last year was, say, $12,000. Is that figure meaningful by itself ? Probably not. An economist might advise throwing in the average income in a typical (neither boom nor depression) year like 1950 as a standard of comparison.

Another tip-look for trends among numbers. Then make your tables as simple as possible to emphasize and clarify these trends.

Assume you are doing a story about auto sales in a small town. You go to the auto title office and collect the data shown in table 1 (with 24 cars sold in July 2001 , 17 in August 2001, and so on).

Table –1

Number of Automobiles Sold in Smith County During the Last Six Months of Each Year 2001-2003

	2001	2002	2003
July	24	28	27
August	17	20	39
September	21	24	41
October	35	34	48
November	38	31	39
December	29	36	46

This table is ponderous and hard to read. Few will stop to interpret its 18 separate numbers.

In refining the table, look for trends. At a glance, you note a sales decline from July to August in both 2001 and 2002. But the reverse holds in 2003 (sales go up in August then). Two years out of three isn't a conclusive batting average, so you'll probably want to ignore August and look elsewhere.

Further scanning shows a substantial increase from the third quarter (July through September) to the fourth (from October on). This holds in each year.

Once you decide to focus on quarters, you may re-cast the table as in number 2. This version is simple. It points up the fourth-quarter sales increase more clearly than does number 1. Also, it takes little space.

Table –2

Number of Automobiles Sold in Smith County During the Third and Fourth Quarter of Each Year, 2001-2003

	2001	2002	2003	Quarterly Totals
Third Quarter (July- September)	62	72	107	241
Fourth Quarter (October-December)	102	101	133	336
Annual totals, last half.	164	173	240	

In nearby text, you can further specify the trend by noting that, for the three years as a whole, sales increased by 39 percent from the third quarter to the fourth. (You may want to attribute this to a new model year starting in October. But this requires someone's interpretation. It doesn't follow directly from the numbers themselves.)

All of this brings us to another tip in detecting trends. Focus on row and column totals. Column totals in table 2 show a very small increase of 5 percent (from 164 to 173) in 2003, but a whopping 39 percent boost (from 173 to 240) in 2003. Here we have "pulled out" for all to see a trend more or less hidden in table 1.

Percentages can help make sense out of numbers. But they are also tricky. You'll need to observe some precautions in using them:

1. Point out the base figure used in computing each percentage. Authors occasionally pull a fast one by shifting bases without letting the reader know. An example shows this. Assume car sales totaled 100 in your town in 2001, 130 in 2002 and 100 in 2003. Here you have a 30 percent increase over the previous

year in 1974, a 23 percent decline in 2001. Reporting only percentages would imply a net increase of 7 percent from 2004 through 2003. Yet sales total 100 in each of those years. The rub comes in use of the 2001 figure (100) as the base in computing the 2001-02 change (30/100=30 percent), the 2002 number (130) in figuring the 2002-03 change (30/130=23 percent). By all means avoid such "sleight of hand".

2. Don't base percentages on a very few cases. This may seem to make a mountain out of a molehill-another type of sleight of hand. For instance, it may sound impressive to say that 60 percent of those in your bridge club are Republicans and 40 percent are Democrats. But such a statement would be unwise (perhaps even deceitful) if it camouflages the fact that your club has but five members !

We now come to two final tips on presenting numbers in tabular form.

First, construct a table before writing copy about it. Once you have a clear, simple table with a message, the copy should almost write itself. Second, place explanatory text near the table or tables to which it refers. It's frustrating indeed to read a table on page 3, then its explanation on page 17. Shuffling back and forth takes time.

Thus far, we have focused on the need to be concrete, factual and clear. This, in turn, helps the reporter realize journalism's two most vital goals-accuracy and completeness. It's impossible to overmphasize these qualities. The public's dependence on the mass media places an awesome responsibility on the reporter's shoulders.

Accuracy

Joseph Pulitzer, one of the most respected-and damned-of all American newspaper editors, emphasized to his staff at the St. Louis Post-Dispatch the importance of accuracy in the slogan: "Accuracy, accuracy, Accuracy." To Pulitzer and to all good journalists, accuracy in content is an obligation of all reporters as well as a practical matter and a question of pride and craftsmanship.

One of the most famous inaccuracies in American journalism crossed the Atlantic on Nov. 7, 1918. Roy Howard, then president of United Press, cabled from France that World War I was over. The UP cable desk in New York flashed the news across the country. Hundreds of papers ran it under banner headlines, triggering many wild celebrations.

Unfortunately for Howard, the armistice wasn't actually signed until Nov. 11. Howard had gotten his information in a conversation with Adm. Henry B. Wilson, Commander of all U.S. Naval forces in France. The UP chief filed his story and went to grab some dinner. While waiting for his drink, he received a frantic message from Wilson that the dispatch was "un-confirmable." Howard's follow-up dispatch, designed to correct the error, did not reach New York until almost noon on Nov.8.

Howard claimed, and Wilson admitted, that United Press really acted in good faith. In fact, one author later suggested that an armistice of some sort may have been signed on No.7 with Kaiser Wilhelm's government, only to lose its official status when the Kaiser abdicated his office.

Guilty of poor reporting or not, Howard came in for great abuse from fellow journalists. The Burlington, Vt., News cancelled its UP service, and other papers threatened to do so. The moral: Even good intentions and reasonable care may not relieve the sting of an inaccurate story.

Accuracy covers a variety of things- accurate notes, accurate typing, correct spelling and grammar, and diligent editing. Some of these activities seem mundane and easy. But all demand the best care and effort a journalist can muster.

Despite deadline pressure, there is no excuse for inacurracy in newswriting. It happens, but it should never be shrugged off and taken for granted. If a woman spells her name Smyth rather than Smith, that is her privilege, and no reporter has the right to change it. If she is 70, saying that she is 69 is not close enough. If she has been arrested and lives at 245 South St., listing her residence as 246 South St. will not make the people who live there very happy.

Completeness

The New York Times slogan, "All of the News That's Fit to Print," stresses a second virtue of good reporting- completeness. The

Times, one of the world's most prestigious papers, is the only American paper that routinely runs presidential speeches and pres conferences word for word, supplemented, of course, by accompanying stories.

At times, the temptation to tell only part of a story is very strong. Partly because of a concern for national security, the American press said very little about preparations for the ill-fated. Bay of Pigs invasion against Fidel Castro's Cuba. **New York Times** staffers argued among themselves long and loud on just how much should be told.

In the end, President John F. Kennedy publicly scolded the **Times** for printing too much. Privately, however, the president reportedly told **Times** managing editor Turner Catledge, "If you had printed more about the operation, you would have saved us from a colossal mistake."

The moral : A reporter should never be satisfied with half a story. There may be times when full reporting would jeopardize personal interests (as when a very young first offender commits a crime) and national interests (as with troop movements during wartime). However, these cases are rare. In any event, holding back information is always an editor's decision. The reporter should never feel comfortable with gaps in a story.

Reporters must be on constant guard for inaccuracies and lack of completeness when depending on other people for information. Witnesses are notoriously inconsistent in their descriptions. In situations in which a murder has been staged in front of a group, for example, the variations are always extreme. Witnesses may estimate the same intruder's height at anywhere from 6-foot-5 to 5-foot-10. Even supposed expert observers can disagree. (A staged murder at a scientists' convention once sent a group of psychologists into utter confusion.)

The reporter must develop a sixth sense about which facts to check and which to accept. At first glance, all this may seem to imply that a good reporter never trusts anyone and would be cynical about everything. Any experienced reporter will say this is absurd. In the first place, one seldom has time to check every fact. Secondly, through dealings with sources, the reporter soon learns who can be trusted.

Thus, courthouse reporters generally will accept a police report of a suspect's place of birth and age rather than taking the time to dig out the suspect's birth certificate. The reporter knows which politicians can be trusted for straight information, which business executives can be depended upon, which teacher will not seek to hide problem areas.

In spite of this, further checking sometimes may be called for. In deciding when to dig deeper, a reporter needs at least three things:

1. A thorough knowledge of the area covered. The reporter must understand the subject matter so well that subtle inaccuracies do not go unnoticed. And only a reporter who has been around a while and knows the community will be likely to get tips or hear rumours leading to good stories.
2. A dash of suspicion and a good deal of care in evaluating sources of information. A reporter may often take the word of an honest, competent police officer who seemingly has nothing to hide. Also, it's important to do as much as possible to help the reader evaluate news sources.
3. Alertness and skill in spotting inconsistencies. The statement that an accident occurred at Palmer and Vine streets may look fine to a casual observer. But it should send the reporter to a city map to see if Palmer and Vine run parallel to each other. Likewise the reporter will want to check further if two people disagree on some information.

Using such intangibles as these, Carl Bernstein and Bob Woodward of **The Washington Post** broke one of the most important news stories in American history –the Watergate scandal leading to the downfall of President Richard M. Nixon. They began feeling the story was other than routine when they found that two address books belonging to the men arrested at the Watergate contained the name and phone number of E. Howard Hunt, with the notations "W. House" and "W. H." A call to the White House number drew a comment from the switchboard operator that Hunt might be in Charles Colson's office. Further digging on Colson led to a great deal of related information, and the story began to mushroom.

On June 22, 1972, just five days after the break-in, President Nixon said publicly that the White House had no involvement whatever in this particular incident. By that time, the two **Post** reporters had noted so many White House related coincidences that they "lingered" over the italicized phrase in Nixon's statement and resolved to push on.

During their investigation, Bernstein and Woodward obtained a list of people occupying offices at the headquarters of the Committee to Reelect the President (CRP). Reasoning that a person usually works close to someone with a related job, the reporters began knocking on the doors of those with offices near John Mitchell and other key people.

In interviewing, it sometimes proved useful (although some might feel it a bit questionable ethically) to imply falsely one already knew something and was simply seeking added detail. In this way, reluctant witnesses were led to believe they could talk-they really weren't spilling many beans, anyhow, if the interviewer knew the essentials.

Speed

Accuracy and completeness are easy if one has lots of time to use the dictionary, atlas, city directory and telephone. Deadline pressure often makes this difficult. However, the good reporter doesn't dash off stories at breakneck speed without care and thought. The key is to save time for writing by moving rapidly in getting to the scene of the story, getting needed information on the phone, taking notes and organizing thoughts. Given all this, speed in actual writing and typing as well as editing copy will follow.

Speed is a quality which most reporters develop gradually. It may require weeks or months on the job to remain calm under pressure. An experienced journalist is rarely pushed to the point of being uncomfortable-working at full speed becomes normal. Understandably, not everyone can become accustomed to daily and even hourly deadlines. As a result, some beginning journalists may be happier on magazines and other publications with fewer and more distantly spaced deadlines.

The point is this: The reporter must be able to work under great pressure and still maintain accuracy throughout. Accuracy is necessary at all times ; speed is necessary some of the time. The good reporter has both.

Ethical Considerations

Journalists work in the most public of all occupations. They are depended upon by millions of readers, viewers and listeners, all of whom are media critics. The degree to which journalists are effective depends upon the degree to which they are trusted by the public . Recent revelations of illegal and unethical activities by government officials, combined with a national trend toward a skeptical consumerism, has made citizens more likely to look at all social institutions, including the media, with a critical eye.

Thus, it has become more and more apparent that journalists must conduct not only their professional lives, but to some degree their private lives, so as to avoid casting suspicion on their performance. This was stressed in a memo from Wes Gallagher, former president and general manager of The Associated Press, to AP staff members.

"You are all aware of the increasing and unprecedented scrutiny which the press, its members and the media in general are receiving today. It comes not only from legal, judicial and governmental elements of society, but from the general public and some members of the media themselves," Gallagher said in the memo. "This is expectable since the media are scrutinizing and questioning the activities of many institutions. It is therefore necessary that the press conduct itself in a way that is above reproach in the eyes of the public as well as in fact."

Gallagher stressed that any compromise in the integrity of the Associated Press "reflects on the news report as a body and on each staff member individually. The basic rule, which does apply to everything in a general way, is that impartiality in reporting, editing and covering the news must be strictly observed."

For these reasons, media groups like AP as well as other journalistic organizations have developed sets of ethical policies to guide reporters in their day-to-day activities. The Code of Ethics of the Society of Professional Journalists, Sigma Delta Chi, is representative of these in most respects.

In Gallagher's memo, as well as the SPJ, SDX code, emphasis is placed upon many ethical considerations which have been a part of journalism for years. Reporters and editors are urged to remember that they are dealing with human beings who do not lose all their rights to be respected even though they have become objects of news. Reporters who remember this and who avoid assuming a superior attitude in their relations with news sources will have little trouble living with the following:

- Provide the right of reply. The journalistic concept of balanced presentation, as well as respect for human beings, dictates that an effort will be made to give individuals the chance to present their side of a story. This is especially true where the focus is on charges which affect reputations. Reporters should attempt to present the reply as part of the original story, but if that is not possible because of time pressures, a separate story should be presented the following day. In some cases, it may be desirable to withhold a story for a day until that reply can be obtained.
- Respect an individual's right to privacy. Sometimes, this is a legal matter, but it should be a journalistic concern long before it achieves that level. Journalists sometimes must make news judgment decisions about whether to present a particular story. They must ask whether the content of the story truly is of value to the public or whether the temptation to present the material is based on little more than curiosity. A classic debate here centers on the degree to which a government official's private life has impact upon his or her public life. Some reporters assume that public officials have opened themselves for total scrutiny; others try to make individual determinations. In either event, it's a troubling area of reporter prerogative.
- Avoid pandering to morbid curiosity. Reporters also must decide how far to go in presenting details in stories which concern sex or crime. No firm rules can be developed, but at some point enough is enough. Readers do need specific details, but reporters

need to ask themselves why additional material is being presented. It is not enough that the information is available; its presentation in a news story must be necessary to the full understanding and not simply satisfy curiosity.

- Make prompt and complete correction of errors. Usually, how corrections are handled is a matter of the newspaper's policy, but reporters who know they have made a mistake should initiate the effort to have the correction made. Reporters are human, and they sometimes do err. Honest, prompt and complete correction of errors is a practice which most readers will respect. Consistent ignoring or hiding of mistakes, in time, will destroy a reporter's or newspaper's reputation. Of course, the best remedy is to devote full attention to avoiding errors, but when they do occur, do something about them immediately.
- Engage in open dialogue with your audience. Journalistic organizations sometimes are accused of being in an ivory tower and of having lost touch with the public they serve. Reporters have little control over such means of communication as letters to the editor, but they do have great opportunity to keep in touch with the public. Reporters provide newspapers or broadcast stations with their most effective link to the outside world. If coverage has little relationship to the needs and desires of the community, reporters must share in the blame.
- Avoid conflict of interest. Gallagher's memo and the SPJ, SDX code both stress the necessity for journalists to be free of any obligation to a news source or potential source which could hinder fair, complete and accurate reporting. Common sense tells us it is very difficult to write a critical story about someone for whom we have developed a special fondness or to whom we are indebted. For this reason, the code stresses that journalists should accept nothing of value from an actual or potential news source. Likewise, involvement in political activities or secondary employment should be done by journalists with extreme caution.

Journalistic organizations know most individual reporters can be trusted. They know that most are dedicated to their profession and would never allow their journalistic performance to be influenced by gifts or involvement. But the unfortunate fact is that members of the public do not necessarily know this. The growing public suspicion could lead society to lose its faith in the media, and this would seriously hamper the social contribution of journalism. That's why both Gallagher and the code stress not only conflict of interest but the appearance of such conflict of interest.

Summary & Conclusions

While it's often taken for granted, language can become unclear and even dangerous unless it's used with care. Such care requires that we be aware of types of meaning and levels of abstraction.

Semanticists have suggested three basic types of meaning. Connotative meanings reside in emotions like love and hate which occur in the word user. Denotative meaning provides information that most if not all people can check, and the emphasis here is on the entity referred to. Structural meaning stems from other symbols.

In general it's wise to write concretely. However, too much concreteness as well as too little can make a news story boring. The good writer moves up and down on the lower rungs of the ladder of abstraction. It's unwise to stay in one place.

The distinction between abstract and concrete words is fairly complex. Abstraction involves:

1. Using a symbol to designate a large, varied class of entities (for example, animals). Such symbols give the reader or listener little information. Further, they can lead to confusion. That's because, when we label a group of things, we tend to emphasize their similarities rather than their differences.
2. Using symbols like democracy for which different people have very different connotative and denotative meanings. This too, can lead to breakdowns in understanding.
3. Using loaded words such as freedom with potent connotative meanings. These meanings are also evoked by concrete words skilfully used. Furthermore, concreteness helps people to be precise about what they mean, thereby avoiding misunderstanding.

The notions of abstraction and meaning get little attention in many journalism courses. Yet they seem as crucial as grammar, spelling, and transition or "flow" in clear, interesting writing.

The impact of journalistic performance, likewise, is dependent upon the broader ethical context in which journalists work. Journalistic codes of ethics stress the traditional journalistic requirement of fair play as well as the necessity that reporters avoid not only conflict of interest but also the appearance of conflict of interest.

◆◆◆

8

Truth & Ideology in News Making

"The art of the reporter should more than anything else be a celebration of the truth.... The reason millions of people watch and listen is because we place the interests of truth above everything else. Trust is our byword. That is the unalterable principle. It is our heritage and our mission, and I would rather sweep the streets of London than compromise on that... The fundamental obligation of the reporter is to the truth. Start messing with that for any reason and you become the moral accomplices of the secret policemen. (Fergal Keane)

These are powerful words, eloquently spoken. At one level, it seems, the implications of Keane's argument are clear: a journalism resolutely committed to 'the truth' must never hesitate to uncover and expose lies, deceit and misrepresentation regardless of the consequences.

At another, more subtly complex level, however, the implications of Keane's declaration quickly prove to be much more challenging to discern. This reference to 'the truth' begs another awkward question: namely, whose definition of what is true is being upheld as 'the truth'? The answer to that question goes to the heart of ongoing debates over whether or not the news we must consider, however, whether or not the news media 'reflect social reality truthfully, or the extent to which journalists can produce a truthful news account. These debates typically restrict the discussion to one regarding how best to separate 'facts' from 'values'. The assumption that 'the truth' resides entirely in the former leaves aside the problem of whether or not such a separation is actually possible in the first place. We should examine therefore how the news media work to define the ideological limits of 'truth' by exploring how journalists produce news accounts which claim to be 'objective' reflections of reality.

In the first instance, our attention turns to consider two competing perspectives on the role the news media play in structuring public awareness and debate about social problems. Specifically, the **'liberal pluralist position'** will be counterpoised against the **'political economy position'** so as to identify several factors pertinent to the larger social context within which journalists operate. Next, we examine a range of insights generated by researchers attempting to explore the ideological dynamics of newswork practices, that is, the day-to-day routines of news production which inform the cultural construction of news as an 'impartial' form of social knowledge. Here the focus is on the extent to which the codified conventions of newswork contribute to the naturalization of the various social divisions and inequalities indicative of modern society, principally by helping to reaffirm these inequalities as being appropriate, legitimate or inevitable in ideological terms.

Structuring Public Debate

The conviction that the citizen's right to freedom of speech is best protected by a market-based mass media system is at the core of the liberal pluralist conception of the journalist's role in modern society. Many of its advocates, who arguably include most journalists themselves, maintain that the news media represents a fourth estate (as distinguished, in historical terms, from the executive, the judiciary and the parliament). Journalism, as a result, is charged with the crucial mission of ensuring that members of the public are able to draw upon a diverse 'market place of ideas' to both sustain and challenge their sense of the world around them. This responsibility for giving expression to a richly pluralistic spectrum of information sources places the journalist at the centre of public life. **Thus it is the news media, to the extent that they facilitate the formation of public opinion, which are said to make democratic control over governing relations possible.**

The performance of this democratic function is contingent upon the realization of 'press freedom' as a principle safeguarded from any possible impediment associated with power and privilege. The news media, according to the liberal pluralists, must carry out the crucial work of contributing to the 'system of checks and balances' popularly held to be representative of democratic structures and processes. More specifically, by fostering a public engagement with the issues of the day, they are regarded as helping to underwrite a consensual (albeit informal) process of surveillance, whereby the activities of the state and corporate sectors are made more responsive to the dictates of public opinion. As arenas of arbitration, the news media are said to allow for clashes over decision making to be expressed, adjudicated and ultimately reconciled in such a way as to ensure that neither cumulative nor continuous influence is accorded to a single set of interests. Liberal pluralist researchers insist that the capacity of a particular news organization to present the necessary 'plurality of viewpoints' is preserved 'by virtue of the clash and discordance of interests which exist between owners, managers, editors and journalists'.

Opposition to the liberal pluralist position, despite its continued salience in public debates about the news media, has been advanced from a number of different angles by researchers adopting a much more critical stance. For these alternative approaches, many of which rely on a political economy framework for their analyses, the basic tenets of liberal pluralism are in need of serious revision. The writings of Karl Marx have provided an important starting point for several of these lines of critique, including a celebrated passage which he co-wrote with Frederick Engels in the **German Ideology** around 1845:

> The ideas of the ruling class are in every epoch the ruling ideas, i.e. the class which is the ruling material force of society, is at the same time its ruling intellectual force. The class which has the means of material production at its disposal, has control at the same time over the means of mental production, so that thereby, generally speaking, the ideas of those who lack the means of mental production are subject to it... In so far, therefore, as they rule as a class and determine

> the extent and compass of an epoch, it is self-evident that they... among other things ... regulate the production and distribution of the ideas of their age: thus their ideas are the ruling ideas of the epoch.

This passage clearly challenges several of the assumptions underlying liberal pluralist arguments. The 'ruling ideas of the epoch', to be loosely understood as the representations of a 'dominant ideology', are not forced on the subordinate classes, nor are they to be reduced (conspiratorially) to 'useful fictions'. Rather, the Marxist position maintains that the capitalist ruling class must work to advance its particular class-specific interests by depicting its ideas, norms and values in universal terms. That is to say, these 'ruling ideas' need to be mobilized as being consistent with the beliefs of ordinary people, as being the only correct, rational opinions available to them. Mass media institutions, whether publicly or privately owned, are controlled by members of this ruling class. Each one of these institutions reproduces these 'ruling ideas', to varying degrees, so as to lend justification to the class inequalities engendered by capitalist society as being reasonable or commonsensical. In this way, the media help to ensure that the danger or radical protests emerging to disrupt the status quo is sharply reduced.

Marx's personal knowledge of journalism was shaped by the ten years he spent, while living in London, as a European correspondent for the **New York Tribune**. An impassioned advocate of a free press, he regarded it as a means to counter forces of oppression for the greater welfare of society. He nevertheless did not write at length about the news media. For political economists engaged with these issues today, then, Marx's preliminary insights need to be recast in relation to journalistic institutions the likes of which he could not have even anticipated in the nineteenth century. Broadly speaking, modern political economists have retained Marx's focus on class power as a determinant factor of social control in order to document the impact of changing patterns of news media power and influence within local, national and (increasingly) global contexts. **Of particular concern are the growing levels of concentration, conglomeration and integration of ownership in this sector, for these dynamics are**

directly linked to a range of issues associated with control over journalistic content.

For example, many political economists argue that news media power is being restricted to an ever smaller number of (usually white and male) hands; that the corporate priority of profit maximization is leading to increasingly superficial news formats where content becomes evermore uniform and the spaces available to report on controversial issues sharply reduced; and, that corporate fears over 'the bottom line' are reshaping judgments about newsworthiness in ways which frequently all but silence alternative or oppositional voices. Such voices - including those in the labour movement, trade unions, feminists, anti-racists, environmentalists, antipoverty activists and other groups committed to progressive social change – are routinely characterized as representing a threat to the interests of 'market sensitive' news organizations. **Thus the implications of reducing news to just a commodity form like any other are profound, particularly when these types of critical voices are struggling just to be heard within the confines of ideological parameters conditioned by the drive for 'efficiency gains' (and with them greater advertising profits).** It is with these kinds of concerns in mind that political economists continue to channel their research into campaigns aiming to bring about a fundamental reorganization of the current dynamics of media ownership and control, a process to be achieved primarily through the radical restructuring of state regulatory policies.

In seeking to provide a conceptual framework to account for the interrelation of these types of dynamics at the level of news content, Herman and Chomsky (1988) have developed a 'propaganda model'. Writing from a US perspective, they argue that there exists within that country's commercial news media an institutional bias which guarantees the mobilization of certain 'propaganda campaigns' on behalf of an elite consensus (propaganda is deemed to be broadly equivalent with dominant ideology in this analysis). Notwithstanding this 'guarantee', however, the economic power of owners of capital over the media does not culminate in the creation of a political vacuum. Rather, in their view, the news media 'permit- indeed, encourage – spirited debate, criticism and dissent, as long as these remain faithfully within the system of presuppositions and principles that constitute an elite consensus'. Liberal pluralist treatments of the news media as autonomous institutions are thereby to be countered by examining the systematic subordination of the media vis – a - vis the functional requirements of dominant classes. To the degree that the powerful are able to coordinate the fluctuating boundaries of public opinion through the exercise of controls over what will be found in media content, class power will be successfully reproduced.

Liberal pluralist notions of a 'free', independent' and 'objective' news media are thus countered by Herman and Chomsky's contention that if the news media perform a societal purpose at all, it is to 'inculcate and defend the economic, social, and political agenda of privileged groups that dominate the domestic society and the state'. Propaganda campaigns may be instituted either by the state itself or by one or more of the top media firms (or even in unison), but in all instances the collaboration of the mass media is a prerequisite. In order to specify the 'secret' at work behind the 'unidirectionality of propaganda campaigns', Herman and Chomsky define its affectivity in terms of a 'multiple filter system'. By drawing attention to these respective' filters', they are seeking to demonstrate the extent to which journalists reiterate uncritically official positions of the state while, simultaneously, adhering to its political agenda. The resultant news product, they maintain, ultimately makes for 'a propaganda system that is far more credible and effective in putting over a patriotic agenda than one with official censorship'.

Briefly, five components 'filters' of this model, each of which interact with and reinforce one another, are identified by Herman and Chomsky as follows:

1. The first filter to be accounted for concerns the commercial basis of the dominant news organizations: specifically, the size and the scale of the investment required to run major news outlets, the concentration and conglomeration of ownership and cross-ownership patterns, and the power and wealth of the proprietors and their managers. **Close ties between the media elite and their political and corporate counterparts ensure that an 'establishment orientation' is ordinarily maintained at the**

level of news coverage (here issues of placement, tone, context and fullness of treatment are particularly important). It is this top tier of major news companies which, together with the government and wire services, 'defines the news agenda and supplies much of the national and international news to the lower tiers of the media'. At the same time, the resultant 'profit orientation' of these organizations, many of which are under intense pressure from stockholders, directors and bankers to focus on 'the bottom line', is a further key aspect of this filter shaping news coverage.

2. **The second filter pertains to the influence of advertising, the principal income source for commercial news organizations, on media content. 'With advertising,** -the free market does not yield a neutral system in which final buyer choice decides. The **advertisers'** choices influence media prosperity and survival.' Historically, media relying on revenue from sales alone have found it very difficult to compete with the resources available to their advertising – subsidized rivals. This dynamic typically leads to such outlets being pushed to the margins, where eventually many are forced to close down. Advertisers are primarily interested in affluent audiences due to their purchasing power', and thus are less inclined to support forms of news and public affairs content which attract people of more modest means. Moreover, there is a strong preference for content which does not call into question their own politically conservative principles or interferes with the 'buying mood' of the audience.
3. **The news media's over-reliance or government and corporate 'expert' sources is cited as the third filter.** Herman and Chomsky describe the symbiotic relationship that journalists have with their information sources, arguing that it is driven both by economic necessity and a reciprocity of interests. These powerful establishment sources provide journalists with a steady, reliable flow of 'the raw material of news', thereby allowing news organization expend their resources more 'efficiently'. The relative authority and prestige of these sources also helps to enhance the credibility of the journalist's account. The routine

inclusion of such 'experts' not only shapes the news agenda, but simultaneously makes it much more difficult for independent, non - official sources to gain access. 'By giving these purveyors of the preferred view a great deal of exposure,' Herman and Chomsky maintain, 'the media confer status and make them the obvious candidate for opinion and analysis.'

4. **Filter number four addresses the role of 'flak' or negative responses to media content as a means of disciplining news organizations.** 'Flak' can be produced either by individuals, state officials in their ceaseless efforts of 'correct' news coverage, or by various advocacy groups, including politically motivated 'media monitoring' campaigns or 'think tank' operations. Such forms of 'flak' can prove costly for news organizations, not only at the level of legal disputes but also in terms of the potential withdrawal of patronage by advertisers due to organized consumer boycotts.
5. The final filter is the role of the 'ideology as a political-control mechanism. This ideology', in Herman and Chomsky's words, 'helps mobilize the populace against an enemy, and because the concept is fuzzy it can be used against anybody advocating policies that threaten property interests. Its corresponding influence on the news media has also had far-reaching implications.

Overall, then, only the 'cleansed residue', having passed through these successive filters, is pronounced 'fit' to call news. This is not to suggest, however, that the news media are monolithic in their treatment of controversial issues. Rather, Herman and Chomsky state: 'Where the powerful are in disagreement, there will be a certain diversity of tactical judgments on how to attain generally shared aims, reflected in media debate.' Nevertheless, views which contest the underlying political premises of the dominant state discourse, especially with regard to the exercise of state power, will almost always fall outside of the parameters demarcated by the limits of elite disagreement. The 'filters' identified above are deemed to be working to reinforce these parameters in ways which make alternative news choices difficult to imagine. This process, they contend,' occurs so naturally that media news people, frequently operating with complete integrity and goodwill, are able to convince themselves that they choose and interpret the news 'objectively' and on the basis of professional news values'.

News value & frames

There is an extensive research literature concerned with 'news values', much of which elaborates upon an innovative study conducted in the mid-1960s by Galtung and Ruge (1981) on the structure of foreign news in the Scandinavian press. In selectively drawing upon these attempts to specify the informal (largely unspoken) rules or codes of newsworthiness, the following factors may be regarded as being significant:

- **Conflict** : 'balanced' journalism dictates that 'each story has two sides'; when these 'sides' are in dispute, a sense of immediacy is likely to result at the same time that potential *interest* is enhanced through dramatization.
- **Relevance** : the event should be seen to impinge, however indirectly, on the news audience's lives and experiences. The **proximity** of the event is a related factor.
- **Timeliness** : recent events are favoured, especially those that have occurred in the previous 24 hours and which can be easily monitored as they unfold in relation to institutional constraints and pressures.
- **Simplification** : the significance of an event should be relatively unambiguous; the diversity or potential interpretations may then be kept to a minimum.
- **Personalization** : an emphasis on human actors 'coping with life on the ground' is preferred over abstract descriptions of 'faceless' structures, forces or institutions.
- **Unexpectedness** : an event which is 'out of the ordinary' is likely to be 'novel' or 'new', thereby enhancing its chances of being caught in the news net. As an old cliché goes: 'Dog bites man isn't news; man bites dog is'.

- **Continuity** : an event should allow for the projection of a sense of where it 'fits in' so as to allow for prescheduling, a significant consideration for a news organization allocating its resources. A related factor is its consonance or conformity to the news worker's (and audience member's) preconceptions about what type of 'news story' it is likely to resemble.
- **Composition** : a mixture of different types of events must be processed on any given day, thus events are chosen in relation to fluctuations in the 'news hole' to be filled. Divisions between, for example, international, national and local news are usually clearly marked in regional newspapers and newscasts.
- **Reference to elite nations** : a hierarchy is often discernible here which gives priority to events is those countries which are regarded as 'directly affecting the audience's well-being', such as the USA and other members of the 'first world'. This is at the expense of those events taking place in other places, particularly developing of 'third world' countries which only infrequently receive newsworthy status (and then only under certain terms: see chapter 7)
- **Reference to elite persons** : activities performed by politicians, members of the monarchy, entertainment and sporting celebrities, corporate leaders, and so forth, are far more salient in news terms than those of 'ordinary people'.
- **Cultural specificity** : events which conform to the 'maps of meaning' shared by newsworker and news audience have a greater likelihood of being selected, a form of ethnocentrism which gives priority to news about 'people like us' at the expense of those who 'don't share out way of life'.
- **Negativity** : 'bad news' is ordinarily favoured over 'good news', namely because the former usually conforms to a higher number of the above factors. As the celebrated media theorist Marshal McLuhan once remarked, advertisements constitute the only 'good news' in the newspaper.

Routinizing the Unexpected

In discussing the day-to-day activities of reporting, journalists and their critics alike often draw upon the metaphor of a 'mirror' to describe how the social world is 'reflected' in news accounts. The pioneering US broadcast reporter Edward R. Murrow once famously stated, for example, that journalism 'must hold a mirror behind the nation and the world' and that, moreover, 'The mirror must have no curves and must be held with a steady hand' This language of reflection is similarly employed in critiques of news coverage to pinpoint evidence of 'bias', that is, to question whether journalists have mirrored reality in an 'objective' manner or, failing that the extent to which they have a allowed certain' distortions' to creep into the reporting process.

Not surprisingly in light of the issues raised in the discussion above, many critical researchers have dismissed the 'mirror' metaphor for being too simplistic. Even its advocates, they point out, have to acknowledge the vast number of 'blind-spots' which render certain types of events virtually invisible. The mirror metaphor is also difficult to sustain due to its inability to account for the ideological dynamics embedded in the newsworker's mediation of the social world. This process of mediation involves not only a series of procedures for knowing the world but, equally importantly, for not knowing that world as well. As Hallin writes of the 'mirroring' qualities of so-called 'objective reporting' of governmental affairs in the USA: "A form of journalism which aims to provide the public with a neutral record of events and which, at the same time, relies primarily on government officials to describe and explain those events obviously has the potential to wind up as a mirror not of reality, but of the version of reality government officials would like to present to the public."

A Hierarchy of Credibility

The very basis upon which the journalist is able to detect 'news events', according to Fishman, rests on a commonsensical understanding that society is bureaucratically structured. It is this perspective which provides specific procedures for locating knowledge of occurrences. Specifically, it furnishes the reporter with a 'map of relevant knowers' for newsworthy topics. A journalist covering a story concerning, say, the possible effects of a nuclear power plant on the health of children in a local community, knows that information officers at the plant, as well as politicians, scientists, nuclear energy lobbyists, health officials, social workers and environmental groups, among others, will be positioned to offer their viewpoints. 'What ever the happening,' writes Fishman, 'there are officials and authorities in a structural position to know.' This 'bureaucratic consciousness', to employ his phrase, indicates to newsworkers precisely where they will have to position themselves to be able to follow the time-line or 'career path' of events as they pass through a series of interwoven, yet discernible phases.

To clarify, H.S. Becker employs the notion of a 'hierarchy of credibility' to specify how, in a system of ranked groups, participants will take it as given that the members of the highest group are best placed to define 'the way things really are' due to their 'knowledge of truth'. Implicit in this assumption is the view that 'those at the top' will have access to a more complete picture of the bureaucratic organization's workings than members of lower groups whose definition of reality, because of this subordinate status, can be only partial and distorted. As H.S. Becker writes, 'any tale told by those at the top intrinsically deserves to be regarded as the most credible account obtainable... Thus, credibility and the right to be heard are differentially distributed through the ranks of the system.' By this rationale, then, the higher up in this hierarchy the news source is situated, the more authoritative his or her words will be for the newsworker processing the bureaucratic account. Newsworkers are thus predisposed to treat these accounts as factual, according to Fishman, 'because journalists participate in upholding a normative order of authorized knowers in society (and) it is also a position of convenience.' After all, the 'competence' of the source should, by this logic, translate into a 'credible' news story.

Of interest in this context is Hallin's analyses of how the dictates of 'objective' reporting serve to ratify a normative order of 'credible' sources, especially when challenges to the status quo are being mobilized. The journalist's world, he argues, can be usefully characterized as being divided into three regions, each governed by different standards of reporting. These regions may be represented as concentric circles.

1. **Sphere of Consensus** : this sphere, Hallin proposes, can be defined as representing' motherhood and apple pie'. That is to say, it encircles those social issues which are typically regarded by journalists (and, they are likely to assume, most members of the public) as being beyond partisan dispute and, as such, non-controversial. Consequently, '[w]ithin this region journalists do not feel compelled either to present opposing views or to remain disinterested observers. On the contrary, the journalist's role is to serve as an advocate or celebrant of consensus values'

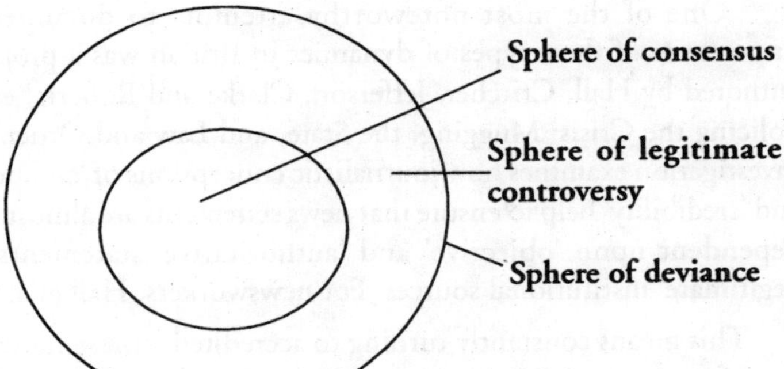

2. **Sphere of legitimate controversy** : in this sphere, there are a range of social issues which are framed by journalists as being the appropriate subject of partisan dispute. The typical types of controversies which unfold during electoral contests or legislative debates, for example, are situated here, the ideological parameters of which are represented by the positions articulated between and within the main political parties (as well as the bureaucracies of the state or civil service). "Within this region,' Hallin writes,' objectivity and balance reign as the supreme journalistic values.'
3. **Sphere of Deviance** : the realm located beyond the above sphere is occupied, according to Hallin by 'those political actors and views which journalists and the political mainstream of the society reject as unworthy of being heard.' Virtually any pretence of journalistic 'neutrality' falls away, he argues, as news organizations perform the work of boundary maintenance. In this sphere, journalism 'plays the role of exposing, condemning,

or excluding from the public agenda those who violate or challenge the political consensus. It marks out and defends the limits of acceptable polítical conflict'

These respective spheres, Hallin is quick to acknowledge, each contain internal gradations, and the boundaries distinguishing them are relatively fluid and changeable. Nevertheless, this model suggests that 'gut instincts' about source credibility are politicized, as the further away al potential source is from the political consensus the less likely it will be that the source's voice will gain media access.

One of the most noteworthy attempts to document the importance of these types of dynamics in Britian was a project co-authored by Hall, Critcher, Jefferson, Clarke and Roberts, entitled Policing the Crisis: Mugging, the State, and Law and Order. Their investigation examines how journalistic conceptions of 'competence' and 'credibility' help to ensure that news statements are almost always dependent upon 'objective' and 'authoritative' statements from 'legitimate' institutional sources. For newsworkers, Hall et a. write:

> This means constantly turning to accredited representatives of major social institutions – M.P.s for political topics, employers and trade union leaders for industrial matters, and so on. Such institutional representatives are 'accredited' because of their institutional power and position, but also because of their' representative' status: either they represent 'the people' (M.P.S., Ministers, etc.) or organised interest groups.

It follows that the 'professional rules' indicative of the routine structures of news production are typically serving to represent the 'opinions of the powerful' as being consistent with a larger 'pubic consensus'. Here Hall et al. proceed to note the irony that 'the very rules which aim to preserve the impartiality of the media, and which grew out of desires for greater professional neutrality, also serve powerfully to orientate the media in the "definitions of social reality" which their" accredited sources" – the institutional spokes [persons] – provide."

The journalist's daily struggle to negotiate the professional demands of newswork, with all of the attendant pressures, produces in Hall et al.'s view 'a systematically structured over- accessing to the media of those in powerful and privileged institutional positions.' It is precisely this issue of how the definitions of certain sources are routinely ' over- accessed' to the detriment of alternative viewpoint which is crucial. Sources who enjoy high status positions in society can assume, in turn, that they are much more likey to become what Hall et all call 'the primary definers' of controversial topics.

Accordingly, the structured relationship between the news media and this hierarchy of institutional definers permits the most powerful of the latter to set down the initial definition or primary interpretation of the news topic to be processed. It is recurrently the case that this interpretation will then be mobilized to 'command the filed' with the likely result that it will, in turn, establish the terms of reference within which all further coverage (as well as any subsequently 'debate') takes place. 'Arguments against a primary interpretation', Hall et al. stress, 'are forced to insert themselves into its definition of "what s at issue"- they must begin from this framework of interpretation as their starting point.' Moreover, this 'initial interpretative frame work is extremely difficult to alter fundamentally, once established'. In this way, then the news media re regarded as playing a vital ideological role in reaffirming the iniquitous power relations underlying society's institutional order.

◆◆◆

9

News as Cultural Politics

A senior politician is only ever a sound-bite away from destruction.

-David Mellor

There is a strong argument that unrelieved coverage of death, crisis and disaster gives a misleading picture of what life is like for most of Britain's citizens most of the time.... that individual news stories become divorced from proper perspective or context... The good news is out there, and the media shouldn't be afraid to report it.

-Martyn Lewis, BBC newsreader

Journalists are among the pre-eminent story-tellers of modern society. Their news accounts shape in decisive ways our perceptions of the 'world out there' beyond our immediate experience. For many of us, our sense of what is happening in the society around us, what we should know and care about from one day to the next, is largely derived from the news stories they tell. Given that we have to take so much on trust, we rely on news accounts to be faithful representations of reality.

We should focus, therefore, on how news discourses help to *naturalize* a cultural politics of legitimacy so as to lend justification to modern society's distribution of power and influence. More specifically, it is the extent to which these news discourses effectively *depoliticize* the dominant meanings, values and beliefs associated with these inequalities, and in so doing contribute to their perpetuation, that will be addressed. Here we raise important questions regarding the ways in which the language of news encodifies as 'common sense' a hierarchical series of normative rules by which social life is to be understood.

News and Hegemony

Gramsci's writings on hegemony have proven to be extraordinarily influential for critical researchers examining the operation of the news media in modern societies. Three particularly significant (and interrelated) aspects of the cultural dynamics of hegemony are the following :

First, *hegemony is a lived process.* Hegemonic ideas do not circulate freely in the air above people's heads; rather, according to Gramsci, they have a material existence in the cultural practices, activities and rituals of individuals striving to make sense of the world around them. That is, hegemony is a process embodied in what Williams aptly describes as 'a lived system of meanings and values', that is, as 'a whole body of practices and expectations, over the whole of living: our senses and assignments of energy, our shaping perceptions of ourselves and our world'. It follows that hegemony constitutes 'a sense of reality for most people in the society' and, as such, is the contradictory terrain upon which the 'lived dominance and subordination' of particular groups is struggled over in day-to-day cultural practices.

Second, hegemony is a matter of 'common sense'. A much broader category than ideology, common sense the uncritical and largely unconscious way of perceiving and understanding the social world as it organizes habitual daily experience. Gramsci stresses that common sense, despite the extent to which it is 'inherited from the past and uncritically absorbed', may be theorized as a complex and disjointed 'infinity of traces', and as such never simply identical with a class-based ideology. 'Commonsensical' beliefs, far from being fixed or immobile, are in a constant state of renewal: 'new ideas', as he notes, are always entering daily life and encountering the 'sedimentation' left behind by this contradictory, ambiguous, 'chaotic aggregate of disparate conseption.

Third, *hegemony is always contested.* Far from being a totally monolithic system or structure imposed from above, then, lived hegemony is an active process of negotiation; it can never be taken for granted by the ruling group. In Gramsci's words, at stake is 'a cultural battle to transform the popular "mentality" and to diffuse the philosophical innovations which will demonstrate themselves to be "historically true" to the extent that they become concretely - i.e. historically and socially – universal.' Consequently, no one group can maintain its hegemony without adapting to changing conditions, a dynamic which will likely entail making certain strategic compromises with the forces which oppose its ideological authority. Dominance is neither invoked nor accepted in a passive manner; as Williams points out: 'It has continually to be renewed, recreated, defended, and modified [in relation to] pressures not at all its own.' Hence Gramsci's contention that common sense be theorized as the site upon which the hegemonic rules of practical conduct and norms of moral behaviour are reproduced and – crucially – also challenged and resisted.

Significantly, then, this shift to address the cultural dynamics of hegemony displaces a range of different formulations of 'dominant ideology', most of which hold that news discourse be theorized as concealing or masking the true origins of economics antagonisms, that is, their essential basis in the class struggle. At the same time, this emphasis on the hegemonic imperatives of news discourse allows the critical researcher to avoid the suggestion that the 'effects' of news discourse on its audience be understood simply as a matter of 'false consciousness'.

The common sense of newspaper discourse

'Journalists believe something is reportable,' according to Ericson *et al.'s* study of Canadian news organizations, 'when they can visualize it in the terms of news discourse.' This process of visualization does not constitute a neutral reflection of 'the world out there'. Rather, it works to reaffirm a hegemonic network of conventionalized rules by which social life is to be interpreted, especially those held to be derivative of 'public opinion' or, at an individual level, 'human nature'. Accordingly, news accounts encourage us to accept as *natural, obvious or commonsensical* certain preferred ways of classifying reality, and these classifications have far-reaching implications for the cultural reproduction of power relations across society.

A newspaper account, far from simply reflecting the reality of a news event, is actually working to construct a codified definition of what should count as the reality of the event. In order to examine these processes of codification, the specific ways in which a newspaper adopts a preferred language to represent 'the world out there' need to be opened up for analysis. That is to say, it is necessary to identify the means by which a particular newspaper projects its characteristic 'mode of address', its customary way of speaking to its audience, on its pages from one day to the next. Shaping this mode of address, are a series of imperatives governing how the 'raw materials' of the social world are to be appropriated and transformed into a news account. An event will 'make sense', they argue, only to the extent that it can be situated within 'a range of known social and cultural identifications' or 'maps of meaning' about the social world. To quote Hall et al in this context:

The social identification, classification and contextualization of news events in terms of these background frames of reference is the fundamental process by which the media make the world they report on intelligible to readers and viewers. This process of 'making an event intelligible' is a social process-constituted by a number of specific journalistic practices, which embody (often only implicitly) crucial assumptions about what society is and how it works. One such background assumption is the consensual nature of society; the process of signification-giving social meanings to events - ***both assumes and helps to construct society as a 'consensus'***. We exist as members of one society because – it is assumed – we share a common stock of knowledge with our fellow men [and women]: we have access to the same 'maps of meanings'. Not only are we able to manipulate these 'maps of meaning' to understand events, but we have fundamental interests, values and concerns in common, which these maps embody or reflect."

It is this seemingly commonsensical belief that 'the consensus' is 'a basic feature of everyday life' that underpins journalistic efforts to codify unfamiliar, 'problematic' realities into familiar, comprehensible definitions about how the world works.

Of primary importance when distinguishing the newspaper's mode of address is its 'professional sense of the newsworthy', an aspect of its 'social personality' conditioned by various organizational, technical and commercial constraints, as well as by its conception of the likely opinions of its regular readers (its 'target audience'). It follows that individual newspapers, even those sharing a similar outlook, will inflect the same topic differently. As Hall *et al.* point out: "The language employed will thus be the newspaper's *own version of the language of the public to whom it is principally addressed:* its version of the rhetoric, imagery and underlying common stock of knowledge which it assumes its audience shares and which thus forms the basis of the reciprocity of producer/ reader."

This form of address, specific to each and every news organization, may thus be advantageously described as the newspaper's distinctive 'public idiom'.

In order to further critique this process of inflection, then, it is necessary to disrupt the very *naturalness* of the ideological codes embedded in the language of newspaper discourse. Such a line of inquiry will need to elucidate the conventionalized rules, strategies or devices which make it recognizable as a distinct genre of 'purely factual' narrative. In the case of a 'hard' news account, for example, it is possible to show that there are certain prescribed forms of narrative logic associated with the telling of a 'hard' news story which stand in contrast with those of 'soft' news stories. The 'hard' news account is defined in opposition to other types of account, such as 'editorials' or 'leaders' which foreground matters of 'opinion'. this genre of discourse will narrativize the social world in a particular manner, that is, in a way which organizes 'the facts' within a distinctively hierarchical structure based on notions of newsworthiness.

Potential readers of this 'hard' news newspaper account are likely to anticipate that it will provide them with a highly formalized construction of the social world. Formalized, that is, in the sense that the 'hard' news item, whether it appears in a tabloid or broadsheet newspaper, typically reinflects the following elements in distinctive ways:

- **Headline** : represents the principal topic or 'key fact' at stake in the account. To the extent that it is recognized as performing this function by the readers, it is likely to influence their interpretation of the account to follow. In this way, then, it helps to set down the ideological criteria by which the reader is to 'make sense' of what follows.
- **News lead** : typically the opening paragraph or two providing a summary or abstract of the account's essential 'peg' or 'hook' which projects, in turn, 'the story' in a particular direction or 'angle'. The five Ws and H (the who, what, where, when, why and how most pertinent to the event) will likely be in the lead or first paragraph: however, as Keeble (1994: 100) observes, 'the "why" factor is a always more problematic.'
- **Narrative order and sequence** : the 'hard' news account almost always follows an 'inverted pyramid style' format. That is, beginning with the news lead, which presents the information deemed to be most 'newsworthy', the account proceeds to structure the remaining details in a descending order of discursive (and usually ideological) significance. By the latter stages of the account, the material being presented could – at least in principle – be dropped without affecting the narrative coherence or sense of the preceding paragraphs. These narrative strategies have become conventionalied to the point that departures from them are likely to disrupt the reader's expectations, yet there is nothing necessary or natural about the rules governing their (in historiecal terms, rather recent) deployment.
- **Vocabulary** : the regular usage of certain types of stylistic devices, including metaphors, jargon, euphemisms, puns and cliches, tends to characterize a newspaper's 'social personality', as well as its 'professional sense of the newsworthy'. The most marked contrasts are usually between the 'popular', tabloid press and the 'quality', broadsheet titles. In general, the former are usually much more colloquial in vocabulary and emotive in judgment (often to the point of being sensational in tone): "A vocabulary of emotional arousal', Holland writes, 'summons laughter, thrills,

shocks, desire, on every page of the *Sun.*' The so-called serious newspapers, in contrast, use terms more likely to be regarded as 'un-emotive' or 'dispassionate', and thereby more consistent with an authoritative appeal to objectivity.

- **Forms of address** : the terms used to refer to, or identify, different news actors indicate a range of important features, including varying degrees of formality ('Tony' versus 'Prime Minister Blair'), the status or power to be attributed to the actor ('monster' or 'fiend' versus 'defendant' or 'alleged perpetrator') or the presumed relationship between the actor and the implied reader of the account (as noted below, made apparent in use of either personalized or impersonalized terms). In the case of the *Sun,* for example, its form of address is personal and direct.

- **Transitivity and modality** : the terms chosen by a journalist to represent the relationship between actors and processes, that is, 'who (or what) does what to whom (or what)', are indicative of transitivity. The journalist's transitivity choices can take on an ideological significance, such as where questions of blame or responsibility are raised. For example, Clark's analysis of tabloid news coverage of rape attacks, shows how the victim (e.g. 'no-sex wife') is recurrently blamed for the crime and not her male attacker (e.g. 'hubby'); or Trew's analysis concerning responsibility for disturbances being attributed to 'strikers' or unions and not employers or the police. Intertwined with relations of transitivity are those of modality, that is, the ways in which journalists convey judgements concerning the relative truthfulness (or not) of the propositions they are processing.

- **Relations of time** : looking beyond the stated place and time ('dateline') of a news account, it is possible to identify the time structure being imposed via the narrativization of the news event in question. 'Hard' news is a highly perishable commodity which is always in danger of becoming 'out of date' consequently, such accounts usually contain an explicit temporal reference (such as 'yesterday') in the news lead. In marked contrast with other types of narratives, especially fictional ones, time in the 'hard' news account is typically represented in a non-linear manner.

The account which respects a chronological ordering of the events it describes is a rare exception to a general rule which holds that 'effects' or 'outcomes' are prioritized over 'causes'. 'Perceived news value,' as Bell writes, 'overturns temporal sequence and imposes an order completely at odds with linear narrative point. It moves backwards and forwards in time, picking out different actions on each cycle.'

- **Relations of space** : interwoven with relations of time are those of space, the latter being represented in a series of ways in the 'hard' news account. Hallin usefully identifies five typical ways in which journalists refer to geographical locations. Specifically, place as authority (the 'here' identified in the account is often listed in the dateline; news gathered 'on the scene' is likely to be deemed to have greater credibility); place as actionable information (relatively rare in 'hard' news; much more likely to appear in 'Weekend', travel or real estate sections where readers are looking for such information in order to do something); place as social connection (through its construction of place, a newspaper can given readers a sense of participation in a distant event, thereby acting as a creator of community); place as setting (invitations to 'experience' the event through detailed descriptions of setting appear only infrequently in 'hard' news because they tend to be considered inappropriate for 'objective' reporting); and, finally, place as subject (the ways in which places themselves become 'news' are often ideologically charged, especially at the level of international politics).
- **Implied reader** : journalists construct news account against a backdrop of assumptions about the social world which they expect the readers to share. It follows that the journalist's orientation to the implied reader, or imagined community of readers, necessarily shapes the form and content of the account. Necessarily implicated in this projection of this ideal reader, who may bear little resemblance to the actual living and breathing reader, are an array of ideological presuppositions concerning relations of class, gender, race, ethnicity, sexuality, age and so forth. Brookes and Holbrook suggest, for example,

that British tabloid news coverage of 'mad cow disease' consistently addressed women as housewives and mothers (evidently a typical feature where 'food scares' are concerned). Personal pronouns are almost always absent in the 'hard' news account, with the exception of the 'I' of an eyewitness or investigative item (this is in sharp contrast to the frequent use of 'we' on the editorial leader page when the newspaper assumes its public voice).

- **Closure** : the achievement of closure with respect to the 'hard' news account is always partial and contingent, that is, it is never fully realized. In narrative terms, the account typically comes to an end abruptly without formal markers signaling closure (in contrast with broadcast news). As noted above, the 'inverted pyramid style' format facilitates the work of the copyeditor, who trims the length of accounts, usually starting from the bottom, in relation to the size of the available 'news hole'. Narrative closure is successful when readers achieve a feeling of completeness, that is, a satisfactory sense that the account has processed an array of facts sufficient to make clear a reasonable and appropriate interpretation of the situation. Thus ideological closure may be said to have been accomplished where readers identify with this dominant interpretation ostensibly encouraged by the account, regarding it to be adequate and factually consistent – for the moment at least – with their personal understanding of the social world.

It is important to note that critical analyses of newspapers, whether tabloid or broadsheet, usually restrict their examinations to the characteristics of the news coverage being generated. This centring of news accounts as the primary focus of inquiry is at the expense of considerations of other forms of content, particularly those types more likely to be seen as mere diversions due to their perceived entertainment value. 'Insofar as acknowledgement is given to entertainment features in the press,' as Curran et al. argue, 'this tends to be grudging and dismissive, as if such content detracts from the central political role and purpose of the press.' As they proceed to point out in their exploration of the non-current affairs sections of newspapers, it is precisely where content is promoted as being 'apolitical' (such as in the realms of human interest as it relates to sport, royalty, celebrities, gossip, competitions, astrology and so forth) that 'ideological significance is most successfully concealed and therefore demands most analysis'. It is also relevant to note that this type of content is regularly disparaged by 'hard' news journalists who are more likely to express concerns over ideology in a different way, namely as a fear that the quality of reporting is being 'dumbed down' by these types of items in the name of boosting circulation figures.

Further studies of 'human interest' or 'soft' news have similarly highlighted how its apparent neutrality reinforces what might be termed the 'dominant political consensus' by encouraging and constraining reader to see events in particular ways. The implications which news coverage of sporting events has for discourses of popular culture, for example, has been the subject of critical attention. Similarly, critiques of editorials or 'leaders', feature articles (including 'opposite editorial' or 'op ed' pages or 'backgrounders') and opinion columns have pinpointed a range of issues, including how the inclusion of this 'subjective', 'interpretative' material helps to underwrite the proclaimed 'objectivity' of 'hard' news accounts. Cartoons have also been singled out for scrutiny, with several studies assessing how issues concerning, for example, 'the economy' national identity and military conflicts, among others, have been subject to political caricature. Also of interest are 'letters to the editor', not least in terms of how the criteria of inclusion in play delimit the ideological boundaries of *legitimate* or *fair* comment.

Another element of both 'quality' and 'popular' newspapers which similarly deserves more critical attention than it has received to date is the news photograph. Hall, in his analysis of news images, suggests that although editors may select a photograph in terms of its formal news values (such as impact, dramatic meaning, unusualness, controversy, and so forth), they are also simultaneously judging how these values will be best treated or 'angled' so as to anchor the intended interpretation for the implied reader. News photographs proclaim the status of being 'literal visual-transcriptions' of the 'real world'; this when as Hall contends, "The choice of this moment of an event as against that, of this person rather than that, of this angle rather than any other, indeed, the selection of this photographed incident to represent a whole complex chain of events and meaning, is a highly ideological procedure. But, by appearing literally to reproduce the event as it really happened, news photos suppress their selective/ interpretive/ideological function. They seek a warrant in that ever pre-given, neutral structure, which is beyond question, beyond interpretation: the 'real world'.

News photographs, in this way, help to reinforce the newspaper's larger claim to be 'objective' in its representations of the social world. "Photography is imbued with the appearance of objectively recorded reality,' writes Banks, 'consequently, editors often seek to use photographs to provide the stamp of objectivity to a news story.'

This appeal to 'objectivity' can be sustained, of course, only to the extent that the reader accepts the photograph as an unmediated image of actual events. What must be denied at all costs, as Taylor argues, is that news images are 'intricately sewn into the web of rhetoric. They are never outside it, and always lend it the authority of witness'. Ostensibly grounded in the 'bedrock of truth', the photograph must naturalize its impossible claim to be making visible 'what really happened' as a neutral, 'historically instantaneous' record of reality. this process of naturalization, is engendered in and through the conceptual rules or frameworks governing the professional practice of photojounalism:'Conventions of framing, composition, lighting, and colour or tonal value guide the translation of newsworthy subjects into the two-dimensional photographic image.' The array of representational devices employed by the photojournalist need to retain their apparent transparency, if the source of drama is to be located in the subject itself and not in the strategies invoked by the photographer. 'Photojournalism, cloaked in its mantle of objectivity, offers the viewer a vision of the world easily consumed and digested, while its naturalism perpetuates its legitimacy as an objective bearer of the news' (Schwarts).

The textuality of television news

The 'moment' of the broadcast news text is clearly a fluid one; its meanings are dispersed in ways which analyses of actual newscasts as static constructs or artefacts cannot adequately address. Turning now to televisual news, of particular interest are the ways in which it seeks to implicate its audience in a specific relationship of spectatorship, ostensibly that of an unseen onlooker or witness. Televisual news claims to provide an up-to-the-miaute (now) marrative which, in turn, projects for the viewers a particular place (here) from which they may 'make sense' of the significance of certain 'news worthy' events for their daily lives. As Hall et al. point out: "The facts must be arranged, in the course of programming, so as to present an intelligible 'story': hence the process of presentation will reflect the explanations and interpretations which appear most plausible, credible or adequate to the broadcaster, his [or her] editorial team and the expert commentators he [or she] consults. Above all, the known facts of a situation must be translated into intelligible audio-visual signs, organised as a discourse. TV cannot transmit 'raw historical' events as such, to its audiences: it can only transmit pictures of, stories, informative talk or discussion about, the events it selectively treats.

Accordingly, it is the codified definitions of reality which are regarded as the most 'natural', as the most representative of 'the world out there', that are actually the most ideological.

Apparent across the range of the different BBC and ITN newscasts are several shared features:

- **Interruption** : the opening sequence, usually composed of a 15-20 second segment of brightly coloured computer-animated graphics, rapidly unfolds to a sharply ascending piece of theme music (the use of trumpets is typical). Its appearance announces the interruption of the flow of entertainment programming by signalling the imminent threat of potentially distressing information (most news, after all, is 'bad news').
- **Liveness** : The opening sequence helps to establish a sense of urgency and, in this way, anchors a declaration of immediacy for the newscast's larger claim to authoritativeness. The news is coming directly to you 'live'; its coverage of 'breaking news' is happening now (even though most of the content to follow will have been pre-recorded).

- **Time-space** : each of these segments privileges specific formulations of temporality (ticking clocks are used by both the BBC and ITN, which signal the up-to-the-minuteness of the news coverage) conjoined with those of spatiality (mages of revolving globes spin to foreground an immage of the British nation as defined by geography, in the case of the BBC; while for ITN's News at Ten, a London cityscape at night is slowly pannel until the camera rests on a close-up of the clockface of the main parliamentary building, the apparent seat of political power).
- **Comprehensiveness** : implicit to this progressively narrowing focal dynamic around time-space is an assertion of the comprehensiveness of the news coverage. The news, having been monitored from around the world, is being presented to 'us' from 'our' national perspective. That is, 'we' are located as an audience within the 'imagined community' (B. Anderson 1991) of the British nation.
- **Professionalism** : the final shot in the succession of graphic sequences (ostensibly sounded by the gong of Big Ben in the case of ITN) brings 'us' into the televisual studio, a pristine place of hard, polished surfaces (connotations of efficiency and objectivity) devoid of everyday, human (subjective) features. A central paradox of broadcast news, as Crisell writes, 'is that if there is one thing more vital to it than a sense of authenticity, of proximity to the events themselves, it is a sense of clear-sighted detachment from them-of this authenticity being mediated through the remote, steriale atmosphere of the studio.'

The camera smoothly glides across the studio floor while, in the case of the ITN Lunchtime News, a male voice-over sternly intones: 'From the studios of ITN (.0 the news (.) with Nicholas Owen and Julia Somerville.' Both newsreaders are situated behind a shared desk, calmly organizing their scripts. Serving as a backdrop for them is what appears to be a dimly lit (in cool blue light) newsroom, empty of people but complete with desks, computer equipment, and so forth. Similarly, for the News at Ten, as the male voice-over declares: 'From ITN (.) News at Ten (.) with Trevor Mc

Donald', the newsreader appears in shot seated behind a desk, typing on an invisible keyboard with one hand as he collects a loose sheaf of papers with his other one (which is also holding a pen). Whether it is ITN or the BBC, it is the institution behind the newsreader which is responsible for producing the news; it is the very 'impersonality' of the institution which, in ideological terms, is to be preserved and reaffirmed by the 'personality' of the newsreader.

As a result, the mode of address utilized by the respective newsreaders at the outset of the newscast needs to appear to be 'dialogic' in its formal appeal to the viewer's attention. This dialogic strategy of co-presence is to be achieved, in part, through the use of direct eye-contact with the camera (and thus with the imagined viewer being discursively inscribed). As Morse observes, 'the impression of shared time, and signs that the speaking subject is speaking for himself [or herself], sincerely'. The impersonally professional space of the studio is, in this way, personalized in the form of the newsreader who, using a language which establishes these temporal and spatial relations of co-presence with the viewer, reaffirms a sense of shared participation.

Nevertheless, these dialogic relations of co-presence are hierarchically structured. The direct address speech of the newsreader (note that the 'accessed voices' will be restricted to indirect speech and eye contact) represents the 'news voice' of the network: the newsreader stands in for an institution charged with the responsibility of serving a public interest through the impartiality of its reporting. For this reason, these relations of co-presence need to be organized so as to underwrite the signifiers of facticity and journalistic prestige, as well as those of timeliness and immediacy.

In addition to the steady gaze of expressive eye contact, the visual display of the newsreader's authority is further individualized in terms of 'personality' (white males still predominate), as well as with regard to factors such as clothing (formal) and body language (brisk and measured). This conventionalized appeal to credibility is further enhanced through aural codes of a 'proper' accent (almost always received pronunciation) and tone (solemn and resolute). Such factors, then, not only may help to create the impression of personal integrity and trustworthiness, but also may ratify the authenticity' of the newsreader's own commitment to upholding the truth value of the newscast as being representative of her or his own experience and reliability. Personalized terms of address, such as ' good afternoon' or 'good evening', may similarly work to underscore the human embodiment of news values by newsreaders as they seemingly engage in a conversational discourse with the viewers.

The newsreader or 'news anchor', as Morse observes, 'is a special kind of star supported by subdued sartorial and acting codes that convey "sincerity,". 'Taken to an extreme, this can lead to 'Ken and Barbie journalism' where, as van Zoomen argues, the charge is made that physical attractiveness of the 'anchor team' is taking precedence over their competence as journalists. Also at issue here is the related trend, particularly pronounced in local news, of 'happy talk'. 'As the name suggests,' van Zoonen writes, 'these are merry little dialogues 'between the anchors showing how much they like each other and how much they love their audiences.' The main purpose behind 'happy talk', according to her interviews with newsworkers, is 'to "people-ize" the news, as one news editor has put it, and to suggest that journalists and audiences are one big happy faimily'.

The immediacy of the implied discursive exchange is thus constrained by the need to project a sense of dialogue where there is only the decisive, if inclusionary, voice of the newsreader. As Stam writes: "The newscaster's art consists of evoking the cool authority and faultless articulation of the written of memorised text while simultaneously 'naturalising' the written world to restore the appearance of spontaneous communication. Most of the newscast, in fact, consists of this scripted spontaneity: newcasters reading from teleprompters, correspondents reciting hastily-memorised notes, politicians delivering prepared speeches, commercial actor representing their roles. In each case, the appearance of fluency elicit respect while the trappings of spontaneity generate a feeling of unmediated communication".

In play are a range of deictic features which anchor the articulation of time ('now, at this moment', 'currently', 'as we are speaking', 'ongoing' or 'today') to that of space ('here', 'this is where' or 'at Westminster this morning') such that the hierarchical relationship of identification for the intended viewer is further accentuated.

Contingent upon these relations of co-presence is what has been characterized as the regime of the 'fictive We'. That is, the mode of address employed by the newsreader, by emphasizing the individual and the familiar, encourages the viewer's complicity in upholding the hegemonic frame. To the extent that the news reader is seen to speak not only 'to us', but also 'for us' ('We' are all part of the 'consensus'), then 'we' are defined in opposition to 'them', namely those voices which do not share 'our' interests and thus are transgressive of the codified limits of common sense. As Stam points out, there needs to be a certain 'calculated ambiguity of expression' if a diverse range of viewers are to identify with the truthclaims on offer: 'The rhetoric of network diplomacy, consequently, favours a kind of oracular understatement, cultivating ambiguity, triggering patent but deniable meanings, encouraging the most diverse groups, with contradictory ideologies and aspirations, to believe that the newscasters are not far from thier own beliefs.' As a result, in attempting to authorize a preferred reading of the news event for 'us', the newsreader aims to frame the initial terms by which it is to be interpreted.

The rules of the hegemonic frame, while in principle polysemic (open to any possible interpretation), are typically inflected to encourage a relation of reciprocity between the viewers' and the newsreader's 'personal' sense of 'news values'. The voice-over of the newsreader, in seeking to specify 'what is at issue' in each of the headlined news stories, beging the work of organizing the news event into a preferred narrative structure for us.

Words are aligned with images to affirm, and then reinforce, the interpellative appeals of the news voice and the strategy of visualization: viewers can 'see for themselves' a range of the elements constitutive of what journalists often call the five Ws and H (who, what, where, when, why and how) of the news lead. Moreover, as Doane writes, 'the status of the image as indexical truth is not inconsequential – through it the "story" touches the ground of the real.' The extent to which these news headlines are made to 'touch the ground of the real' is thus dependent upon the degree to which hegemonic relations of reciprocity are established such that it is obvious to viewers that these are the most significant news events of the day for them to know about, and that it is self-evident how they are to be best understood.

Here it is also important not to overlook the larger performative task of the opening sequences for the newscast. That is to say, attention also needs to be directed to their dramatic role in attracting and maintaining the interest of the viewer and, moreover, the sense of reassurance they offer through their very repetition from one weekday to the next (a sharp contrast is provided by the headline of a news bulletin which suddenly 'interrupts' regular programming. News headlines seek to incorporate the extraordinary into the ordinary; the strangeness of the social world (and hence its potential newsworthiness) is to be mediate within the terms of the familiar. A news event can make sense to the viewers only if they are able to situate it in relation to a range of pre-existing 'maps of meaning' or forms of cultural knowledge about the nature of society.

The framework of interpretation set down by the news headline thus not only tends to nominate precisely 'what is at issue' and how its significance is to be defined, but also must reaffirm the viewers' sense of what is consequential, or at least relevant, in the context of their daily lives. The language utilized in the opening sequences, both verbal and visual, may therefore be analysed as one way in which the newscast indicates the normative limits of the sense of newsworthiness it attributes to its audience. Clearly, then, once a mode of inquiry elects to seize upon the embeddedness of the newscast in the now and here by prioritizing for critique precisely those elements which are usually ignored in analyses of this type, new aspects of the political struggle over the social relations of signification will be brought to the fore for further exploration encouraged to make the appropriate, rational inferences, in order to reaffirm journalistic procedures for handling contrary facts which are otherwise discrepant to the news frame ? In my view, once this 'setting of limits' on the narrativization of meaning has been denaturalized to the point that the polities of its naturalness are rendered explicit, analyses may proceed to identify in news discourse the slippages, fissures and silences which together are always threatening to undermine its discursive authority. In other words, this type of research may be able to contribute to the empowerment of those counter-hegemonic voices seeking to contest the truth politics of news discourse, not least by helping to first disrupt and then expand the ideological parameters of 'the obvious facts of the matter'.

◆◆◆

10

Humanizing the News

Reporters and editors have tended to define certain things they do as "feature stories." Journalism professors and students frequently talk about "feature stories." Everyone seems to accept the terminology, but there is little agreement on what it means. A "feature story" is some what like the taste of an apple or the sound of a breeze rustling through the trees. Everyone can recognize it, but no one can define it precisely.

This is not to say that anyone who uses the term is wrong, but that it's difficult to specify such a type of story because almost all copy in your daily newspaper can be termed a "feature story." The expression "Humanizing the News" is used here to emphasize that we're talking about a process, not a static object. What we tend to call a feature story is the result of the process of inserting the human element into any story and the utilization of certain writing techniques. That human element involves many things, but most of them can be lumped under two broad characteristics: human interest and incongruity.

"Human interest" is any event or idea that appeals to human beings more or less naturally and not necessarily because it has significance to their everyday activities. It is somewhat standard to say that are three main categories of human interest-sex, children and animals. That's true, but let us also add themes such as self-interest, sympathy, corruption, progress, conflict, disaster, hero worship, adventure, spirituality and success.

Any human interest element must be based solidly in human emotion. Notice that each of the elements in the above list can be tied directly to some emotion, some potentially very strong and natural human feeling. A common mistake is to assume that when one speaks of emotion with regard to the feature writer, the reference is primarily to sorrow or tragedy. Human interest is much broader; the emotion of joy, especially when involved with humor, probably appears more frequently than sorrow or tragedy. There was a time when newspapers concentrated on the "tear-jerker" type of story, but such emphasis has declined.

Another element, in addition to emotion or human interest, is incongruity, or the unexpected. It is related to the "whodunit" story or the suspended interest and surprise ending organization. People like the challenge of guessing the ending, and they enjoy being surprised.

Incongruity plays an important role in writing the feature story, for reporters may add to the effectiveness of the story if they have enough skill with the language to make it work for them in surprising the reader. The most obvious example of this skill is the pun. The automatic response to a good pun in a groan, but most people appreciate such talent with the language.

Let's now take a case in which such situation incongruity and verbal incongruity combine to produce an eye-catching feature lead. First, a summary lead based upon the results of a trial in a municipal court:

Bert Cedrick, 32, of 14 Bartholomew Lane was sentenced to 30 days in city jail by Police Judge Oakley Addis yesterday after he and another man were picked up for fighting outside the Inside Inn.

This is a very straightforward statement, containing all the "five W's and H." But it is the lead of an unimaginative reporter who missed a good opportunity. The fight had been over ownership of a battered brass cornet In an effort to determine who actually owned the instrument, Judge Addis has asked each of the two men to play it in court. Cedrick couldn't, and the other man, Raymond Ogden, could. Ogden's sentence was suspended. Another reporter, recognizing the unexpected quality of such a procedure and adding skill with the language, wrote this lead:

The charge wasn't piracy in a case before police Judge Oakley Addis yesterday, but it had something to do with activity on the high C's.

This second lead is sharp an interesting. It shows some imagination. The reporter who has the ability to recognize such situations and to use them effectively in writing will be more likely to hold the reader's interest.

Types of Feature Treatment

With regard to their feature qualities, newspaper stories may be placed on a continuum which distinguishes the emphasis on news values as opposed to human interest values. On one end of that continuum would be the so-called "straight" news story which seeks only to pass along a set of facts in a very straightforward manner. On the other end would be what is labeled the "human interest story' which may contain a little news value but is interesting because of its emotional qualities. At various places between these two would fall the type of story called the "news feature" which is a combination of the two. The news feature may represent use of a sparkling human interest lead on a story which, for the most part, is rather straight, or it may be a complete feature approach to a story which could be written as a straight news story.

Strictly human interest stories are written for entertainment and need not contain information which is newsworthy by the usual standards. Such stories-often called "brighteners" or "brites"-are interesting because they are amusing, tragic, pathetic, happy –in brief, because they elicit some emotional response from the reader. Frequently, their subject matter is so unusual that they plead for a reporter to put them of paper. Sometimes, they are in the form of anecdotes which have unexpected, humorous endings, As such, they usually are written as concisely and to the point as possible.

Human interest stories appear in newspapers frequently, but news features provide the greatest number of examples of humanizing the news. This is because the news feature is a story which has both newsworthiness and human interest or incongruity and which has been written in the "feature way." It could have been written as straight news if the reporter had elected to write it that way. But an enterprising reporter has adapted the writing style to take advantage of both.

By Bob Olmstead

Chicago Sun-Times

CHICAGO – Now you may think a piano is a musical instrument. And the dictionary may define the piano as a musical instrument.

But the Chicago Board of Education recently spent $183.75 researching the question and has come to the firm legal opinion that it's not.

The question came up when Mrs. William L. Rohter, a board member often critical of what she considers sloppy accounting practices, noticed that the school budget lists pianos as a discussion of legal expenses, Mrs. Rohter complained that she had learned that the school's legal department spent $ 183.75 to find out what a piano is-but never told her the answer.

A legal aide dug around and handed her a two-page opinion which concluded that a piano is a piece of furniture because the budget has always classified it that way.

This is crazy, said Mrs. Rohter. A piano's a musical instrument. Everybody knows that.

Even Webster's New International Dictionary, second edition, says: "Piano: a stringed instrument of percussion..."

Not so, said the board of education. A piano's a piece of furniture and always has been.

Mrs. Rohter went to the Chicago schools' music director and asked him "What do teachers do with a piano?"

He looked at her rather strangely and said, "Why, we teach music with it."

Armed with this expert opinion, Mrs. Rohter went back to the board of education and demanded that it change its mind and its budget. The board said it would research the question.

The significance of all this –if any-is that the money for a piano could come from two different tax funds-the building fund and the textbook fund.

A year ago, the school system's accounting practices were criticized by its own accountants, Arthur Anderson & Co., as being so arbitrary as to be nearly useless in reflecting reality.

Mrs. Rohter maintains that –if the piano example is any indication-the budget's conductor may have changed, but the melody lingers on. (Reprinted with permission from Chicago Sun-Times)

Humanizing Your Writing

Now let us turn our attention to the techniques used in humanizing the news. It's at the same time very easy and frightfully difficult, because almost anything goes.

In feature writing, rules are broken deliberately or new ones created if the situation calls for it. When rules are broken, however, the breaking must be done to serve a specific function; it must add some element to the story which is needed. And, like the clown on a tightrope, reporters must first have a very firm grasp of the rules before they can break them effectively. In newspaper writing, creativity simply for the sake of creativity and not for the benefit of the readeı usually produced bad copy.

But if reporters know the rules and have reasons for breaking them, they may, for example: write stories is first, second or third person instead of the usual standard third person; use slang; provide a summary statement at the end of the story; use any form of story organization which seems most acceptable, usually avoiding the inverted pyramid, or use almost any writing technique.

Let us now be more specific about the "feature way" of writing in the context of feature leads, language, writing style and story organization.

Feature Leads : It would be well to remember first that the "five W's and H" summary lead has two primary functions: (1) to summarize the story by giving the essential fact or facts of the story, and (2) to attract attention. Of the two, emphasis is on (1), the summary of the story. It is expected that attracting attention will be accomplished by the content of such a summary.

The feature lead serves the same functions, but reverses the order of their importance. That is, it seeks, first, to attract attention and stimulate interest through a variety of techniques and second, to provide information about the story itself. Because of this, the only content requirement of a feature lead is that it, at a minimum, gives a hint of what the story about. There must be some direct connection between the lead and the story itself, naturally, but this connection may be a very loose one. One would not, for example, write a lead simply for the purpose of attracting attention (perhaps a joke) and then launch into a story which was not related in any way.

As an example, we might remember the lead on the police court story presented earlier. It has as its main purpose to attract attention, and the information it provides the reader is minimal. He tells only that the story concerns something that happened in police court (we're not sure that and that it involved Police Judge Oakley Addis is some way. In spite of this limited amount of information, however, the lead is very likely to attract the reader into the story, if for no other reason than to find out what the story is all about.

Other examples of leads which might do the same hting for the same story are the following:

A short tune ended on a sour note for Bert Cedrick yesterday in police court before Police Judge Oakley Addis.

Lady Justice faced the music in police court yesterday, including some sour notes, but in the end she reached her decision by playing it by ear.

Bert Cedrick is signing the blues in jail today because the couldn't play them on a cornet yesterday in police court.

Bert Cedrick has been in jail before, but he never thought he would get 30 days just because he wasn't musically inclined.

Note that each of these leads, in spite of different approaches to the subject, makes some reference to the incongruity of the situation. Note also how most of them use familiar idea or statement in a s somewhat different or unexpected context. And note that they are all short. Good writers have found that the short, compact, to-the-point lead is much more effective than one which rambles. Human interest and incongruity have their greatest impact when presented in a concise manner. It is seldom that a good feature lead will exceed three typewritten lines.

It was stated earlier that leads are the most difficult part of the story to write, and this is especially true for feature leads. Even the most experienced reporters frequently go through a number of false starts before they find the lead which satisfies them. Sometimes reporters under pressure of a deadline will use a lead which they feel is not quite right. But if they have time, they will work with the lead until the proper idea and wording fall into place. It's matter of allowing your imagination to play upon the human interest or incongruous elements in the story, then seeking the correct words to express the ideas you formulate. If words and ideas mesh, you're ready to move into the body of the story; if the idea comes, but not the words, don't be afraid to toss out that idea and seek another; if the idea won't come, write a lead which may be acceptable although not quite what you would like, then complete the story and return to rework the lead if time permits. Feature leads take work; good feature leads usually are made, not born.

Feature Language : The difference between feature and news writing is evident in the language which the reporter uses. This does not mean common usage of profanity or vulgarities, for most reporters still must tailor their writing for family readership. It does mean that the language in a feature story usually is more relaxed, more relaxed, more casual, than in straight news. A feature story should be written in as near conversational style as you can create. It should sound like a story being told by someone to a group.

Conversational style can involve many things. It may mean the use of incomplete sentences or, for the right reason, improper grammar. It may mean the use of slang, colloquialisms or a particular dialect (although it is only fair to warn the beginning reporter that writing in dialect is difficult and is not effective unless done properly). Sometimes, it will involve using such obvious conversational gimmicks as "It seems that..." This, for example, might fit very well at the beginning of the second paragraph of the police court story, following the lead with: "It seems that Bert Cedrick and Raymond Ogden were in police court charged with disturbing the peace..." Reporters also might find some reason to use nonwords such as "uh" or "ah" to indicate pauses in the speech, or they might deliberately stop in mid-sentence, then start again, to indicate a false start: "I really want...uh... I mean, I think I would like... at least, it sounds like an interesting idea to me."

Remember that selection of common, well-known words and simple sentence structure are musts for conversational style. Most persons speak this way. And, when judicious, but limited, use of other techniques is added, the result stands a good chance of being effective. But don't overdo such use of conversational gimmicks to create an effect. Too many reporters have a tendency to place too much emphasis on the gimmicks and too little on word choice and sentence structure. The result often is a very forced, uncomfortable, sometimes unreadable, and certainly unacceptable piece of writing.

If a play on words, such as a pun, suits your purposes, and if you have a good one, it is a legitimate tool. Sarcasm and satire fit into certain situations, although they must be used carefully, and the feature writer must avoid misusing freedom of subjectivity. Understatement and overstatement also may add to a feature story. The following lead, for example, effectively uses understatement to provide an eye- catching lead:

Officers Karl Macklin and Barry O'Dell knew that something was out of the ordinary yesterday when, driving along West branch Avenue, they saw two lions trotting toward Koon's Butcher Shop.

Even though all of these techniques are available to the feature writer, sue them with caution. They tend to be most effective when used verbally because the speaker can use inflection-a shifting of tone of voice-to indicate real meaning. But no such device is available in written communication, so the reader may not understand the real intent. When feature writers are using irony, a pun, sarcasm, satire, understatement or overstatement, they must make certain that the meaning is very clear to the reader. Lack of understanding or misunderstanding by the reader destroys the effectiveness of any type of writing.

Let' return now to the police court story to see how the reporter uses many of these techniques to present a well-written, interesting story:

The charge wasn't piracy in a case before Police Judge Oakley Addis Monday, but it had something to do with activity on the high C's.

It sems that Bert Cedrick, 32, of 14 Bartholomew Lane and Raymond Ogden, 41, of 3 Morrison Ave. were in police court on charges of disturbing the peace. They had been picked up by Policeman Harold J. Rembro Sunday night while fighting over an old brass cornet.

Each of the men claimed ownership of the battered instrument and accused the other of stealing it.

"It's my horn," Cedrick told the judge. "I used to play in a dance band."

Ogden disagreed: "You can see it belongs to me. I can tell it by that dent."

Jedge Addis laid his finger thoughtfully along the side of his nose and pondered the contradicting claims. Then, showing the wisdom of Solomon, he turned to Cedrick.

"Blow it," the judge ordered, handing the cornet to the man.

Cedrick did, and the result was anything but musical. A crackly, mournful off-key sound filled the room.

"Now you blow it." the judge told Ogden.

Ogden smiled and confidently placed the cornet to his lips. He blew a high, sweet, clear note, gave a demonstration of triple-tonguing and appeared about ready to launch a concert when the judge interrupted.

"Give him the horn, "Addis instructed. "Thirty days for disturbing the peace. Sentence suspended."

To Cedrick the judge was stern.

"Thirty days in jail," he said

Lead : Designed principally to attract attention and give a hint of the story content.

Lead Transition : Use of conversational style to provide smooth flow from lead into narration of the event; also introduces principal characters.

Statement of the conflict.

Use of Dialogue : Much of the remainder of the story is presented in direct quotation form, with descriptive passages providing transition and detail.

Use of short sentences and paragraphs highlight the drama of the situation.

Conclusion : Climax of the story. This information would be in the lead of an inverted pyramid version of this story.

Writing Style : Important to the presentation of straight news, writing style is crucial to the feature story. It includes the relaxed, casual approach discussed earlier; it also includes a greater reliance upon short direct quotations and greater amounts of dialogue. But the general point to remember is this: Feature writing must be dramatic writing; that is, it must be written in a style which is compatible with the mood of the content. This idea is borrowed from music. In a sense, all music is mood music since it elicits some psychological response. Rapid-moving, staccato music tends to create a psychological atmosphere of excitement, of movement, of haste. Slow music utilizing greater flow creates the mood of peace and quiet, of meditation, of relaxation.

Writers of novels and short stories have been applying this technique for years. They know that language and sentence structure and even paragraph structure can convey a particular mood if handled correctly. What they have discovered is that long sentences which flow smoothly seem to create an atmosphere of thoughtfulness, of deliberation, of calm. On the staccato phrasing with much punctuation. In this way, writing style can team with content to create the proper mood for the story.

As an example of such pacing in short-story writing, let us review a brief passage from William Faulkner's "Barn Burning":

Then he was free. His aunt grasped at him but it was too late. He whirled, running, his mother stumbled forward on her knees behind him, crying to the nearer sister: "Catch him, Net! Catch him!" But that was too late too, the sister (the sisters were twins, born at the same time, yet either of them now give the impression of being, encompassing as much living meat and volume and weight as any other two of the family) **not yet having begun to rise from the chair, her head, face, alone merely turned,** presenting to him in the flying instant an astonishing express of young female features untroubled by any surprise even, wearing only an expression of bovine interest.....

The variety of rhetorical pacing within this one paragraph and even within individual sentences lends to it a quality which feature writers should seek. In the first place, although Faulkner's sentences are very long and complex, they are broken up into short phrases and contain much punctuation, thus creating the mood of breathless excitement which he intended. This can best be seen in the italicized portions, especially at the beginning of the paragraph. In the middle, especially the parenthetical statement in the second sentence, are passages which do not convey such excitement, but moments of meditation. The ability to use a dramatic style of writing this way helped make Faulkner a great writer, although the newspaper writer seldom will make such extensive use of a Faulkner-type style.

But these principles do fit the newspaper story-especially the feature-very well. Notice, for example, how the writer of the following interesting, but unspectacular, story used the same techniques although in a more modest fashion:

Lead : Designed to catch interest and give hint of what story is about

Setting the scene for the narration

Still setting the scene, this time from main action of the story

Taking a slow pace in effort to show the relaxed moment of the story

Speeding up tempo, using short sentences to emphasize the speed and excitement of the situation.

Slowing down again, to emphasize pace and to build suspense

Slowly building to the climax

Punch line, presentation of the climax

Tag line, reporter's conclusion, seeking to subtly emphasize incongruity

For Blackie, a hard-working Labrador retriever, it was all a matter of first things first at lake Wahoo early yesterday.

One of the participants in an ill-fated. duck-hunting expedition, William Steppe of 42 N. Charles St., related the unusual experience this way:

Shortly after daybreak, Steppe, Blackie and the dog's owner, George R. Stanley of 2 Barberry Lane, were in a small boat on the lake.

Five ducks had been bagged in the early morning hours before things slowed down. The sky was empty, so Steppe and Stanley relaxed, laid down their guns and started to light cigarettes while Blackie gazed intently at the sky.

Suddenly, a lone duck appeared on the horizon. The two men grabbed their guns, took quick aim, fired ... but missed. Blackie became excited. In his readiness to retrieve, he tipped the boat over. Dog, men and five dead ducks were dumped into the icy waters.

Although weighted down by their heavy clothing and very, very cold, the two men managed to reach the capsized boat. They clung to it.

But Blackie knew what to do. In a very businesslike manner he went about his job, carrying the five dead ducks individually to shore. Only when all had been retrieved and were safely on the bank did he return to the boat to see what could be done for the men.

The men were almost exhausted when Blackie took hold of a rope attached to the front of the boat and pulled them ashore.

Steppe and Stanley are in pretty good shape today, although both are suffering from colds and Stanley barely missed a case of pneumonia.

Blackie? He's fine, and there's a possibility he may enjoy a sirloin steak for his efforts. The men haven't quite been able to make up their minds yet.

One final point about writing style is that feature writers are allowed more leeway to be somewhat subjective. They are much more likely, for example, to be descriptive to the point of presenting some degree of personal opinion. They may reach conclusions about a subject or an individual in a feature, such as the tag line in the Labrador retriever story. They may even go beyond subjectivity at times, even to the extent of presenting material which, it taken literally, in untrue.

The freedom to use exaggeration to the point of untruth must not be taken too far. The literary license of the statement must be so obvious that no reader is likely to misinterpret it. Reporters never have the right to create facts. They must stick with the situation as it is, avoiding any degree of fiction except that which is rhetorical and is bound to be understood that way.

Story Organization : This will be brief because there are few guidelines. A story can be organized in any logical manner which satisfies the reporter's purpose. To say there are few rules, however, is not to say there is no organization. It means simply that reporters decide the best pattern in which to write the story and then organize the facts according to that pattern.

This may involve use of the inverted pyramid, although incidences are rather rare. It may be suspended-interest organization in which the writer deliberately withholds the important element for the end. It may be pure chronology. In some cases (usually longer stories), reporters may elect to use "flashbacks" as they seek to tie present with the past. The only requirement is that the presentation be logical so that the sequence is clear to the reader. If the reporter accomplishes his or her purpose and the reader can follow the description to that purpose, the organization is just right for the story regardless of what form it has taken.

The Personal Approach : Although it may fall in either the human interest or the news feature category, one type of story which always has been common in newspapers is the personality feature.

Names make the news, journalists say, so they make efforts to write about people, either in the form of separate stories or by approaching an event or other subject matter through one or more persons.

The personality feature story tends to be based on interview material, but, unlike the standard interview story, the source is asked to talk about herself or himself instead of some subject on which he or she is an authority. Reporters seek to go as deeply as possible into the source's personality; after reading the story, one should have the feeling of knowing the source personally.

Reporters have latitude with information they present in personality stories, sometimes being more subjective than they would be for standard news presentation. Among others, reporters may take any or all of the following approaches:

- Interview the source. An obvious technique, of course, but if time is available, reporters prefer to spend much more time in the interview situation than they would for a straight news story. Many specific questions are asked, but reporters like to spend time in informal conversation with the source. This adds depth to the information received, permits the reporter to gain a better understanding of the source's personality and gives the reporter more solid, meaningful, direct quotations.
- Observe the source's surroundings. Individuals surround themselves with things they prefer, and often these will give the reporter clues about their personality. Frequently, of course, it is not possible for reporters to go to the source's home or office, but when it can be done it may be very fruitful and give the reporter ideas for meaningful question and perhaps even ideas for descriptive passages in the story.
- Interview others about the source. This is done regularly in sports stories and in stories about the deaths of famous persons. But it is a technique which should be expanded. One cannot always gain a full perspective by dealing only with the individual involved. Sometimes, family members, friends or business associates will have a helpful insight into the source's personality.
- Observe the source in action. A source's words may or may not be substantiated by his or her life. If Mary Ann Mulberry says

she believes each person has a responsibility to help others, the reporter would be advised to try to find out how well she fits this philosophy into her life. If she does, the reporter will gain specific examples for the story; if she does not, the reporter will have gained deeper insight into her personality. "Talk" stories are desirable, but "talk and action" stories are much more meaningful.

- Develop personal viewpoints about the source. This technique is used rarely but, under the right circumstances, it can add to a personality story. Reporters who spend much time with a source may be in a position to make comments which they are unable to get from others. Such a subjective technique should be used with extreme caution. It is seldom that reporters can get away with statements of bald opinion which cannot be substantiated. Most frequently, when reporters make comments in this type of story, those comments are designed to broaden points which are presented from other sources of information.
- First-person description. Reporters sometimes find it desirable to enter into the story as participants because the reporter-source relationships get important points across. This is one of the few occasions in which use of the first-person "I" is acceptable in newspaper copy. A word of caution is in order, however, because reporters must remember that any use of this technique must have the source, not the reporter, as the central character in the passage.

In writing the personality story, and, in fact, many feature stories, reporters tend to broaden the use of literary technique and place much greater emphasis on writing style. Facts are not de-emphasized, but their impact is heightened by good writers who effectively use description, significant passages of direct quotations (sometimes in the form of dialogue) and anecdotes which pound home an important point.

Note, for example, how Lois Cress of the **Denver Post** effectively intertwines several of these techniques in the following word picture of a woman who had achieved her 100th birthday:

By Lois Cress

Denver Post Senior Staff Writer

Mrs. Ellie Harris Fields doesn't "feel equal" to going to the polls this year because "I have a bad heart." But she takes the matter of voting seriously.

"We are citizens of the United States," she said," "and we should be interested in everything that takes place in the United States. We're in a country where, if the administration doesn't suit us, we can vote it out. I am an American through and through- not always satisfied, but it's my country."

Tiny Mrs. Fields spoke solemnly and thoughtfully, remembering that she has been interested in politics since she was a small girl sitting with her family around the table discussing the subject back in Hannibal, Mo., where she was born 100 years ago.

"I love politics," she said, seated is a soft chair in her room at the Hayes Residential Care Home, 2346 Gilpin St. an adult foster-care home, where she may pursue her interests and come and go as she pleases.

Her eyesight is poor and her hearing impaired, but she turns up her radio to get the news of world events.

Mrs. Fields calls her first 100 years "eventful." "You know, to live 100 years, you could write a book," she said. "I've had a lot of sorrow. I've never allowed it to make me bitter. I've had some happy days.'

Mrs. Fields said she lost her health while teaching in Hannibal. "I went to St. Louis and went into the music world. I was the organist for one of the large churches and gave music lessons." She also studies hairdressing.

She was married twice, once to "a Denver man, an undertaker," Curtis Harris. They were married only two years, five months before he died. She was single for 20 years before marrying again. Her second husband was B.W. Fields, "an old schoolmate (from Hannibal) I hadn't seen for 43 years."

Her life with Fields in the Nevada desert apparently left an indelible impression on Mrs. Fields' memory. Periodically, Mrs. Fields accompanied her husband about 76 miles into the open desert, where he completed necessary assessment work to hold the claims to gold and silver mining property.

"We were 32 miles from any human beings. All I heard was the bark of hounds. We had a little house four or five feet out-the rest inside the mountain. It had a dirt floor, just one room.

"Have you ever been in the desert? Oh, it's the most beautiful place. In the spring, the flowers-and no water-where do they come from? Oh, the sunsets and sunrises...I would be on the desert today if I had anyone to be with me."

Now, as far as family is concerned, Mrs. Fields is alone. But even alone, she feels especially "blessed."

While she was reminiscing, the Rev. Richard Kerr, pastor of Holy Redeemer, stopped by with a box. She had told him in midsummer that she thought she would need a new dress for her 100th birthday. As was his custom, he went shopping for her, choosing "her favorite color-black" set off with a paisley scarf. It was the first time he had chosen her favorite. Until this purchase, he had been steering her wardrobe from the backs and navy blues into bright colors.

"He has such good taste," Mrs. Fields said after he left. (Reprinted with permission from **The Denver Post**)

Personalizing a newspaper story has another meaning to reporters, however, and does not have to go as far as the personality story. Frequently, reporters face a situation in which they could write a straightforward account of an event, but they decide the story is best told through the eyes of experiences of a participant or example. The facts of the story still are important; the story could stand on its own merits, but the reporter adds interest by personalizing the approach.

In the following **St. Louis Post**-Dispatch story, William C. Lhotka's major purpose it to explain to his readers that the median barrier will be built. Notice how he adds human interest to the early part of the story by concentrating on a personal experience.

By William C. Lhotka

Jefferson City Correspondent of the Post-Dispatch

Jefferson City- The plea of a bereaved father for the construction of a median barrier along Lindbergh boulevard in west St. Louis Country where his daughter was killed has prompted an immediate response from the Missouri Highway Commission.

"If that barrier had been put there, my daughter would be alive today and these tragedies would have been avoided," Harvey Rothberg of Ladue told the six-member panel yesterday. "I want you to put the safety of the public ahead of any special interest group that might consider it unsightly."

Rothberg said his 17-year-old daughter, Laurie, had been killed in June "because a Lincoln Continental went berserk, crossed the center line, proceeded down the wrong lane and, without braking, crashed into our car. My daughter swerved and fortunately saved the lives of her friends. But the car was struck on the driver's side and she was killed instantly."

The struck on the driver's side and she was commission voted to proceed as rapidly as possible in carrying out plans for the median barrier, from Clayton Road south to Manchester Road. The four-lane highway is already divided by a median wall from Clayton Road north to St. Charles Rock Road.

The commission rejected a request from a group of west country residents for major modifications to those plans. (Reprinted with permission from the **St. Louis Post Dispatch**)

Postscript

Feature writing requires greater thought and effort than standard news story form. It does this because the reporter must make several subtle decisions about leads, language, style and organization. There are few guidelines which direct the writing. Thus, don't be misled into thinking that feature writing is fun because it is easy; it is fun, but primarily because of the challenge which reporters face. It they overcome this challenge, feature writing is extremely satisfying.

And reporters who develop the talent to use the principles of feature writing in all stories will have a most valuable tool. Much of what is dull and uninteresting in news stories stems from reporters' inability to use techniques which would make those stories interesting. Of course, straight news writing, being what it is, cannot be written in precisely the same way as a feature story. But a more casual style, a more informal approach, skill in language choice, use of drama, personalization and an appreciation of human interest all could add to the readability and interest of more regular news stories.

◆◆◆

11

Interviewing for News

Information is the merchandise of a journalist. While some of it is gathered from records and some from observation, most of it is gathered in person-to-person conversations. For that reason every journalist needs to develop interviewing skills.

Interviewing is an imperfect process. As in the city water-works system, there is plenty of leakage. When the city pumps a million gallons of water, not all of it reaches the customers. Some evaporates, some leaks through decaying pipes. Some people illegally siphon some of the water.

Information leaks out, too as it is passed from source to interviewer to editor to reader. The source may not want you to know everything. The source may be telling you everything, but you may not understand the subject. Unrecognized differences in cultural and ethnic backgrounds can influence meaning. When someone says "blue" to you, a colour flashes in your mind's eye. However, it may not be the same shade of blue that is in the mind's eye of the speaker. Shades of meaning often leak out of the information pipeline.

In such an imperfect system of information gathering and transfer, we can reduce-though not eliminate-the leaks. Consequently, you must work hard to refine your skills. You simultaneously ask questions, digest responses, record answers, cajole the source, gauge reactions and look for details. This is no work for the unprepared.

Preparing for the Interview

A reporter was assigned to interview Vivien Leigh, who was attending the premiere of the reissue of "Gone With the Wind."

When he opened the interview by asking her what part she played in the film, Miss Leigh, whose portrayal of Scarlett O' Hara is a classic indignantly ended the conversation with good reason. A reporter who begins an interview without the proper preparation is like a student taking a final exam without studying. Both may make it, but luck, rather than skill, may have more to do with it.

The success of the interview depends as much on what you do before you ask the first question as it does on the questioning and writing. You should research both the subject and your source. A.J. Liebling, a famous journalists, author and press critic, didn't know much about horse racing, but his first question in an interview with jockey Eddie Arcaro was, "How many holes longer do you keep your left stirrup than your right?" Arcaro responded enthusiastically to the knowledgeable question. Liebling's research gave him the key to open the interview. A source who thinks the reporter is knowledge able about the subject of the interview is more likely to speak frankly and fully than one who must explain everything as the conversation progresses.

Liebling was able to overcome Arcaro's skepticism with a single question. Syl Jones had considerably more difficulty with William Shockley, who won a Nobel Prize for his work developing the transistor. Jones, however, wanted to talk to him for Playboy magazine about much more volatile topics: Shockley's theory of black genetic inferiority and his revelation that he had participated in a Nobel-laureate sperm bank. Burned many times by the press, Shockley was exceedingly cautious.

Shockley often turned down reporters' requests for interviews because he believed they didn't know enough about genetics. By hone, Shockley quizzed Jones, a science and medical writer, about genetics. The quizzes involved complicated mathematical analyses of statistics designed by Shockley in support of his theories. After a few weeks of grilling, he agreed that Jones was competent enough to interview him.

But first Shockley wanted even more information. He asked for personal information, everything from where Jones was born to where he went to school. Jones told the rest of the story in **Playboy**:

Long before this point in the process, most other reporters had written Shockley off as a book and had given up. I was tempted to do the same. But something intrigued me: Never once did he ask my race or make any kind of racist remark, and he had no idea I was black. I didn't tell him, because I was hoping for a confrontation....

When a white photographer and I showed up at Stanford for the interview, Shockley instinctively reached to shake the photographer's hand with the greeting," "Hello, Mr. Jones." It was a wrong guess that seemed almost to stagger him. Obviously stunned by my blackness, he insisted that I submit to one final test, concocted on the spur of the moment, concerning the application of the Pythagorean theorem to some now long-forgotten part of his dysgenic thesis. Somehow, I came up with a satisfactory explanation, and Shockley had no choice but to grant me the interview.

Let's hope you never have to overcome those kinds of barriers.

Consideration of Story Type

How you prepare for the interview depends in part on what kind of a story you intend to write. You may be doing a news story, a personality profile or an investigative piece. In each case you check the newspaper library and search the data bank, talk to other reporters and, if there's enough time, read magazine articles and books.

To prepare for a news story, you pay more attention to clips about the subject of the story than to those about the personality of the individual to be interviewed. To prepare for a Profile, you look for personality quirks and the subject's interests, family, friends, travels and habits. To prepare for an investigative piece, you want to know both your subject matter and the person you are interviewing.. In all these stories, do not overlook other reporters and editors who know something about the person or subject. Let's look at each of these three types of stories more closely.

The News Story

One day Paul Leavitt made a routine telephone call to a law enforcement source. Leavitt, then assistant city editor for the **Des Moines (Iowa) Register**, was working on a story. He knew the source from his days as a county government and courts reporter for the **Register**.

He expected the story, and the interview, to be routine. Polk County was building a new jail. Leavitt wanted to find out about the progress on the new building. The source begged ignorance. He said," Oh, Leavitt, I don't know. I haven't had time to keep up on that, what with all these meetings on the Pope's visit.

Leavitt didn't say anything right away. A less astute reporter might have let the source know he was surprised. The Pope in **Des Moines**? Are you kidding? Instead, Leavitt remembered a story he had read about an Iowan who had extended an invitation for John Paul II to stop in Iowa during his American visit. Leavitt didn't think the Iowan had much of a chance. When the Vatican had announced the Pope's visit, people from every state were bartering for a chance to bask in the worldwide limelight.

Still, the source's slip of the tongue seemed genuine. Leavitt finally replied, "Oh, yeah, that's right. When's he coming, anyway?"

October 4," the source said.

As the conversation progressed, Leavitt waved frantically to the **Register's** managing editor. A major story was brewing.

"I started asking him some more questions," Leavitt recalls," then it dawned on him that he probably wasn't supposed to be talking about this. But it was clear from what he said that the Pope was definitely coming to Iowa. He even had the hours."

Before the conversation ended, Leavitt had learned of a meeting among the Secret Service, the Vatican, the U.S. State Department and Iowa law enforcement officials to discuss the trip. He also had learned when the Pope would arrive, were he would arrive, where he would celebrate Mass and when he would leave.

As a result, the **Register** stunned its readers the next morning with a copyright story saying the Pope would speak in Des Moines on Oct. 4. The story was printed three weeks before the Vatican released its official itinerary of the visit. Other area reporters scoffed at the story . One newspaper even printed a story poking fun at the thought of John Paul II hobnobbing in an Iowa cornfield.

Leavitt and the **Register** were vindicated. As scheduled, the Pope arrived Oct.4-and celebrated Mass in an Iowa cornfield.

Remembering his conversation with the source, and how a routine question turned into a bona fide scoop, Leavitt said, "I don't even remember what the original question was."

Leavitt probably would not have got on the story had he not remembered the earlier story about the invitation and known something else about interviewing: When a source unwittingly gives you a scoop, sometimes it is best to act as if you already know it. That may encourage the source to give you more information.

The Profile

A reporter who decided to write a profile of a local free-lance writer prepared differently. Because the reporter had used the writer as a source in an earlier story, she knew something about the writer. But she needed to know more. So she looked in contemporary Authors and found biographical information. She also asked the writer to send her copies of some of the articles she had written. Before the reporter went to see the free-lancer, she had read several of her articles. She also interviewed the editor at one of the magazines that bought the writer's material.

The reporter was prepared. Or so she thought. She had to pass one more test. The free-lance writer was an animal lover, and when the reporter arrived, she first had to make friends with a handful of dogs. Fortunately, she loved dogs. That immediately established rapport with the free-lancer. The resulting story was full of lively detail:

Joan Gilbert is a free-lance writer.

Joan Gilbert stretches lazily to soft sunbeams and chirping birds. She addresses casually in blue denim shorts and a plaid, short-sleeved blouse. She and her favourite work companions, five playful dogs, file out the door of her little white house to begin their day with a lazy walk in the surrounding woods. When she returns, she'll contentedly sit down at her typewriter. Such is work.

The Investigative Piece

The casual atmosphere of the Gilbert interview is not always possible for the investigative reporter. Here, the adversary relationship determines both the preparation required and the atmosphere of the interview itself. An investigative reporter is like an attorney in a courtroom. Wise attorneys know what the answers to their questions will be. So do investigative reporters. Preparation is essential.

In the early stages of the investigation, you conduct some fishing expedition interviews: Because you don't know how much the source knows, you cast around. Start with persons on the fringes. Gather as much as you can from them. Study the records. Only after you have most of the evidence do your confront your central character. You start with a large circle and gradually draw it smaller.

When Glenn Bunting, a reporter for the **San Jose (Calif.) Mercury News**, heard complaints about the low caliber of workers turned out by a government- funded training agency, he quietly did a little checking. Before he had gone too far, he had a friendly interview with the administrator, who did not know the real purpose of Bunting's inquiries.

Then Bunting went to work. He tracked the trail of money. He examined bank statements and cancelled cheques, government audit reports, purchase orders and weekly time cards-all public records because the agency got its money from the government. He interviewed counsellors and job-training instructors, law officers and others who did business with the agency. By the time Bunting was ready to talk to the administrator again, he already had most of his story confirmed. This is how the story of the interview began:

Robert Bernal was getting angry.
Confronted with evidence of wrong-
doing project DARE, his face
turned red and his voice grew louder.
"Why are you attacking me?" he
asked. "You don't believe me, but
everything I've told you is the truth. I
haven't told you any barefaced lies
But he had.

Among other things, Bunting was able to show that Bernal had earned a "degree" not from Stanford as he claimed, but from San Quentin Prison. Confronted with the evidence, Bernal told Bunting, "You never lose the stigma of being in prison. You have a tendency to build up a facade, a degree of phoniness-even saying that you have a college degree."

Bunting was able to pierce the deceptions because he had drawn the circle around Bernal tighter and tighter before he went into the interview.

Other Preparatory Considerations

All this homework is important, butit may be something as trifling as your appearance that determines whether you will have a successful interview. You would hardly wear cutoff shorts into a corporation president's suite, and you wouldn't wear a three-piece suit to talk to underground revolutionaries. It is your right to wear you hair however you wish and to wear whatever clothes you want, but it is the source's prerogative to refuse to talk to you. Most reporters choose to blend in with the environment.

The environment, too, is important. Most interviews are conducted in the source's office. Especially if the story is a profile or a feature, it usually is better to get the source away from his or her work. If you are doing a story about a rabbi's hobby of collecting butterflies, seek a setting appropriate to the topic. Suggest meeting in the rabbi's den or even outside.

In some interviews, it would be to your advantage to get the source on neutral territory. If you have some questions for the mayor or other public official, suggest meeting in a coffee shop at a quiet time. A person has more power in his or her official surroundings.

It is important, too, to let the source know how much time you need and whether you expect to return for further information. And if you don't already know how the source might react to a tape recorder, ask when you are making the appointment.

You have now done the appropriate homework. You are properly attired. You have made an appointment and told the source how much time you need. Before you leave, you should write down a list of questions you want to ask.

They will guide you through the interview and prevent you from missing important topics altogether. The best way to encourage a spontaneous conversation is to have your questions prepared. You'll be more relaxed. Barbara Walters once told a reporter that she writes as many as 500 questions on index cards, then selects the best ones for use during the interview. The thinking you must do to write the questions will help prepare you for the interview. Having questions prepared relieves you of the need to be mentally searching for the next question as the source is answering the last one. If you are trying to think of the next question, you will not be paying close attention to what is being said, and you might miss the most important part of the interview.

Preparing the questions for an interview is hard work, even for a veteran like Isabel Hilton, European affairs editor of **The Independent** in London. She was promised an interview with Gen. Alfredo Stroessner, the dictator who fled Paraguay and was living in Brazil. Many had tried to interview Stroessner, but only Hilton had been invited. Writing about the experience later, Hilton recalled, "I found myself worried. I imagined myself forgetting to ask the most obvious question, paralyzed by the absurdity of the situation." She added, "That night I went through my notebooks. I couldn't think of a single thing I could ask him that he would possibly want to tell me."

While you may ask all of your prepared questions in some interviews, in most, you probably will use only some of them. Still, you have benefited from preparing the questions in two important ways. First, even when you don't use many, the work you did thinking of the questions helped prepare you for the interview. Second, your sources who see that you have a prepared list often are impressed with your seriousness.

On the basis of the information you have gathered already, you know what you want to ask. Now you must be careful about how you ask the questions.

Phrasing the Question

Listen to an accomplished courtroom lawyer ask questions. How the question is structured often determines whether the lawyer will win the case. Journalists face the same challenge. Reporters have missed many stories because they didn't know how to ask questions. Quantitative researchers have shown how just a slight wording change affects the results of a survey. It you want to know whether citizens favour a city plan to beautify the downtown area, you can ask the question in several ways:

- Do you favour the city council's plan to beautify the downtown area?
- The city council plans to spend $3 million beautifying the downtown area. Are you in favour of this?
- Do you think the downtown area needs physical changes?
- Which of the following actions do you favour?
    - Building a traffic loop around the downtown area.
    - Prohibiting all automobile traffic in an area bounded by Providence Road, Ash Street, College Avenue and Elm Street.
    - Having all the downtown storefronts remodelled to carry out a single theme and putting in brick streets, shrubbery and benches.
    - None of the above.

How you structure that question may affect the survey results by several percentage points. Similarly, how you ask questions in an interview may affect the response.

By the phrasing of the question, many reporters signal the response they expect of prejudices they have. For instance, a reporter who says, "Don't you think that the city council should allocate more money to the parks and recreation department?" is not only asking a question but is also influencing the source or betraying bias. A neutral phrasing would be, "Do you think the city council should allocate more money to the parks and recreation department?" Another common way of asking a leading question in this: "Are you going to vote against this amendment like the other legislators I've talked to?"

Sometimes a reporter unwittingly blocks a response by the phrasing of the question. A reporter who was investigating possible job discrimination against Hispanics conducted several interviews before she told her city editor she didn't think the Hispanics with whom she talked were being frank with her. "When I ask them if they have ever been discriminated against, they always tell me no. But three times now during the course of the interviews, they have said things that indicate they have been. How do I get them to tell me about it?" she asks.

"Perhaps it's the way you are asking the question," the city editor replies. "When you ask someone whether they have ever been discriminated against, you are forcing them to answer yes or no. Don't be so blunt. Ask them if others with the same qualifications at work have been advanced faster than they have. Ask if they are paid the same amount as whites for the same work. Ask them what they think they would be doing today if they were white. Ask them if they know of any qualified Hispanics who were denied jobs."

The city editor was giving the reporter examples of both closed- and open-ended questions. Each has its specific strengths.

Open-Ended Questions

Open-ended questions allow the respondent some flexibility. Minorities may not respond frankly when asked whether they have ever been discriminated against. The question calls for a yes-no response. But an open-ended question such as "What would you be doing today if you were white?" is not so personal. It does not sound as threatening to the respondent. In response to an open-ended question, the source often reveals more than he or she realizes or intends to.

A sportswriter who was interviewing a pro scout at a college football game wanted to know who the scout was there to see. When the scout diplomatically declined to be specific, the reporter tried another approach. He asked a series of questions:

- "What kind of qualities does a pro scout look for in an athlete?"
- "Do you think any of the players here today have those talents?"
- "Whom would you put into that category?"

The reporter worked from the general to the specific until he had the information he wanted. Open-ended questions are less direct and less threatening. They are more exploratory and more flexible. However, if you want to know a person's biographical data, don't ask "Can you tell me about yourself?"

Closed-Ended Questions

Eventually the reporter needs to close in on a subject, to pin down details, to get the respondent to be specific. Closed-ended questions are designed to elicit specific responses.

Instead of asking he mayor, "What did you think of the conference in Washington, D.C.?" you ask, "What did you learn in the session 'Funds You May Not Know Are Available'?" Instead of asking a previous employee to appraise the chancellor-designate's managerial abilities, you ask, "How well does Uehling listen to the people who work for her?" "Do the people who work for her have specific job duties?" "Does she explain her decisions?"

A vague question invites a vague answer. By asking a specific question, you are more likely to get a specific answer. You are also communicating to your source that you have done your homework and that you are looking for precise details.

Knowing exactly when to ask a closed-ended question or when to be less specific is not something you can plan ahead of time. The type of information you are seeking and the chemistry between the interviewer and the source are the determining factors. You must make on-the-spot decisions. The important thing is to keep rephrasing the question until the source answers it adequately.

Establishing A Rapport

Tad Bartimus, AP's regional reporter for the Rocky Mountains, has interviewed hundreds of people, beginning with former President Harry S Truman while working for her hometown weekly at age 14. She approached the ex-president and said, "Excuse, me sir, but I'm from the local paper. Could you please talk to me?"

"Well, young lady, what would you like to know?" Truman responded. Years later, Bartimus recalled, "For the first time in my life, I was struck dumb. What did I want to know? What was I supposed to ask him? How do you do this interviewing stuff, anyway?"

Bartimus knows the answers to those questions now. One piece of advice she offered her colleagues in an article for AP World was to share and care. "I try never to go to an interview as a hostile antagonist. I am merely a reporter asking questions, with no axe to grind. I am a person with a family, a home, an unbalanced chequebook, a weight problem and a car that goes 'thonka-thonka-thonka' when it's cold. Unless my interview subject is Ivana Trump or Meryl Streep or Richard Nixon, my life is probably, at least in one way or two ways, similar to the person of who I'm asking the questions."

Wariner urges reporters to reveal themselves as people. "A little empathy goes a long way to defuse (the) fear and hostility that is so pervasive against the press," she says.

Rapport- the relationship between the reporter and the source- is crucial to the success of the interview. The relationship is sometimes relaxed, sometimes strained. Often it is somewhere in between. The type of relationship you try to establish with your source is determined by the kind of story you are doing. Several approaches are possible.

Is it Betrayal?

Are all these techniques "morally indefensible," as author Janet Malcolm calls them in her book, "The Journalist and the Murderer." Malcolm says the journalist is "a kind of confidence man, preying on people's trust and betraying them without remorse."

Malcolm was writing about the relationship between Joe McGinnis, a successful non-fiction author, and Jeffrey MacDonald, a doctor who was convicted of murdering his wife and two daughters. McGinnis had written permission to be party to all the discussions relating to MacDonald's defense before and during the trial as well as access to MacDonald's papers. In return, MacDonald was to share the income from the book.

MacDonald entered into the agreement to get a sympathetic hearing and to raise money for his defense. McGinnis, who lives with MacDonald for a time, showed him great empathy in conversations and letters, even after he had decided that MacDonald was guilty. In his book, "Fatal Vision," McGinnis described MacDonald as a "pathological narcissist."

MacDonald sues McGinnis for fraud. The trial ended with a hung jury, but five of six jurors favoured MacDonald's position, according to Malcolm. The case later was settled with a $325,000 payment to MacDonald.

Malcolm's thesis-that not just McGinnis but all journalists betray their sources-started a firestorm of debate in the profession . In an article in **Columbia Journalism Review**, author Nora Ephron, for instance, said she was "astonished" that anyone took issue with Malcolm. Author David Halberstam accused Malcolm of going after the subject with a sledgehammer. "I think 'betrayal' is a very, very strong and ugly word," he said. Author J. Anthony Lukas described the reporter-source relationship as "mutually manipulative."

Two critical differences exist between the McGinnis-MacDonald relationship and those involving most journalists. First, McGinnis had a contract giving him access to the information. The legal relationship created a partnership, even though McGinnis protected his artistic rights in the contract. McGinnis was working with MacDonald and sharing the profits. Most journalists are working for their publication not their sources. Second, the relationship lasted years, not hours or days as it does for most journalists. Beat reporting comes the closest to the long-term relationship between McGinnis and MacDonald. Even beat reporters, however, are not partners with their sources in the news-gathering effort. It is one thing to remain disinterested, as most journalists try to do; it is quite another to mislead a source, as Malcolm claims McGinnis did.

Still, journalists must be aware of the debate and adopt techniques that are defensible. Some techniques that are defensible for public officials who have betrayed their office may not be defensible with sources who are private citizens.

Interview Approaches

For most news stories and personality profiles, the reporter has more to gain of the subject is at ease. Often that can be accomplished by starting off with small talk. Ask about a trophy, the plants or an engraved pen. Bring up something humorous you have found during your research. Ask about something you know the source will want to talk about. In other interviews, if you think the subject might be skeptical about your knowledge of the field, open with a question that demonstrates your knowledge.

Reporter who can show sources what they have in common also have more success getting information. When Janet Chusmir was a reporter for the **Miami Herald**, she was assigned to interview the parents of Bernardine Dohrn. Dohrn was a suspect in an anti-war protest bombing and a fugitive. Many reporters, including some from the **Herald**, had tried to talk to the parents. None had succeeded.

Chusmir went to their home and knocked on the door. She identified herself and told then why she was there. They said they didn't want to talk. She said she understood because the was a parent, too. She asked for a glass of water. They complied with her request. She edged into the house and sat down to drink the water. While she sat there, they chatted about, among other things, why the parents didn't want to be interviewed. Before she left, she had enough information for a story. Although the request for water bought the reporter some time, it was her ability to talk to them sympathetically parent to-parent that made her successful.

On another occasion, Chusmir was among a group of reporters who showed up expecting to witness kidnappers return a mother's child. The kidnappers never showed up. The police slipped the mother into the back seat of a police car and edged through the crowd. As the car went by her, Chusmir tapped on the window. The mother rolled it down slightly, "I hope you find your child," Chusmir said. The woman told her to call. Chusmir did and got an exclusive story.

One of the mistakes reporters make is not being empathetic, Chusmir says. "I genuinely feel for these people. I think sources can sense that."

Rapport also depends on where you conduct the interview, Many persons, especially those unaccustomed to being interviewed, feel more comfortable in their workplace. Go to them. Talk to the business person in the office, to the athlete in the locker room, to the conductor in the music room. In some cases, though, you may get a better interview elsewhere if the source cannot relax at the workplace or is frequently interrupted. Reporters have talked to politicians during car rides between campaign appearances. They've gone sailing with businesspeople and hunting with athletes. One reporter doing a feature on a police chief spent a weekend with the chief, who was painting his home. To do a profile, which requires more than one interview, vary the location. New surroundings can make a difference.

Scott Kraft of the Associated Press once did a story on a couple who for more than two years drove the streets of Los Angeles looking for the man who raped their 12-year-old daughter. The search was successful.

"When I knocked on their door in May, I wanted them to know that I would be careful and honest, and I wanted them to tell me everything, even though it would probably be difficult," he wrote in Editor & Publisher.

Kraft conducted interviews in three locations. The first was in the family's living room. The second was in a car as they revisited the places where the family searched. The third was by phone. Kraft said the mother talked more candidly on the phone after her children had gone to school.

There are times when the reporter would rather have the source edgy, nervous or even scared. When you are doing an investigation, you may want the key characters to feel uneasy. You may pretend you know more than you actually do. You want them to know that the material you have is substantive and serious. Seymour Hersh, a Pulitzer Prize-winning investigative reporter, uses this tactic. Time magazine once quoted a government official commenting on Hersh: "He wheedles, cajoles, pleads, threatens, asks a leading question, uses little tidbits as if he knew the whole story. When he finishes you feel like a wet rag."

In some cases, however, it is better even in an investigation to take a low-key approach. Let the source relax. Talk around the subject but gradually bring the discussion to the key issues. The surprise element may work to your favour.

So may the sympathetic approach. When the source is speaking, you may nod or punctuate the source's responses with comments such as "That's interesting." Sources who think you are sympathetic are more likely to volunteer information. That was the key to Chusmir's success. Researchers have found, for instance, that a simple" mm-hmmm" affects the length of the answer interviewers get.

Other Practical Considerations

Where you sit in relation to the person you are interviewing can be important. Unless you deliberately are trying to make those interviewed feel uncomfortable, do not sit directly in front of them. Permit your sources to establish eye contact if and when they wish.

Some people are even more disturbed by the way a reporter takes notes. A tape recorder ensures accuracy of quotes, but it makes many speakers self conscious or nervous. If you have permission to use a tape recorder, place it in an inconspicuous spot and ignore it except to make it is working properly. Writing notes longhand may interfere with your ability to digest what is being said.

Techniques for Ensuring Accuracy

Accuracy is a major problem in all interviews. Both the question and the answer may be ambiguous. You may not understand what is said. You may record it incorrectly. You may not know the context of the remarks. Your biases may interfere with the message.

You have no control over some of the things that may affect the accuracy of the answers you receive in an interview. In 1946 two researchers conducted an experiment in which a group of people were asked, "Do you think there are too many Jews holding government offices and jobs?, The interviewers were divided into four groups: Jewish in appearance with a Jewish name; Jewish in appearance; non-Jewish in appearancel and non-Jewish in appearance with a non-Jewish name. Ten percent more people answered yes to the non-Jewish-appearing interviewer than they did to the Jewish-appearing interviewer with a Jewish name. Some respondents tailored their answer to what they believed the interviewer wanted to hear.

Some possibilities for making errors or introducing bias are unavoidable, but others are not. To ensure the most accurate and complete reporting possible, you should use all the techniques available to obtain a good interview, including observing, understanding what you hear and asking follow-up questions. Let's examine these and other techniques.

Observing

Some reporters look but do not see. The detail they miss may be the difference between a routine story and one that is a delight to read. Of course, it was not delightful to read about the flood damage in Hattiesburg, Miss, but reporter Sharon Wertz's observation as she listened to one of the victims brought the agony home to readers:

> "You know," Cheryl says, covering her anguished face with her hands, her shoulders shaking, "we canceled our flood insurance two months ago. The premiums went up.... Who would have thought this would happen?"
>
> She wipes her reddened eyes.
>
> "I'm sorry," she says, sniffing.
>
> "We're really lucky to be alive."

Gabriel Garcia Marquez, a Colombian writer and Nobel laureate, has experience on both sides of the interview. He, too, counsels the interviewer to listen and observe. "Today one has the impression that the interviewer is not listening to what you say, nor does he think it important, because he believes that the tape recorder hears everything. But he's wrong; it doesn't hear the beating of the heart, which is the most important part of the interview."

These same powers of observations serve the investigative reporter. Is the subject nervous? What kinds of questions are striking home? The mayor may deny that he is going to fire the police chief, but the reporter who notices the chief's personnel file sitting on an adjacent worktable may have reason to continue the investigation.

People communicate some messages non-verbally. Researchers have been able to correlate some gestures with meanings. For instance, folded arms often signal inapproachability; crossed ankles often signal tension. Many non-verbal messages, however, may not be the same for all ethnic and cultural groups. Reporters should read more about the subject.

Understanding

Understanding what you see is crucial to the news-gathering process. So is understanding what you hear. It is not enough merely to record what is being said; you must also digest it. The reporter who was investigating job discrimination was listening but not understanding. Her sources were telling her about incidents of discrimination, but all she heard were their denials.

Sometimes what you don't hear may be the message. The reporter who was trying to find out if the mayor was going to fire the police chief asked several questions about the chief's performance. What struck the reporter during the interview was the mayor's lack of enthusiasm for the chief. That unintentional tip kept the reporter working on the story until he confirmed it.

The **Miami Herald's** Chusmir listened, too. Once when she was interviewing Joan Fontaine, the actress, Chusmir mentioned that she had a daughter about the same age as Fontana's. Fontaine asked, "Is she jealous of you?" Listening closely, Chusmir correctly deduced that Fontaine was revealing a problem of jealousy in the family, and interview took an unexpected turn.

Asking Follow-Up Questions

It you understand what the source is saying, you can ask meaningful follow-up questions. There is nothing worse than briefing your city editor on the interview and having the editor ask you, "Well, did you ask..."Having to say no is embarrassing.

Even if you go into an interview armed with a list of questions, the most important probably will be the ones you ask in response to an answer. A reporter who was doing a story on bidding procedures was interviewing the mayor. The reporter asked how bid specifications were written. In the course of his reply, the mayor mentioned that the president of a construction firm had assured him the last bid specifications were adequate. The alert reporter picked up on the statement:

"When did you talk to him?"

"About three weeks ago," the mayor said.

"That's before the specifications were published, wasn't it?"

"Yes, we asked him to look them over for us."

"Did he find anything wrong with the way they were written?"

"Oh, he changed a few minor things. Nothing important."

"Did officials of any other construction firms see the bid specifications before they were advertised?"

"No, he was the only one."

Gradually, on the basis of one offhand comment by the mayor, the reporter was able to piece together a solid story on the questionable relationship between the city and the construction firm.

Other Techniques

Although most questions are designed to get information, some are asked as a delaying tactic. A reporter who is taking notes may fall behind. Emily Yoffe, a senior editor of **Texas Monthly**, will say, "Hold on a second-let me get that" or "Say that again." Other questions are intended to encourage a longer response. "Go on with that" or "Tell me more about that" encourages the speaker to add more detail.

You don't have to be stalling for time to say you don't understand. Don't be embarrassed to admit you haven't grasped something. It is better to admit to one person you don't understand than to advertise your ignorance on news print in front of thousands. **Once you have written the story, check with your sources. Check the concepts. Catch your errors before publication. You'll impress your editors, you will serve your readers better, your newspaper will have more credibility, and your sources will be happy to talk to you the next time.**

Another device for making the source talk on is not a question at all; it is a pause. You are signaling the source that you expect more. But the lack of a response from you is much more ambiguous than "Tell me more about that." It may indicate that you were skeptical of what was just said, that you didn't understand, that the answer was inadequate or several other possibilities. The source will be forced to react. The only problem with this, says the AP's special correspondent Saul Pett, "is that it invites the dull to be dull at greater length."

Many dull interviews become interesting after they end. There are two things you should always do when you finish your questions: Check key facts, figures and quotes and then put away your pen but keep your ears open. You are not breaching any ethical rule if you continue to ask questions after you have put away your pen or turned off the tape recorder. That's when some sources loosen up. Many reporters find they get their best material after the formal interview has ended and they are having a cup of coffee with the source.

Before you leave, ask if there's anything you forgot to ask. Put the burden on the source. You are also doing your subject a favour by giving the person a chance to contribute to the direction of the interview. You may have missed some important signals during the conversation, and now the source can be more explicit about what he or she wanted to say. Sometimes this technique leads to entirely new subjects.

Quickly review your notes and check facts, especially dates, numbers, quotes, spellings and titles. Besides helping you get it right, it shows the source you are careful. If necessary, arrange a time when you can call to check other parts of the story or clear up questions you may have as you are writing.

As a matter of courtesy, tell the source when the story might appear. You may even offer to send along an extra copy of the article when it's completed.

Remember that, although the interview may be over, your relationship to the source is not. When you have the story written, call the source and confirm the information. Better to discover your inaccuracies before you print than after.

◆◆◆

12

Structuring the News Story

A carpenter needs three things-building materials, tools and a blueprint which outlines the completed house. The journalistic equivalents of these would be a set of facts which merit treatment in a story (building materials), journalistic tools and some sort of plan which tells reporters in a general way what is acceptable journalistic presentation.

This last need, the blueprint, is provided in the form of a set of standard principles which have come to be known as the "inverted pyramid." The beginning reporter should understand the inverted pyramid but also remember that it is a principle, not a set of unbreakable rules. Carpenters use blueprints, but not all houses look alike; there is plenty of room for variation in appearance. Journalists use the inverted pyramid, but not all news stories look alike; there is plenty of room for the use of individual technique.

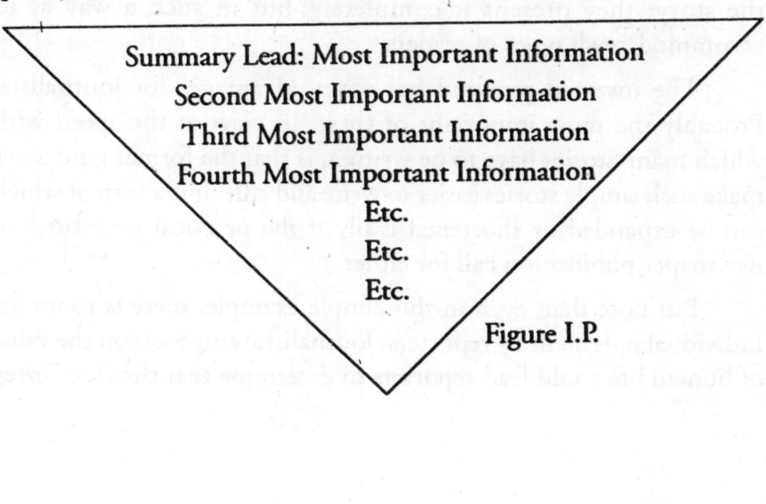

Figure I.P.

Story structure, in fact, is difficult to define precisely because it always depends upon the facts available and the reporter's judgments about those facts.

The inverted pyramid gets its name from the diagram presented in figure I.P. and its basic principle is this: Individual facts in a news story are presented in descending order of importance. The broad top of the pyramid represents the "lead" in which reporters seek to summarize the most essential information in the story. In using this structure, reporters present that fact or group of facts which they consider most significant, then organize the remainder of the information according to its decreasing importance. In this way, at least in theory, each succeeding paragraph contains information which is less significant than that which preceded it. Following the lead will be the second most significant fact or explanatory material; then comes the third most significant, and so on to the end of the story. In theory, although not always in practice, if the story has to be cut, one should be able to omit the final paragraph as the least significant.

The purpose of this type of structure is to present the news quickly, clearly and readably to help the reader easily understand the content. Its basic logic grows out of the different ways in which readers approach a news story. Some are so interested in the subject they read every word the reporter writes; others read only a few paragraphs; many read only the headline and the lead. To provide all of these readers with maximum benefit, reporters seek to stack the deck from the top down. They do not deliberately waste the latter portions of the story; they present it completely, but in such a way as to accommodate all types of readers.

The inverted pyramid has other advantages for journalists. Probably the most important of these, in view of the speed with which many stories have to be written, is that the format guidelines make such simple stories easier to write and edit. It is a format which can be expanded or shortened easily if the practical necessities of newspaper publication call for either.

But note that, even in this simple example, there is room for individual judgment by reporters. Journalistic emphasis on the value of human life could lead reporters to determine that the fact Torrey was not hurt merited earlier emphasis in addition to Jones' death. Thus, the opening statement could be written just as correctly this way:

One local resident was killed and another escaped injury in an automobile collision at the intersection of 23rd Street and Washington Boulevard at about 12:15 a.m. today.

Sometimes reporters, using the same inverted pyramid on a set of facts, will differ in their evaluation of the importance of those facts. There is no single "best" formula, and different emphasis frequently will appear. Take, for example, the following stories which appeared on the same day, both in morning newspapers:

Williamburg, Mich. (AP)-

The well suspected of causing natural gas eruptions in this tiny, half evacuated community has been capped, Amoco Production Co. officials said yesterday.

It would probably be at least three days until the danger is passed, state officials said, and precautions were still being taken to prevent an explosion.

Amoco, a subsidiary of Standard Oil of Indiana, dumped more than 1,300 barrels of heavy mud-water into the 6,200-foot well shaft Tuesday in unsuccessful efforts to block the gas flow. Still heavier mud was used yesterday.

Amoco has denied its well is the source of the gas, but state officials say they believe the well is responsible.

A series of natural blow-holes that began bubbling up in the area a week ago has forced evacuation of about 250 residents. State officials said the eruptions started three days after Amoco drillers lost control of the nearby well.

"If the gas pressure starts going down then we know the matter is solved, and we know the Amoco well caused it," an official said.

Williamburg, Mich. (U.P.)

- Highly flammable natural gas shot out of old craters with new intensity Wednesday as geologists worked to plug an oil well blamed for the geyserlike eruptions bursting from the earth in this resort village for a week.

The danger of fire increased because there was less water and silt mixed into the gas, officials said.

"Some of the first craters are blowing practically pure gas at this point," William Mullendore, a spokesman for the Michigan Department of Natural Resources, said. "It is increasing the fire hazard."

At the same time, the fact that "older" gas craters had been cleared of water and silt meant there was better venting of the gas from the earth and thus less chance of the craters spreading beyond the four square mile area to which they have been confined.

About 60 families had already been moved out of the immediate danger zone.

A spokesman for Amoco Production Co., a subsidiary of Standard oil of Indiana, said the company sealed an oil well four miles south of the town that state geologists have blamed for the craters.

The Associated Press writer led with the well's capping, a fact which the UPI writer relegated to the final paragraph. Which is correct? That's a matter of judgment. The facts in the two stories essentially are the same, but the reporters evaluated their significance differently.

This matter of judgment makes it very difficult to write many stories in the perfect inverted pyramid. It works only in certain situations and has definite limitations. For one thing, it is sometimes necessary to include rather lengthy passages of background material even though they don't deserve high play when viewed in isolation. They are placed in a story to aid understanding of other points which are important.

The necessity of such judgment explains why some say objectivity is impossible in news writing. The personal effect of reporters on the copy is reduced, however, by the fact that, with experience, journalists begin to think in rather standardized ways about relatively straightforward types of stories. Beginning reporters should be very familiar with the guidelines provided by the inverted pyramid and should seek to apply them to most stories they write. It is not the only story structure, as we shall see, but it is the one used in newspapers for the presentation of most news stories.

The Lead

The most recognizable characteristic of this type of structure and the one which should be mastered first is the "lead" or beginning of the news story. There are several types of leads, but the one most often used with the inverted pyramid is known as the "summary lead" because it seeks to summarize the story in a few lines. Because it transmits the essence of the news at the beginning of the story, the summary lead is not an introduction like that learned in English composition classes. It is a brief bulletin, summary, climax of the story, all in one concise package.

Usually, in most simple stories, the lead wraps the story into a small, neat bundle by attempting to answer all or most of these familiar questions: Who? What? Where? When? Why? How? Take, for example, the following lead:

Three young Northville residents were killed last night when their car skidded on rain-slick U.S. 101 near Centerville and plunged over a 40-foot embankment.

Police identified the victims as...

This summary lead gives the bulk of the information so completely it could almost stand alone. It tells: Who? "Three young Northville residents"; What? "Were killed"; Where? "on U.S. 101 near Centerville"; When? "last night"; why? "their car skidded on wet pavement"; How? "lunged over a 40-foot embankment." The lead is a complete summary of the story.

Of course, these six ingredients do not apply in every story, and they don't fit into every first paragraph. The Who? question, for example, might not exist in some types of stories, such as one about a landslide in which there were no property damages, personal injuries or deaths. The reporter, again, evaluates the available information to determine if one of the standard ingredients does not apply. This must be done cautiously, however, for every story should at least answer the questions: What? Where? and When? If there are no answers to these, chances are there's no story.

Since the trend today is to make opening paragraphs as brief and to the point as possible, reporters frequently will find themselves evaluating the "five Ws and H" to determine which to place in the first paragraph and which may be saved for later, usually the second paragraph. For example, in the lead above, the writer chose to identify the accident victims as "three young Northville residents," saving the specific identifications for later. Here, the lead will consist of at least two paragraphs. Any of the basic elements may be reserved for later use in this manner.

But the principles of the summary lead dictate that reporters present the information quickly; thus, it is the exceptional story in which the lead information must be spread over more than two paragraphs. In situations in which going beyond tow paragraphs in justified, it usually is the case that the writer has chosen to "featurize" the lead, that is, to write a first sentence of paragraph which is designed more to attract attention and create interest.

The summary lead takes two main forms, depending on the amount of information the reporter decides to include. This first will result when the reporter determines that there is one major point which should be the focus of the lead. That point is then hit immediately and directly, and the lead would look like this:

The city of Centerville will build a new recreation complex-including a regulation-sized swimming pool-on the current site of the city parking lot, Mayor Bert Jemieson announced at City Council's meeting last night.

This lead emphasizes the one main element of the story, including the answers to most of the "Ws and H" questions and provides additional specific information on the swimming pool. But if City Council had taken several equally important actions at the meeting instead of one, the lead probably would have been of the second type which seeks to summarize several major points:

City income taxes will be raised by 1 percent next year so the city can build a new recreation complex, make needed improvements to the water treatment plant and pave all streets in the Edgewood Section.

City Council made these decisions last night...

Note that this lead mentions four major decisions, admittedly a more productive meeting than most, but nevertheless an example of how it is possible, and desirable to pull a number of items together into one relatively brief summary lead. Of course, the reporter does have the alternative of writing several separate stories, but doing so depends on the paper's policy.

Facts may be summarized in many different ways, so no formula is appropriate to every summary lead. Reporters make extensive use of the principles of emphasis discussed earlier. In this way, the reporter highlights certain pieces of information by placing them first in the lead. Thus, again using the "five Ws and H,," it is possible to write the same summary lead in different forms. For example:

Emphasis on "Who"

Officials from the Idaho office of Security will open an investigation within the next week into the financial activities of the three organizations responsible for purchasing state highway equipment.

Emphasis on "What"

An Investigation into the financial activities of the three organizations responsible for purchasing state highway equipment will be opened by the Idaho office of Security within the next week.

Emphasis on "Where"

The three Idaho organizations responsible for purchasing state highway equipment will be subjects of an Office of Security investigation, beginning within the next week.

Emphasis on "When"

Within the next week, officials from the Idaho Office of Security will open an investigation into the financial activities of the three organizations responsible for purchasing state highway equipment.

Emphasis on "Why"

Charges of financial irregularities in the three organizations responsible for purchasing state highway equipment have prompted officials from the Idaho Office of Security to set up an investigation, to begin within the next week.

Emphasis on "How"

A three-person committee will be named within the next week to conduct an investigation into the financial activities of three organizations responsible for purchasing state highway equipment.

All six of these leads provide the same information in different forms, the only real difference being the emphasis. And that emphasis is rooted in the reporter's determination of which element is most significant and the mechanical placement of that element at the beginning of the paragraph. The remainder of the information is placed in what seems a logical arrangement. But note that all the leads satisfy the general requirements of the summary lead.

Such lead emphasis, however, is not arbitrary. The decisions are based on accepted principles of news judgment and the inverted pyramid. For example, the "Who" is stressed only under special circumstances because the statement or action usually is the important fact of a story, not who does it or who says it. Some journalists make it standard practice to avoid starting a lead with a name. Another element which seldom deserves emphasis is "When." In fact, the "When" example above would not be accepted by most reporters and editors. Not only is it vague, but the time element of the investigation cannot rank as more significant than the investigation itself. Many reporters say this applies not only to leads, but to all sentences, and they avoid starting any sentence with the time element.

The practice of putting nonessential information in the place of emphasis in the lead is known as "backing into the lead" or "burying the lead." It is rejected by reporters because it does not present the important information first. The beginning reporter should go to considerable effort to hit the main point clearly and immediately. He or she should avoid leads like the following which present secondary information first and get to the major point only later.

In an on-the-street survey conducted by the Midtown Chronicle at the intersection of Court and Rainey streets yesterday, it was discovered that **Midtown residents solidly support the women's rights ordinance presented last week by City Council.**

A speech was delivered to the annual meeting of the American Association of General Practitioners in Memorial Auditorium last night by Harry S. Stone, special advisor to the Department of Health, Education and Welfare, in which he said that **socialized medicine in inevitable in the United States.**

Harry S. Stone, special advisor to the Department of Health, Education and Welfare, told the American Association of General Practitioners in Memorial Auditorium last night that **socialized medicine is inevitable in the United States.**

In each of these examples, it should be obvious that the most significant element is the highlighted section at the end. The information presented first is necessary, but not so significant that it merits the prime location. The good reporter would have written leads which looked more like these:

Midtown residents solidly support the women's rights ordinance presented last week by City Council, according to an on-the-street survey conducted yesterday by the **Midtown Chronicle.**

Socialized medicine is inevitable in the United States, a Department of Health, Education and Welfare advisor told members of the American Association of General Practitioners in Memorial Auditorium last night.

The speaker, Harry S. Stone, added that....

Let's now look at other examples of how reporters would use a set of facts in constructing good leads. All of the following spot news leads would result naturally from the process we have discussed here.

Facts

- New organization will be formed on University of Minnesota campus.
- Will be known as Students, Inc.

- Purpose will be to represent students on matters pertaining to them.
- Will work with university administrators, faculty, the city, etc.
- Organizational meeting Friday at 7 p.m. in 227 Student Union.
- Information comes from John Stimmis, a senior in history and one of the founders.
- Fire in Middletown.
- Pleasant Valley Nursing Home.
- Modern, brick, one story.
- Cause of fire unknown.
- 21 elderly residents killed.
- 27 others injured.
- 50 persons known in building at time of fire.
- YMCA Board of Directors.
- Will meet Friday at Middletown Hotel..
- Noon luncheon meeting.
- Two major items on agenda.
- One is passage of next year's operating budget.
- Other is a capital repair fund drive.
- Woman killed in auto accident.
- Jane Lee Albers of Middletown.
- She was 26 years old.
- Pronounced dead at Middletown Hospital
- 1:15 a.m. today
- Car she was driving plunged over a 40-foot embankment on U.S. 50, three miles west of Middletown.
- Hospital officials said she died of internal injuries.

Leads

An organizational meeting will be held at 7 p.m. Friday in 227 Student Union for a new group, Students, Inc., which will seek to represent students in disputes.

Or

Students, Inc., a new University of Minnesota campus organization designed to represent student opinion, will hold an organizational meeting at 7 p.m. Friday in 227 Student Union

Twenty-one elderly persons were killed and 27 injured as fire swept through the Pleasant Valley Nursing Home in Middletown yesterday. Two residents still are missing.

Next year's operating budget and a capital repair fund drive will be discussed by the YMCA Board of Directors at its noon luncheon meeting Friday at the Middletown Hotel.

A 26- years-old Middletown woman was dead on arrival at Middletown Hospital at 1:15 a.m. today after the car she was driving plunged over a 40-foot embankment on U.S. 50, three miles west of town.

Skill at writing leads may be attained only through practice and through careful analysis of one's own writing and the writing found in newspapers. Beginning reporters should read their local newspaper and at least one major metropolitan newspaper very carefully, making a regular study of leads an important part of their daily reading. In making such analyses, be very aware of the requirements of emphasis and completeness. Additionally, ask the following questions: Might the lead stand alone, if necessary? Is the lead conclusive? Is a good headline suggested by the lead content? If the answer to any of these questions is in the negative, check the lead more closely to make certain it is satisfactory.

The discussion to this point has concerned summary leads. There are other types, but mastery of the summary lead must be the first task of the beginning reporter. If he or she can develop the talent to construct a smooth-flowing lead which contains complete information, that's a big step toward journalistic proficiency.

The Lead Transition

Since the news story lead is designed as a summary of the essential facts of a story and not as an introduction to the presentation of the details, reporters must pay special attention to providing transition between the lead and the running copy. This is the lead transition. It may be only a word or two, or it may be a paragraph or two, but its importance to the unity of a newspaper story cannot be overstated.

A common fault in newspaper writing is failure to adequately connect the summary lead with the body of the story, making it appear as if the lead is little more than a head line and the story actually begins on its completion. Note the lack of such transition in this lead:

> A proposal for the establishment of a city Racial Relations Commission was presented last night by one of the candidates for mayor in the November election.
>
> "The situation of racial minorities has become worse than at any time in history," Republican Samuel R. Peabody said.

The information presented probably captures the essence of Peabody's statement quite well. But the presentation is lacking in flow for two reasons. First, although the relationship between the two paragraphs is logical, the statements are not tied together in any functional way. From a literary standpoint, therefore, the paragraphs are disconnected. Second, readers may have grown to expect certain information quickly because they have become accustomed to the "five Ws and H" which constitute the summary lead. The most obvious missing element is "Where". Such omissions leave gaps over which readers, at least subconsciously, must stumble in their efforts to grasp the full meaning of the lead.

Now note this revised version:

> A proposal for establishment of a city Racial Relations Commission was presented last night by one of the candidates for mayor in the November election.
>
> Speaking to members of the City Republican coordinating Committee, Samuel R. Peabody urged such a commission because "the situation of racial minorities in this city has become worse than at any time in history,"

These paragraphs satisfy the two major requirements of the lead transition: that it provide information which has been withheld from the lead itself and that it direct the reader's thought smoothly from the summary lead to the details in the body of the story. In this case, it does so by adding the expected information, and through the use of repetition which provides functional transition.

Filling in identifications which are too detailed for the lead is a common practice in the lead transition For example:

> Three young Northville residents were killed last night when their car skidded on rain-lick U.S. 101 near Centerville and plunged over a 40-foot embankment.
>
> Police identified the victims as Harry R. Kinney, 18, of 1314 S. Main St.; Ruth R. Golding, 17, of 32 Roosevelt Drive, and Peter S. Wazkowski, 18, of 805 Cherry Blossom Lane.
>
> The accident occurred when.

Provision of identification in the lead transition usually in restricted to situation in which the list is short. If the story had been about an airplane crash in which 43 persons were killed or about a group of 72 high school students who were being honoured for academic excellence, the reporter would not have provided the list immediately. It would have been saved for a later portion of the story or made into a separate related story called a sidebar.

Reporters also will provide elaboration or clarification of a lead statement:

The local chapter of Theater Arts, Inc., has issued a call for persons to try out for parts in "Oklahoma!" which will be presented in Memorial Auditorium in July

Persons interested in trying out for the roles for five women and six men remaining to be cast may report at 7 p.m. Thursday to the Theater Workshop, 657S. Virginia St.

The reporter, writing the following lead, omitted all but the "What" from the opening paragraph, placing the remainder in the lead transition. Notice also the use of "with this warning" which serves as functional transition between the two paragraphs.

"If the railroad tracks are not moved from their present location adjacent to the city park, I predict that sooner or later we are going to have an accident which will shock the whole city."

With this warming, Tracy T. Townsend, president of the Centerville PTA, urged last night in a speech to the Lions Club in the Gibson Hotel that the community unite in an effort to have the tracks relocated.

Organizing the More Complex Story

Obviously, a news story about a minor automobile accident or a meeting of the local Rotary Club differs significantly in structure from a story about the renovation of ten downtown blocks. The facts in relatively simple stories may be arranged in declining order of significance, but that is difficult to do in more complicated multi-incident situations. Thus, as stories become more complicated, the organization becomes more complicated, the organization becomes more complicated, involving more shifting from topic to topic. Reporters must find ways to present complex information within the context of the inverted pyramid principle.

The application of that principle to the multi-incident story boils down to this: Reporters seek to introduce no new important material after they have reached the half-way point of the story. Strict adherence to the inverted pyramid when writing a complex story could result in the pushing down of some significant points if reporters provided all available discussion on each topic before introducing the next. To get around this, reporters tend to divide the material into segments, present the highlights of each segment very early and then return later to each for presentation of details.

Thus, many alternative approaches exist, depending on the reporter's judgment, but let us analyze three types of approaches here. By way of example, we will return to the city council meeting mentioned earlier in which there were four major topics of interest: (1) that income taxes will be raised by 1 percent, (2) that a new recreation complex will be constructed (3) that improvements will be made to the city water treatment plant and (4) that all streets in the city's Edgewood Section will be paved.

The reporter's first question must be whether these story elements are of equal significance or whether they may be given priority. If the elements are determined to be of equal significance, the reporter probably would use the one-paragraph, limited-detail summary lead which would present each topic. This lead would be followed by the lead transition, then an explanation of each of the four items. Introduction of each item in the lead has satisfied the inverted pyramid principle because the remainder of the story consists of explanation of what already has been mentioned. No new topics of discussion, in this case, are raised after the lead. The story would look something like this:

City income taxes will be raised by 1 percent next year so the city can build a new recreation complex, make necessary improvements to the water treatment plant and pave all streets in the Edgewood Section.

These decisions were made by City Council last night in what officials termed the "most productive" meeting of council in years.

The income tax boost-the first for the city since 1965 - will raise an estimated $5 million, Treasurer Albert Williams told council members at the meeting. He and Mayor Bert Jamieson labeled this amount the minimum required for necessary city progress.

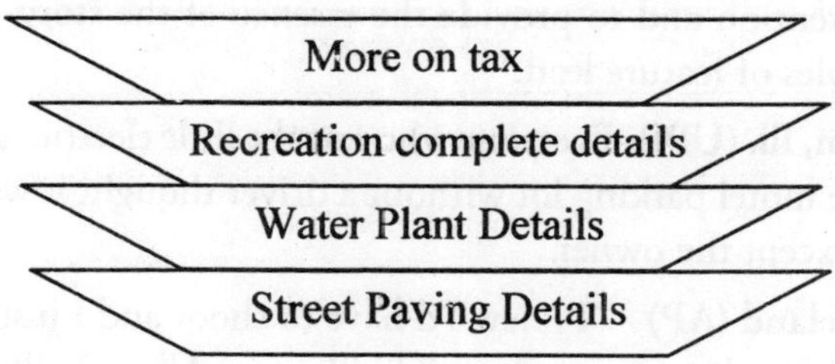

Multi-Incident : summary lead. Its purpose it to pull together all four of the significant points the reporter wants to emphasize. Its use means that all significant topics of discussion have been raised.

Lead Transition : Provides the essential point that the material in the first paragraph results from a City Council meeting and leads the reader smoothly into presentation of details of each point.

Details of First Item : At this stage, the reporter may present all available information about the tax raise.

Details of each other Item : Full explanation of each is given with reporter providing transition when story moves from one to another.

This form of multi-incident organization may be given an additional variation if the reporter decides the mention of each component in the lead is not enough. It may be the case that among the details to be presented on each topic, some should be presented earlier than other. In the previous example, the reporter has no means whereby differentiation of detail significance may be accomplished. To solve this problem, the reporter subdivides all available material on each item into highlights and details. Once that has been accomplished, the reporter would utilize the same summary lead as a type of table of contents and, briefly present the highlights of each.

The feature lead, on the other hand, may be used in almost any form. Narrative leads, in fact, could be defined as feature leads. But whatever their form, feature leads have two major characteristics: They will seek to emphasize human interest, and they will stress some type of incongruous situation. Many reporters seek to develop the talent to use a catchy feature lead or news stories, to capture the readers' attention and to provide the essence of the story. Here are two examples of feature lead:

Salem, Ill. (UPI) -Everyone who saw the little electric car driving around the motel parking lot without a driver thought it was funny; everyone except the owner.

Cleveland (AP) - "I knew I'd have to shoot and I just prayed I wouldn't shoot them somewhere I'd kill," said Albert Williams.

Frequently, when reporters use either of the type of leads, they shy away from the inverted pyramid construction and use a suspended interest or narrative from of organization. Either is proper if circumstances are right. In suspended interest construction, reporters use a narrative or feature lead, deliberately avoid giving too much information early and lead the reader through the details to a climax or surprise ending. Under most circumstances, this type of story is short and of the feature variety. The narrative story may be opened with a summary, narrative or feature lead, then be structured chronologically (or sequentially) through the event being described. The tendency, again, is for these stories to be short.

Concluding the Story

Unlike academic theses and English class papers, the newspaper story seldom has a conclusion as a separate entity. Ending the story usually is very simple; when you have said everything you want to say, quit writing. The inverted pyramid construction is based on the philosophy that the last paragraph will be the least important. If the structure has been handled properly everything worth saying will have been said by the time the reporter reaches the story's end.

Young reporters frequently want to do one of two things at the end of a story. Sometimes they provide the reader with a summary statement, but they should remember that if a summary merits use, it probably should be the lead, not the conclusion. On other occasions, your reporters want to provide the reader with personal opinion, ignoring the journalistic principle of objectivity. In short, remember that no form of concluding statement is necessary for most news stories.

Structuring the News Story

In their day-to-day writing, experienced reporters seldom will consider consciously each of the principles of story structure which have been discussed here. Years of experience have made their application automatic. The beginning reporter, on the other hand, must be very deliberate in· evaluating available information and in determining how to write the story. He or she must be acutely aware of every step in the process.

Using a set of familiar facts contained in the story of Red Riding Hood; let us now consider an example of how this process should work.

First, does the story of Red Riding Hood have news value? According to the criteria of news worthiness, it does. What happened to her might happen to any little girl delivering goodies to her grandmother's house in the Woods. A mother might say, "That could have been my daughter instead of Red Riding Hood." The facts have human interest because they concern a little girl, a hero and a villain. They also involve a dramatic rescue and considerable excitement. It might also be said that the story could serve a social good by warning other parents to be careful of allowing their daughter to walk alone in the woods. It is therefore, safe to say that a reporter would write a story if confronted with the facts of this incident.

Remembering that the lead should present the climax of the story is summary form by answering the questions posed by the "five Ws and H," reporters would determine that the lead should concentrate on the following: Who? "sportsman"; What? "saved Red Riding Hood's life"; where? " at her grandmother's house"; when? "a long time ago" (but for current purposes, let us assume that the story will be in a newspaper of the time; thus, we can say "yesterday"); Why? "the wolf was about to eat her"; How? "he shot the wolf." An alternative who? approach could concentrate on Red Riding Hood instead of the sportsman. To do this, however, the lead would have to be written in passive voice ("Red Riding hood was saved...") and newspapers prefer use of active voice ("sportsman *saved* Red Riding Hood"). In spite of such a preference, either approach is valid.

Stringing these elements together, the reporter could write the following lead: A sportsman saved the life of Red Riding Hood at her grandmother's house in the woods yesterday when he shot of wolf which was about to eat her.

This summary lead satisfies all the requirements and thus is acceptable in content. But it is somewhat dry and lifeless in its presentation. The good reporter would add life to the writing by emphasizing the action, by adding to the human interest and by filling in the fate of the grand mother. When doing this, however, the reporter must remain within the length limitations of the newspaper lead. Given these considerations, the reporter could revise the lead is this manner:

Quick action by an unidentified sportsman saved the life of a 10-year-old girl yesterday when he shot and killed a wolf which had eaten her grandmother and was about to eat her.

The information omitted from this lead would be placed in the second paragraph. For example, the Where? element should be mentioned quickly. Red should be identified by a listing of her parents' names and home address (standard practice for a young person). The grandmother should be fully identified. And more specific information about the activities of the wolf should be provided. If the information were available, the sportsman certainly should be identified. But let us assume in this instance that he remained anonymous. Seeking to provide this is information as well a smooth transition from the lead to the body of the story, the reporter could continue:

The young lady, Red Riding Hood, daughter of Mr. And Mrs. James Hood of 1313 Forest Lane, said she was delivering some cakes and butter to her sick grandmother when the wolf, disguised as the elderly woman, declared he was going to eat her.

The grandmother, Mrs. Sarah Hood, 79, of 32 Elm Lane apparently had been eaten before little Red arrived, according to police.

After leading the reader smoothly through the first three paragraphs, the reporter would seek to provide the details of the incident in as concise - yet interesting - a way as possible. The major effort in the body of the story would be to arrange the facts according to descending importance. The reporter would try to get across all the news material within the first half of the story; in the second half, secondary, but needed, explanatory material would be provided. The logic of factual organization would be dictated by the type of inverted pyramid structure being followed and determination of the purpose for using certain facts.

In writing, the reporter would seek to use techniques which would highlight the mood of the story, thus supplementing the content. This means he or she would vary sentence and paragraph length, would use dialogue when possible and would omit superfluous details. At all times, the principles of grammar, word choice, sentence construction, paragraphing and style would be kept in mind.

Te final product could look something like this.

Hunter Kills Wolf, Saves
Life of 10-year-Old Girl

Quick action by an unidentified sportsman saved the life of a 10-year-old girl yesterday when he shot and killed a wolf which had eaten her grandmother and was about to eat her at her grandmother's house in the woods.

The young lady, Red Riding Hood, daughter of Mr. and Mrs. James Hood of 1313 Forest Lane, said she was delivering some cakes and butter to her sick grandmother when the wolf, disguised as the elderly woman, declared he was going to eat her.

The grandmother, Mrs. Sarah Hood, 79, of 32 Elm Lane, apparently had been eaten by the wolf before little Red arrived, according to police.

Red told police she had met the wolf previously in the woods as she was walking from her home to her grandmother's house. She said he had been very polite at that time and had told her to give his "love" to her grandmother.

Summary Lead : Statement of the essence of the story.

Organization : is single-item inverted pyramid.

Lead Transition : Provides full identification for the secondary ID in the lead. It also strives for transition between lead and details in body of the story.

Body : Quoting police and central figure, presents details of incident according to inverse importance.

Apparently, the wolf had determined her destination in that conversation, police said, and then taken a shortcut, getting there before the girl, eating her grandmother and taking the grandmother's place in bed.

The young lady said she had lingered during the walk, playing in the woods, so the wolf easily could have arrived ahead of her.

When she arrived at the house, the wolf apparently mimicked the grandmother's voice, telling her to come in. Once inside, she told police, she noticed that something was wrong. She said she asked the wolf about his long arms.

"The better to hug you, my dear," the wolf reportedly told her.

Then she asked about the wolf's very large ears and was told: "The better to hear you."

Red told police she then noticed the wolf's large teeth and, knowing her grandmother did not have such teeth and becoming more frightened, asked about them.

"The better to eat you up now," the wolf is reported to have cried as he grabbed the young lady.

At that instant, a shot rang out and the wolf fell dead. The sportsman checked on the condition of the child and, finding she was not injured, left immediately. Police arrived moments later, having been called by a passer-by.

Police are attempting to identify the hunter.

The funeral for the grandmother, Mrs. Hood, is pending.

Direct Quotations liven up presentation.

Final Detail is elaboration of lead statements.

Last Two Paragraphs provide transition to next day's stories.

No Formal Conclusion

Summary

The structure of most newspaper stories is according to the principles of the inverted pyramid which stipulate that the most significant information should be presented first in the story and followed by the remainder of the information according to inverse significance. The usual way to accomplish this is through use of the summary lead which may be either a statement of the single most significant fact or a combination of several judged by the reporter to be most significant. While there are other types of structures and leads, they are reserved for special situations in which the reporter determines that the summary lead and inverted pyramid are not the most appropriate.

◆◆◆

13

50 Common Errors in Newspaper Writing

1. **Affect, effect.** Generally, AFFECT is the verb; FFECT is the noun. "The letter did not AFFECT the outcome." "The letter had a significant EFFECT." But EFFECT is also a verb meaning to bring about. Thus: "IT is almost impossible to EFFECT change."
2. **Afterward, afterwards.** Use AFTERWARD. The dictionary allows use of AFTERWARDS only as a second form. The same thinking applies to TOWARD and TOWARDS. Use TOWARD.
3. **Alright All right.** That's the way to spell it. The dictionary may list ALRIGHT as a`legitimate word but it is not acceptable in standard usage, says Random House.
4. **Allude, elude.** You ALLUDE to (or mention) a book. you ELUDE (or escape) a pursuer.
5. **Annual.** Don't use first with it. If it's the first time, it can't be annual.
6. **Averse, adverse:** If you don't like something, you are AVERSE (or opposed) to it. ADVERSE is an adjective: ADVERSE (bad) weather, ADVERSE conditions.
7. **Block, bloc:** A BLOC is a coalition of persons or a group with the same purpose or goal. Don't call it a BLOCK, which has some 40 dictionary definitions

8. **Compose, comprise.** Remember that you COMPOSE things by putting them together. Once the parts are put together, the object COMPRISES or includes or embraces the parts.
9. **Couple of. You need the OF.** It's never "a couple tomatoes."
10. **Demolish, destroy.** They mean to do away with completely. You can't partially demolish or destroy something, nor is there any need to say TOTALLY destroyed.
11. **Different from.** Things and people are different FROM each other. Don't write that they are different THAN each other.
12. **Head up.** People don't HEAD UP committees. They HEAD them.
13. **Drown.** Don't say someone was DROWNED unless an assailant held the victim's head under water. Just say the victim DROWNED.
14. **Due to, owing to** , because of: We prefer the last.

    Wrong: The game was canceled DUE TO rain.

    Stilted: OWING TO rain, the game was canceled.

    Right: The game was canceled BECAUSE of Rain.

    reproduced with permission of the Associated Press Managing Editors Association.
15. **Ecology, environment.** They are not synonymous. ECOLOGY is the study of the relationship between organisms and their ENVIRONMENT

    Right: The laboratory is studying the ECOLOGY of man and the desert.

    Right: There is much interest in animal ECOLOGY these days.

    Wrong: Even so simple an undertaking as maintaining a lawn affects ECOLOGY.

    Right: Even so simple an undertaking as maintaining a lawn affects our ENVIRONMENT.
16. **Either**: It means one or the other, not both.

    Wrong: There were lions on EITHER side of the door.

    Right: There were lions on EACH side of the door.

17. **Fliers, Flyers:** Airmen are FLIERS. Handbills are FLYERS.
18. **Flout, flaunt.** They aren't the same word; they mean completely different things, and they're very commonly confused. FLOUT means to mock, to scoff or to show disdain for, FLAUNT means to display ostentatiously.
19. **Funeral service.** A redundant expression. A funeral IS a service.
20. **Hopefully.** One of the most commonly misused words, in spite of what the dictionary may say. HOPEFULLY should describe the way the subject FEELS.

    For instance:

    Hopefully, I shall present the plan to the president. (This means I will be hopeful when I do it.)

    But it is something else again when you attribute hope to a nonperson. You may write: Hopefully, the war will end soon. This means you hope the war will end soon, but it is not what you are writing. What you mean is: I hope the war will end soon.
21. **Imply and infer.** The speaker implies.

    The hearer infers.
22. **In advance of, prior to.** Use before; it sounds more natural.
23. **It's, its.** ITS is the possessive, IT'S is the contraction of ITIS.

    Wrong: What is IT'S name?

    Right: What is ITS name? ITS name is Fido.

    Right: IT'S the first time he's scored tonight.

    Right: IT'S may coat.
24. **Lay, lie.** Lay is the action word; lie is the state of being.

    Wrong: The body will LAY in state until Wednesday.

    Right: The body will LIE in state until Wednesday.

    Right: The Prosecutor tried to LAY the blame on him.

    However, the past tense of LIE is LAY.

    Right: The body LAY in state from Tuesday until Wednesday.

    Wrong: the Body LAID is state from Tuesday until Wednesday.

The past participle and the plan past tense of LAY is LAID.

Right: He LAID the pencil on the pad.

Right: He HAD LAID the pencil on the pad.

Right: The hen LAID an egg.

25. **Leave, let:** LEAVE ALONE means to depart from or cause to be in solitude. LET ALONE means to be undisturbed.

    Wrong: The man had pulled a gun on her, but Mr. Jones intervened and talked him into LEAVING HER ALONE.

    Right: The man had pulled a gun on her, but Mr. Jones intervened and talked him into LETTING HER ALONE.

    Right: When I entered the room I saw that Jim and Mary were sleeping, so I decided to LEAVE THEM ALONE.

26. **Less, fewer.** If you can separate items in the quantities being compared, use FEWER. If not, use LESS.

    Wrong: The Rams are inferior to the Vikings because they have LESS good linemen.

    Right: The Rams are inferior to the Vikings because they have FEWER good linemen.

    Right: The Rams are inferior to the Vikings because they have LESS experience.

27. **Like, as.** Don't use LIKE for AS or AS IF. In general, use LIKE to compare with nouns and pronouns; use AS when comparing with phrases and clauses that contain a verb.

    Wrong: Jim blocks the linebacker LIKE he should.

    Right: Jim blocks the linebacker AS he should.

    Right: Jim blocks LIKE a pro.

28. **Marshall, marshal.** Generally, the first form is correct only when the word is a proper noun: John Marshall. The second form is the verb form: Marilyn will MARSHAL her forces. And the second form is the one to use for a title: FIRE MARSHAL Stan Anderson, FIELD MARSHAL Erwin Rommel.

29. **Mean, average, median:** Use mean as synonymous with AVERAGE. Each word refers to the sum of all components

divided by the number of components. MEDIAN is the number that has as many components above it as below it.

30. **Nouns.** There's a growing trend toward using them as verbs. Resist it. HOST, HEADQUARTERS and AUTHOR, for instance, are nouns, even though the dictionary may acknowledge they can be used as verbs. If you do, you'll come up with a monstrosity like: "Headquartered at his country home, John Doe hosted a party to celebrate the book he had authored."

31. **Oral, verbal:** Use ORAL when use of the mouth is central to the thought; the word emphasizes the idea of human utterance. VERBAL may apply to spoken or written words; it connotes the process of reducing ideas to writing. Usually, it's a VERBAL contract, not an ORAL one, if it's in writing.

32. **Over and more than.** They aren't interchangeable. OVER refers to spatial relationships: The plane flew OVER the city. MORE THAN is used with figures: In the crowd were More Than 1,000 fans.

33. **Parallel construction.** Thoughts in series in the same sentence require parallel construction.

    Wrong: The union delivered demands for an increase of 10 percent in wages and to cut the work week to 30 hours.

    Right: The union delivered demands for an increase of 10 percent in wages and for a REDUCTION in the work week to 30 hours.

34. **Peddle, pedal.** When selling something, you PEDDLE it. When riding a bicycle or similar form of locomotion, you PEDAL it.

35. **Pretense, Pretext:** They're different, but it's a tough distinction. A PRETEXT is that which is put forward to conceal a truth.

    He was discharged for tardiness, but this was only a PRETEXT for general incompetence.

    A PRETENSE is a "false show"; a more overt act intended to conceal personal feelings.

    My profuse compliments were all PRETENSE.

36. **Principle, principal.** A guiding rule or basic truth is a PRINCIPLE.

    The first, dominant, or leading things is PRINCIPAL. PRINCIPLE is a noun; PRINCIPAL may be a noun or an adjective.

    Right: It's the PRINCIPLE of the thing.

    Right: Liberty and justice are two PRINCIPLES on which our nation is founded.

    Right: Hitting and fielding are the PRINCIPAL activities in baseball.

    Right: Robert Jamieson is the school PRINCIPAL.

37. **Redundancies to avoid:** Easter Sunday. Make it EASTER. Incumbent Congressman. CONGRESSMAN.

    Owns his own home. OWNS HIS HOME.

    The company will close down. THE COMPANY WILL CLOSE.

    Jones, smith, Johnson and Reid were all convicted. JONES, SMITH, JOHNSON and REID WERE CONVICTED.

    JEWISH RABBI. JUST RABBI 8 p.m. tonight. All you need is 8 TONIGHT or 8 P.M. TODAY.

    DURING THE WINTER MONTHS.

    DURING THE WINTER

    Both Reid and Jones were denied pardons. REID AND JONES WERE DENIED PARDONS.

    I am currently tired. I AM TIRED.

    Autopsy to determine the cause of death. AUTOPY.

38. **Refute.** The word connotes success in argument and almost always implies an editorial judgment.

    Wrong: Father Bury REFUTED the arguments of the proabortion faction.

    Right: Father Bury responded to the arguments of the proabortion faction.

39. **Reluctant, reticent.** If he doesn't want to act, he is RELUCTANT. If he doesn't want to speak, he is RETICENT.
40. **Say, said.** The most serviceable words in the journalist's language are the forms of the verb TO SAY. Let a person SAY something, rather than declare or admit or point out. And never let him grin smile, frown or giggle something.
41. **Slang.** Don't try to use "with-it" slang usually a term is on the way out by the time we get it in print.
42. **SPELLING.** It's Basic. If Reporters Can't Spell And Copy Editors Can't Spell, We're In Trouble. Some Ripe Ones For The Top Of Your List:

    It's CONSENSUS, Not Concensus.
    It's RESTAURATEUR, Not Restauranteur
    It's DIETITIAN, Not Dietician.
43. **Temperatures.** They May Get Higher Or Lower, But They Don't Get Warmer Of Cooler.

    Wrong: Temperatures Are Expected To Warm Up In The Area Friday.

    Right: Temperatures Are Expected To Rise In The Area Friday.
44. **That, Which.** THAT Tends To Restrict The Reader's Thought And Direct It The Way You Want It To Go; Which Is Nonrestrictive, Introducing A Bit Of Subsidiary Information.

    For Instance:

    The Lawnmower That Is In The Garage Needs Sharpening. (Meaning: We Have More Than One Lawnmower. The One In The Garage Needs Sharpening.)

    The Lawnmower, Which Is In The Garage, Needs Sharpening. (Meaning: Our Lawnmower Needs Sharpening. It's In The Garage.)

    The Statue That Graces Our Entry Hall Is On Loan From The Museum. (Meaning: Of All The Statues Around Here, The One In The Entry Hall Is On Loan.)

The Status, Which Graces Our Entry Hall, Is On Loan. (Meaning: Our Statue Is On Loan. It Happens To Be In The Entry Hall.)

Note That Which Clauses Take Commas, Signaling They Are Not Essential To The Meaning Of The Sentence.

45. **Under Way,** Not Underway. But Don't Say Something Got Under Way. Say It STARTED Or BEGAN.

46. **Unique Something that is unique is the only one of its kind.** It can't be very unique or quite unique or somewhat unique or rather unique. Don't use it unless you really mean unique.

47. **Up. Don't use it as a verb.**

    Wrong: the manager said he would UP the price next week.
    Right: The manager said he would RAISE the price next week.

48. Who, Whom. A tough one, but generally you're safe to use WHOM to refer to someone who has been the object of an action. WHO is the word when the somebody has been the actor:

    A-19 year-old woman, to WHOM the room was rented, left the window open. A-19-year-old woman, WHO rented the room. left the window open.

49. **Who's, whose.** Though it incorporates an apostrophe, WHO's is not a possessive. It's a contraction for WHO IS WHOSE is the possessive.

    Wrong: I don't know WHO'S coat it is.
    Right: I don't know WHOSE coat it is.
    Right: Find out WHO's there.

50. **Would:** Be careful about using WOULD when constructing a conditional past tense.

    Wrong: If Soderholm WOULD NOT HAVE HAD an injured foot, Thompson wouldn't have been in the lineup.

    Right: If Soderholm HAD NOT had an injured foot, Thompson wouldn't have been in the lineup.

This concludes the APME listing. Here are a few others:

1. **Accept-except** : ACCEPT means to take or receive, EXCEPT as a verb means to exclude, and EXCEPT as a preposition means with the exception of . Thus, "Virginia ACCEPTED the gift for her mother." "If you Except the third point, the compromise will be ratified." "All made statement EXCEPT the mayor."
2. **Agree to-agree with** : You may AGREE TO a proposal and AGREE WITH another person.
3. **Compare to-compare with** : COMPARE TO should be used only to suggest likenesses between two objects, COMPARE WITH to suggest likenesses and differences. Thus, "The typical 10 year-old boy is often COMPARED To a howling hyena." "In COMPARING the book WITH the original manuscript, she found several variations."
4. **Compound adjectives** : The list is endless, but he rule is to use a hyphen when two or more words come together to form one adjective to modify another word. The HYPHENS in such cases are ESSENTIAL to meaning. "He jumped over a four-foot fence." "The 3-year-old girl was honored at a party." "The back-and-forth motion made him nauseated."
5. **Consensus** : It's redundant to say CONSENSUS OF OPINION. The word CONSENSUS means general agreement and automatically contains the idea of opinion. Thus, "The CONSENSUS was that White's argument was the correct one."
6. **Council-counsel** : COUNCIL means assembly, official group; Counsel means advice or adviser. COUNSEL also is a verb, meaning to give advice. Thus, "The city COUNCIL will meet tonight." "The lawyer gave me good COUNSEL." "He COUNSELED me to be cautious."

Dangling Modifier : This results from carelessness in clarifying the object of a modifier and usually leads to confusion of meaning. For example, "Absentmindedly stepping from the sidewalk, an automobile hit me" actually means the automobile stepped from the sidewalk and hit me.

◆◆◆